**Fiscal Management and Planning
in Local Government**

Fiscal Management and Planning in Local Government

James C. Snyder
University of Wisconsin–
Milwaukee

Lexington Books
D.C. Heath and Company
Lexington, Massachusetts
Toronto

Library of Congress Cataloging in Publication Data

Snyder, James C
    Fiscal management and planning in local government.

    Bibliography: p.
    Includes index.
    1. Local finance. 2. Fiscal policy. I. Title.
HJ9105.S6   352'.1   76-43218
ISBN 0-669-01055-3

Published simultaneously in Canada.

Printed in the United States of America.

International Standard Book Number: 0-669-01055-3

Library of Congress Catalog Card Number: 76-43218

Contents

List of Figures

List of Tables

Preface

This text has been written primarily in response to several contemporary conditions: (1) the critical need for rational fiscal management and planning at the local government level; (2) the growing trend to integrate the "planning process" into the overall function of local government management; and (3) the need for an introduction/survey text in the area of fiscal management that addresses the practical needs as perceived by planners, managers, and elected officials, as well as the academic needs of undergraduate and graduate students in such areas as urban planning, urban affairs, and public administration.

Local governments are increasingly finding themselves in situations where the demand for public goods and services exceeds the supply. Increases in population, income, and urbanization, along with rising expectations, have clearly increased the need for, and thus the demand for, more extensive local government activity. The depth and scope of public services has expanded dramatically in recent decades, and there appears to be no reason to believe that this trend will not continue in future decades. In addition to increases in demand, relatively high rates of price inflation (particularly public worker wage inflation) have led to higher costs of production. However, local government revenue structure and production capacity have remained relatively constrained. The federal government, with reliance on the income tax, and the states, with reliance on sales and income taxes, have generally been able to provide expanded services in a growing economy without significant increases in tax rates. Local governments, however, rely heavily on the property tax, the revenue of which lags behind economic growth. Thus, local governments have had to impose higher tax rates. These factors have produced a condition called "fiscal crunch," where local governments simply cannot finance the desired level of public service. The local problem is further compounded by the fragmentation and overlapping of political jurisdictions—leading to the segregation of persons by income and wealth, disparities in fiscal capacity, diseconomies of scale, and a lack of overall planning and management for public resources. All of this produces a great deal of confusion on the part of the citizen relative to benefits he or she receives for the tax dollar, and of uncertainty on the part of government relative to revenue and expenditure decisions. In this general situation, it is clear that sound fiscal management and planning practice is critically needed at the local government level.

Indeed, there appears to be a trend towards increased levels of management and planning in local government. Public sector "planning," traditionally confined to relatively narrow land use and transportation contexts, has expanded to include a more comprehensive set of functions including physical, social, economic, environmental, and other concerns. In addition, planning is increasingly being integrated into the overall process of management. Whereas planning traditionally belonged to an "independent" planning commission that "advised" elected officials and professional managers, planners are now found in the offices of mayors and managers, legislative staffs, and major functional departments and programs. One aspect of this change is the consolidation of certain planning and finance functions. Planning without regard for financial consequences, and financing without the benefit of planning, are equally questionable. Nevertheless, historically this has been the situation in local government. Therefore, the strong trend now is to combine planning and finance into units of "planning and budget," "policy analysis," "program analysis," and the like. As planning and finance become integral parts of the management function, there is a need for planners to more fully understand financial matters, and financial personnel to appreciate the planning process. Elected officials and management staff must be versed in both.

The third rationale for this text involves an apparent gap in the existing literature. Many excellent public finance texts are available, but most are oriented towards public sector economics for professional and academic economists. Many useful texts and reports are also issued by the Municipal Finance Officers Association, the International City Management Association, and other professional organizations. However, these works tend to deal with the more specific information required by singular professions in the field. There is a need for a survey or overview text that ties planning and finance together, but one which simplifies technical aspects and can be useful to a broad audience of elected officials, managers, planners, department heads, program directors, and others interested in local government.

This text presents fiscal management and planning in the above context. It is organized into three parts: Foundations, Practice, and Techniques of Analysis. Part I, Foundations, deals with the more theoretical bases of local government finance. Chapter 1, The Market System, is essentially a review of "microeconomics"—that part of the social science of economics that deals with the behavior of individual decision-making entities within the economy, rather than with the performance of the "whole" economy. A basic understanding of this material is prerequisite to the subject of this text, because fiscal management and planning involves making decisions on behalf of the economic entity of local government. Readers without previous training in economics may want to use this chapter as an introduction and guide to further inquiry into more complete texts, whereas those with economic training may use the material as a review.

Although no specific mathematical background is required, some understanding of "marginal concepts" is necessary. Therefore, some readers may want to skip forward to the first part of Chapter 12, Marginal Analysis, for an explanation of this important concept. Chapter 2, The Public Sector, addresses the rationale and functions of the public sector of the economy. Chapter 3, Management and Planning, addresses the processes of management and planning in local government, including the presentation of a model that treats planning as an integral part of the management process. These three chapters collectively establish a contextual overview from which the more practical aspects of fiscal management can be approached.

Part II, Practice, addresses particular aspects of fiscal management in a local government context. Although emphasis is given to the municipal form of government, the principles are sufficiently general to allow application to nearly all local governments—regional, metropolitan, county, city, town, township, village, or special district. Chapter 4, Fiscal Management and Planning, covers the financial elements of the overall management system that were established in the previous chapter. Organizational structure, roles and responsibilities, and specific fiscal planning tasks are described—from basic economic research to capital and operating programs. The preparation of the budget, the last stage in the fiscal planning process, is sufficiently detailed to require separate treatment in Chapter 5. Both traditional and contemporary forms of budgeting are covered.

Chapter 6, Revenue, addresses basic revenue structure, principles of taxation, economic effects, and each major source of local government revenue. Intergovernmental Relations, including a description of typical fiscal problems and potential solutions, is addressed in Chapter 7. Chapter 8, Debt Financing, covers the economic structure of public debt, debt instruments and planning. Chapter 9, Accounting Systems, presents a brief description of the purposes, structure, and functions of accounting systems in local government.

Part III describes certain techniques of analysis to provide the reader with a guide to (1) recognizing situations where analysis can be useful, (2) conducting basic analysis and problem solving relative to fiscal situations, and (3) interpreting analyses conducted by staff experts and/or consultants. Although some measure of comprehensiveness is attempted, the reader should be aware that large and complex problem situations may warrant efforts of analysis beyond those presented here. Nevertheless, this material should provide a sufficient foundation for a large part of the fiscal analysis that might be conducted at the local level, as well as presenting an introduction and reference to more specialized works. Chapter 10, Structuring the Analysis, deals with the task of converting a decision problem into an analysis format. A general descriptive "systems model" is used for this purpose.

Chapter 11, Program Evaluation, is devoted to the specific techniques of policy and program evaluation; Chapter 12, Marginal Analysis, presents the basic concept and application of marginal analysis techniques. Chapter 13, Investment Analysis, covers the techniques for analyzing investments that exhibit costs and/or benefits over an extended period of time as well as short-term investment of surplus cash. Example analyses are used throughout these four chapters.

This text has been designed primarily for use as introductory material for managers and planners in local government. It should also be useful to elected officials and other interested persons who require an overview of good fiscal management and planning practice. The text can also be used for graduate or undergraduate courses in public administration, urban planning, and related fields. The material is sufficient for a one-quarter course on its own, or for a two-quarter sequence when supplemented by selected readings from the included references, current periodicals, and case study problems.

Finally, a significant share of credit for this material must go to my students and colleagues and to practitioners in local government with whom I have worked. The identification of problems to be addressed, the priorities for content, and many specific and useful suggestions have come from them. Errors and omissions are solely the responsibility of the author.

James C. Snyder

Part I:
Foundations

1

The Market System

This chapter presents a basic overview of the market system—the private sector of the U.S. economy. The emphasis is on "microeconomics," that part of the discipline of economics that deals with the behavior of individual decision-making units within the economy. An understanding of this "individual" economic behavior is prerequisite to the study of sound financial management practice. The market system, as presented, can be considered as classic in that it focuses on the attributes of a theoretical perfect market, which in reality does not exist. However, the classic construct has sufficient validity to warrant its use as a basis for an understanding of the functions of the private and the public sectors of our economy. The material is organized in the form of a review; some readers may want to refer to more complete economic texts.[1]

Economic Goals and Functions

All societies have goals relative to the quality of life of their members. One of the basic components of the quality of life is economic welfare, and thus all societies have basic economic goals. Economic goals include:

1. maximum income—a high level of wealth in goods and services, including the range of goods and services
2. equitable distribution of wealth—a "fair" distribution of goods and services among members of society.

Economic systems exist to provide mechanisms for the realization of these goals. The basic functions of an economic system include:

1. the allocation of resources
2. the selection of methods of production
3. the distribution of wealth
4. stabilization and growth

Allocation

Economic systems must provide a mechanism for the utilization of the resources of land, labor, and capital in the production of goods and services.[2] Because

3

these resources are limited, there exists a condition of "scarcity," which simply means that a society cannot have everything it wants at a given time. The system must make choices; it must allocate resources among competing demands. This leads to the concept of "cost." The cost of utilizing a resource for a particular use can be measured in terms of the benefit foregone by not using the resource in an alternate use (thus the term "opportunity cost"). For example, consider the resource of crude oil. If a society allocates more crude oil to the production of gasoline, less crude oil will be available for heating oil and other products. The "opportunity cost" of more gasoline is the benefit foregone by having less heating oil and fewer other products. (As discussed later, the opportunity cost may or may not be accurately measured by the dollar price of the respective products.)

At the state and local levels a governmental unit must allocate its limited resources to a variety of activities via the budget. If it increases the size of the public safety budget, then there is less in the budget for other activities. Within a given level of resources (or budget) the "real" cost, or opportunity cost, of allocating more resources to public safety activities is the benefit foregone by allocating less to other activities. The economic system must include a mechanism for allocating scarce resources among competing productive activities in such a way that the total benefit to society is maximized.

Production

An economic system must also provide a mechanism for selecting the best, or most efficient, methods of production. Usually there is a variety of alternative methods or techniques for producing a particular good or service, each with a different set of resource requirements. For example, within a given budget, police services can be provided via a heavy emphasis on police personnel (labor) with less emphasis on communications, transportation, and other equipment (capital), or by fewer police personnel and more equipment. Likewise, solid waste can be collected by one person with a sophisticated truck or by three people with a simple truck.

Efficiency in resource utilization is defined as the ratio of outputs to inputs; the most efficient method of production is that which yields the highest ratio or the greatest return per unit of utilized resources. Because the various resources (land, labor, and capital) can all be measured in common terms of cost (the dollar), alternative methods can be evaluated. Selection from among alternatives usually takes the form of maximizing the ratio of outputs to inputs, maximizing the output for a given cost (budget), or minimizing cost for a given level of benefit.[3]

Stabilization and Growth

Questions of stabilization and growth generally fall into the area of macro-economics (concern with the whole economy). Stabilization relates to the full utilization of resources, price stability, and the international balance of payments; growth relates to the rate of increase in productive capacity. Provision of these functions falls to the economy as a whole, with policy responsibility largely at the federal level. At the local government level, growth and stability fall into the area of urban and regional economics, with such concerns as the maintenance of an adequate economic base (quantity and mix of base employment industries), population and area growth, development and use of regional resources, and transportation. As such, these concerns fall outside the scope of this book but are discussed elsewhere.[4]

Distribution

The wealth, or goods and services, produced by a society must be distributed among its members. The basic economic goal involves an equitable distribution. Thus, "equity" must be defined. Equity has something to do with "fairness" or the relationship between one person's wealth relative to his effort and another person's wealth and effort. Equity generally does not require equality of wealth, but it does require that equal effort receive equal reward, and that unequal effort receive unequal reward (horizontal and vertical equity). However, what is fair to one person may not be fair to another, and thus the question requires a value judgment. The extent of equity may vary from extreme differences in wealth to absolute equality of waelth. Economic systems can affect distribution but they cannot make value judgments. Thus, the level of equity must be determined via the political system and affected in the economic system.

Economic Systems

Economic goals can be pursued in a variety of ways. The variations are often viewed on a continuum between the extremes of capitalism and socialism. However, the "isms" usually carry noneconomic connotations and perhaps a different terminology is appropriate. First, goods must be divided into private goods and public goods.[5] The private production of private goods is "capitalism"; the public production of private goods is "socialism." The public production of public goods is just one of the functions of government in either case.

Systems can also be differentiated by the primary decision mechanism: individual or central. A free market economy is defined as a system of markets where individual households and firms participate in market decisions and thus affect the allocation of resources. A central or planned economy is defined as an economy where allocation decisions are made by some central authority. Individual decisions are direct (e.g., you buy a candy bar; you eat it), but can lead to situations where a collection of "individual rational decisions" does not equal a "collective rational decision." For example, each individual's decision to use his or her land to best advantage may not produce the best collective land use pattern for a city, and each automobile driver's decision to keep his or her gas tank full may lead to an overall short-run gasoline shortage. Central decisions presumably reflect individual decisions through voting or some other process, but suffer from being indirect or removed from the individual. An individual may vote for a candidate who will not take office until next year, and who may subsequently change his or her mind on issues. Another major difference between market and central decisions involves "one person—one vote" and "one dollar—one vote." Voting systems assign equal weight to each voter, whereas the market system allows more votes to the rich than to the poor.

Most economic systems lie somewhere between the extremes of these dimensions. For instance, the United States economy is generally characterized as a capitalist-market economy. The majority of land and capital resources are owned and utilized by private individuals and groups, and markets exist where individual decisions affect the pattern of allocation. However, the U.S. economy is not pure in either sense. Substantial resources are owned and utilized by government and substantial economic decisions are made by government. The USSR is characterized as a socialist-central economy, although some private ownership and some markets exist, and many economic decisions are affected by individual decisions. Other countries (such as Yugoslavia) may lie somewhere between with different mixes of private and public production, ownership, and decision processes.

The Market System

The economy of the United States utilizes a mix of private and public sector components, relying heavily on the private production of private goods and the public production of public goods. Consider first the private sector. A simple model of the system (Figure 1-1) involves two categories of actors (households and business firms) and two categories of markets (the factor market and the product market).

A "household" is an individual or group of individuals with certain economic objectives as well as ownership of some resources of land, labor, and capital. A "business firm" is an organization with certain economic objectives, which is owned by an individual or group of individuals, and which transforms resources (factors of production) into products and services. The "factor market" is the mechanism whereby factors of production are exchanged for money;

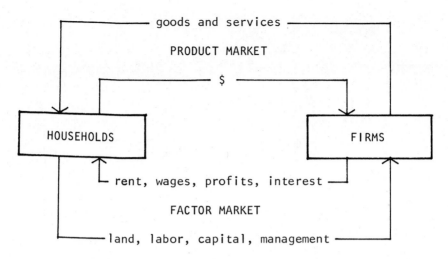

Figure 1-1. Simple Model of the Market System

the "product market" is the mechanism whereby goods and services are exchanged for money. Money is the medium of exchange, allowing for the measurement and holding of value.

The system operates as follows. Households and firms participate in both markets. The households sell their resources of land, labor, and capital to business firms in the factor markets, while receiving rent, wages, interest, and profits in return. The business firms transform these resources into goods and services, and sell these products to households in the product markets, thereby receiving money in return. In both markets, buyers exhibit a desire to buy, expressed as "demand," and sellers exhibit a desire to sell, expressed as "supply." Exchange between buyers and sellers requires that an exchange rate be agreed upon. That exchange rate is the "price" of the product or factor (e.g., its wage, rent, interest, or profit). A pure competitive market system has many buyers and sellers, none of which are powerful enough to control prices. Rather, prices are set as a result of the actions of all the buyers and sellers automatically and without outside or central intervention.

Market Functions

The market system (assuming perfect operation) provides for all of the previously identified economic functions. Allocation of resources is signaled by consumer demand. Firms produce those products and services which consumers are willing and able to buy. Society allocates its resources to the mix of uses that maximizes the welfare of households and the profits of firms. Methods of production are selected via the assignment of cost to every resource. The market sets the price of resources in a way that reflects the opportunity cost of the resources. Resources are utilized in mixes that reflect the productivity (that is, output per unit of input or cost) of each resource. Stabilization and growth are accomplished through several mechanisms. First, the market limits current consumption to current production. Second, the medium of money allows for the holding of value and for levels of consumption under production. Thus, savings and investment are possible. Third, the market affects the distribution of income and wealth, although there is always the question of the extent of equity. Resources, including labor, are simply rewarded in amounts relative to their productivity.

Conditions for a Perfect Market

This presentation of a classic market system assumes a "perfect competitive market." In reality such a market does not exist. However, as a theoretical concept, several conditions must be present:

1. many buyers and sellers in the markets
2. ease of entry and exit of firms
3. perfect information for buyers and sellers
4. perfect mobility of resources
5. maximization goals for households and firms relative to welfare and profits
6. absence of public goods and externalities

If these ideal conditions were to exist, a perfect competitive market system would perform all the required economic functions and achieve the basic economic goals of maximum welfare and equitable distribution, with the major condition that "equitable" is defined as "reward relative to productivity."[6]

Microeconomics

Microeconomics deals with the behavior of individual economic entities or decision making units such as the household or firm. Macroeconomics deals with the performance of economy as a whole and with aggregates of units. This demarcation is a matter of convenience only, and thus most economic problems, and certainly matters of public finance, have roots in both areas. However, the context here is one of laying the groundwork for individual public management decisions, and thus the material is weighted towards the "micro" aspects. This section does not attempt comprehensiveness, but rather attempts to review some of the more important basic principles of microeconomics. Those who have previously studied microeconomics may use the material as review; those without previous experience may use the material as a brief overview and guide to further study with other texts.[7]

Demand

"Demand" is the economic term applied to the amount of a good or service that a population desires to purchase in a given time period. The demand for a good or service may, or may not, equal the amount purchased. For instance, the population of a city may want to buy 100 electronic calculators per week when only 50 are available and sold. The demand is 100; the amount purchased is 50. The demand for a good or service depends on six interrelated factors:

1. population preferences,
2. population size,
3. population income,
4. distribution of income,
5. price of the good or service,
6. prices of other goods or services.

Changes in demand caused by changes in the preferences and tastes of the population are difficult to quantify. Preferences for particular goods vary in intensity and duration, and depend on a variety of personal and social factors (e.g., status, style, innovation, and bandwagon effects). This uncertainty is partially countered by, and to some extent controlled by, the mechanisms of advertising and public information. At best, changes in demand caused by changes in preference can be estimated from the interpolation of long-run trends in consumption (e.g., the current trend in recreational activities towards tennis and bicycling).

The size of the population is somewhat easier to estimate. Demand refers to the aggregate amount desired, and thus an increase in population (assuming constant rate of employment) leads to a corresponding increase in purchasing power and an increase in demand. The level of income and the distribution of income also affect demand. A low-income population spends much of its income on the basic necessities of life such as food, clothing, and shelter. A higher income population spends a smaller percentage of income on necessities and a higher percentage on nonessential goods and services. Although an increase in income yields a higher demand for most goods, some goods (i.e., inferior goods) may exhibit a lower demand. For instance, as incomes increase in a small town, the demand for central water and sewer systems may increase while the demand for wells and septic tanks may decrease. The distribution of income also affects demand; a city with a narrow range of income would exhibit different demands than a city with a wide range of income.

The price of a good or service, as well as the prices of other goods and services, affects demand. Because a variety of goods and services exist at any given time, households can satisfy their wants in a variety of ways. Each product has a price and gives a relative amount of satisfaction to the household. The household allocates its income among available products to achieve the highest level of satisfaction. If the price of a particular good is increased, then that good will be relatively less attractive in terms of benefit received per dollar spent, and so the household will shift expenditures away from that good to other goods. Likewise, a decrease in the price of a particular good will make that good relatively more attractive, and households will shift expenditures to that good and away from other goods. Thus, price changes lead to changes in demand and in the allocation of consumer dollars.

The prices of other goods and services also influence the demand for particular goods. If two goods are "substitutes," then an increase in the price of one will lead to an increase in demand for the other, and vice versa. If two goods are "complements," then an increase in the price of one will lead to a decrease in demand for the other, and vice versa. For example, an increase in the price of gasoline may lead to an increase in demand for mass transit (substitutes) and a decrease in demand for large automobiles (complements).

Demand Schedules and Curves. Demand schedules and curves show the relationship between the quantity desired in a given time period and the price of the good or service, with all other factors held constant. For example, consider a recreational park with an entrance fee. The quantity demanded is measured as the number of admissions per unit of time, and the price is measured as the admission fee. Table 1-1 and Figure 1-2 show such a schedule and curve.

The demand curve is constructed from the schedule and shows all of the price-quantity combinations at a given moment. The law of demand holds that the price and the quantity demanded are inversely related; the quantity demanded increases as price decreases, and decreases as price increases. This demand curve represents the demand of all persons for a particular good at a

Table 1-1
Demand Schedule

Price ($)	Quantity/Time
.50	1,000
1.00	800
1.50	600
2.00	400

PRICE

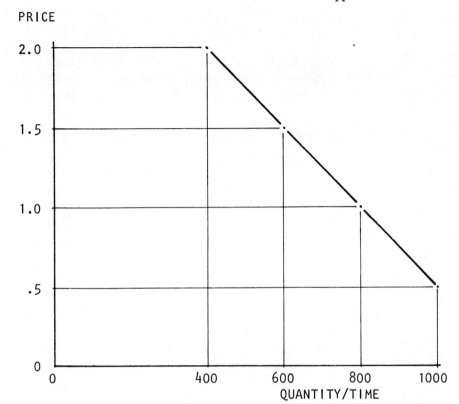

Figure 1–2. Demand Curve

particular time. It is downward sloping for several reasons. First, each good has "diminishing marginal utility." That is, the first unit of a good is valued more highly than successive units. Figures 1–3 and 1–4 show the relationships among quantity, total utility, and marginal utility for a typical good.

The total utility of a good is related positively to the quantity of the good; total utility increases with quantity. However, total utility increases at a diminishing rate; the utility contributed by successive units decreases with quantity. For example, a household may place relatively high values on initial quantities of water, automobiles, and money, and less value on subsequent quantities of those items. Four automobiles are valued at some level below four times the value of one automobile. An additional $100 of income means more to a poverty income family than to an executive who earns $400,000 per year.

Also, preferences and incomes vary among individuals, and thus some persons are willing to buy a product at a very high price, whereas some people will only buy at a lower price. In Figure 1–2, four hundred persons would buy tick-

12

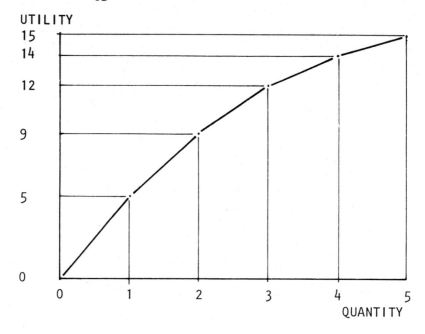

Figure 1-3. Total Utility

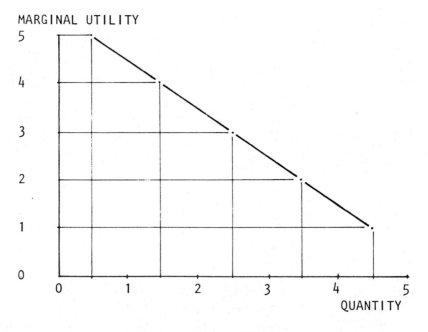

Figure 1-4. Marginal Utility

ets at $2.00, two hundred more at $1.50, two hundred more at $1.00, and so on. In a perfect market however, the price is fixed at one point. Buyers above that point buy at a price below what they were willing to pay, and buyers below that point do not buy.

The effects of factors other than price are shown as "shifts" in the demand curve. A shift to the right indicates an increase in demand; a shift to the left, a decrease. For example, an increase in preferences for a particular good can shift the curve to the right, and a decrease can shift the curve to the left. An increase or decrease in population size has a similar effect. Figure 1–5 shows some of the possibilities.

When referring to a "change" in demand, one must differentiate between "movement along" the demand curve (a change caused by price) and a "shift" in the demand curve (a change caused by some other factor). In reality, all factors are operating simultaneously and the demand curve is always moving. Demand functions can be estimated in a number of ways, most of which involve some empirical (historical or cross-sectional) observation of actual price-quantity combinations. That is, each observation can be represented by a single point on a demand graph (Figure 1–6). Each observation represents a quantity-price combination actually purchased, and therefore depends on the supply of goods as well as demand factors. Thus a series of observations from different time periods may form a series of points.

Statistical techniques can be utilized to identify, isolate, and quantify the effects of various factors, and thereby to estimate and project the demand function. In Figure 1–6, both supply and demand have increased in each time period, with price remaining relatively stable. Another way of showing these observations involves plotting the quantity purchased against time, as in Figure 1–7. Although this type of curve is sometimes called "demand," it actually shows the changes in the quantity produced and consumed. Such an approach is particularly useful in projecting long-run changes in demand.[8]

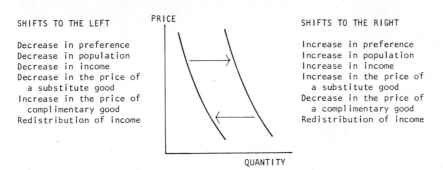

SHIFTS TO THE LEFT

Decrease in preference
Decrease in population
Decrease in income
Decrease in the price of
  a substitute good
Increase in the price of
  complimentary good
Redistribution of income

PRICE

SHIFTS TO THE RIGHT

Increase in preference
Increase in population
Increase in income
Increase in the price of
  a substitute good
Decrease in the price of
  a complimentary good
Redistribution of income

QUANTITY

Figure 1-5. Shifts in the Demand Curve

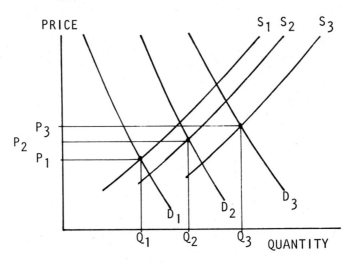

Figure 1-6. Demand as Price-Quantity Combinations

Supply

Supply is the economic term applied to the amount of a good or service that firms desire to sell in a given time period. As with demand, the amount actually

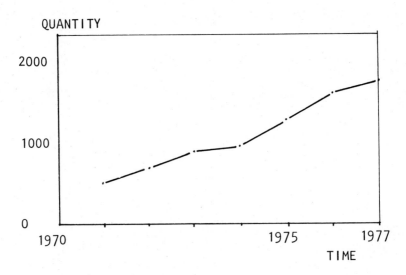

Figure 1-7. Demand over Time

sold may or may not equal the supply. For example, firms may want to sell 100 electronic calculators per week and yet only 50 are purchased. The "supply" is 100 while the "amount purchased" is 50.

The supply of a good or service depends on five interrelated factors:

1. goals of firms
2. state of technology
3. costs of the factors of production
4. price of the good or service
5. prices of other goods and services

Organizations are established and operated for a variety of reasons, but in the case of the firm there is assumed to be one dominant goal—profit maximization. The amount of a good supplied by a firm will depend on the profit derived from that good, and a firm will produce a mix of goods in such a way as to maximize profits. The amount supplied will also depend on the state of technology. More advanced technology allows more output from a given amount of resources. As technology is introduced, a greater quantity of output can be produced at a lower cost, and thus the production of that good or service becomes relatively more attractive. A decrease in the costs of the factors of production (land, labor, and capital) for a particular good will lead to an increase in the supply of that good. Likewise an increase in costs of factors will lead to a decrease in supply. Finally, the price of a good and the prices of other goods affect supply. An increase in the price of a good, all other things being equal, will lead to an increase in supply. That is, an increase in the price of a good will increase the profitability of that good relative to other goods, and firms will shift production efforts to that good. Likewise, a decrease in the price of a good will lead to a decrease in the supply.

Supply Schedules and Curves. Supply schedules and curves show the relationship between the quantity supplied in a given time period and the price of the good, all other factors held constant. For example, consider the number of taxi-hours of service in a city relative to the fare rate. Table 1–2 and Figure 1–8 show the supply schedule and curve.

The supply curve is constructed from the supply schedule and shows all of the price-quantity combinations at a given time. The curve represents the total quantity of a particular good that will be supplied by all firms. The law of supply holds that quantity supplied is directly related to price; an increase in price will lead to an increase in supply, and a decrease in price will lead to a decrease in supply.[9] As with demand, one must differentiate between a change in supply (shift of the supply curve) and a change in the quantity caused by a change in price (movement along the supply curve). Problems of observation and estimation of supply are similar to those discussed under the section on Demand and therefore are not repeated here.

Table 1–2
Supply Schedule

Fare Rate	Taxi-hours
$1.00	1,000
2.00	1,500
3.00	2,000
4.00	2,500

Elasticity

The previous two sections have reviewed the theoretical base for changes in supply and demand in terms of increases and decreases. "Elasticity" provides a

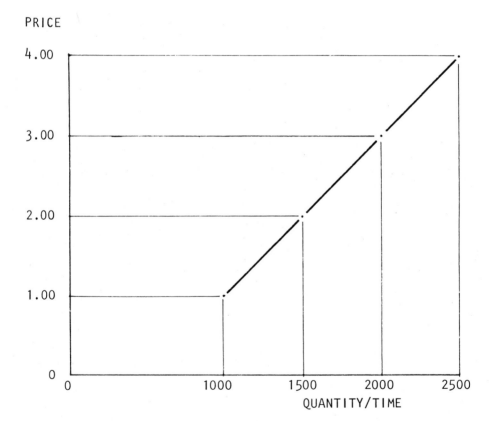

Figure 1–8. Supply Curve

measure of relative quantity of change, or responsiveness of change in one factor relative to a change in another factor. The price elasticity of demand is defined as the percentage change in quantity demanded, divided by the percentage change in the price. Graphically it is simply the slope of the demand curve at a single point on the curve, or between two points on the curve.[10]

Other common elasticity measures are income elasticity of demand and price elasticity of supply. If the elasticity is less than 1.0, the demand (or supply) is relatively "inelastic," and if the elasticity is greater than 1.0, it is relatively "elastic." Demand curves with different elasticities are shown in Figure 1-9.

Price elasticities are important because they indicate changes in total expenditure. Price elasticities of demand of 1.0 or "unity" will leave total expenditures unchanged regardless of a change in price. However, if the elasticity is less than 1.0, a rise in price will increase total expenditure, while a decrease in price will decrease total expenditures. Likewise, if the elasticity is greater than 1.0, a rise in price will decrease total expenditure, while a decrease in price will increase total expenditure. Thus, if the demand for gasoline is relatively price-inelastic, a percentage increase in price will result in a smaller percentage decrease in the amount demanded, and in a larger total expenditure for gasoline.

Price and Market Dynamics

The determinants of supply and demand have been reviewed with emphasis on the quantity demanded and supplied relative to price and other factors. When supply and demand are considered together, "price" is the common element that provides the mechanism for agreement and exchange between buyers and sellers. Buyers and sellers form the market. Exchange will take place if both buyer and seller are able to receive more in value than they relinquish. Firms will sell only

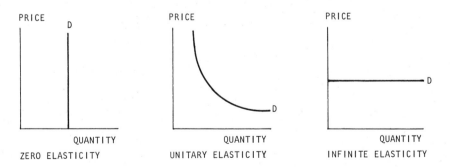

Figure 1-9. Elasticity

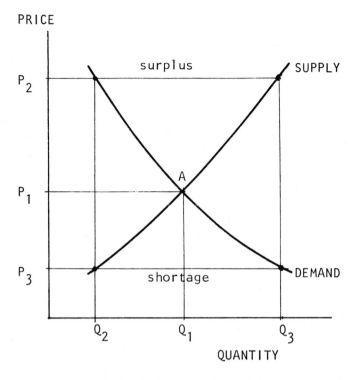

PRICE

P₂

surplus   SUPPLY

A

P₁

P₃   shortage   DEMAND

Q₂   Q₁   Q₃

QUANTITY

Figure 1-10. Determination of Price

if price exceeds the cost of factors, and households will buy only if value received exceeds price. Thus in every transaction, there is a net increase in value. Price is determined by the intersection of the supply and demand curves (Figure 1-10). At this point (A) the quantity demanded equals the quantity supplied, and the price is determined. Factor prices (wages, rents, and interest) are determined similarly in the factor markets. P_1 and Q_1 represent the price and quantity "equilibrium." If the price were at P_2, the quantity demanded (Q_2) would fall short of the quantity supplied (Q_3) and a surplus would exist. The price would fall, profits would fall, and eventually firms would leave the market until equilibrium was restored. If the price were at P_3, a shortage would exist, prices would rise, firms would enter the market, and again equilibrium would be restored. Similar dynamics take place if the quantity moves away from equilibrium. This situation is called a "stable equilibrium" because market forces automatically tend to seek the equilibrium point.[11] The important aspect of the system is that it is self-correcting, a factor that forms one of the classical arguments for minimum government involvement in the market economy.

Consider again the statement that there is a net increase in value for every transaction. Assume a market situation as shown in Figure 1-11. The supply and demand curves are given, with price at P_1 and quantity at Q_1. Notice that Q_2 quantity would have been produced at a price as low as P_2, but because the price is set at P_1 for all units of the good, every unit up to Q_1 receives revenue above that which is required for its production. At Q_2, the amount of the price up to P_2 is termed "transfer payment," because that amount is necessary to transfer resources from other uses to production of this good. The amount between P_1 and P_2 is termed "economic rent," and is that amount received in price that exceeds transfer earnings. This economic rent represents positive value to the producer. Notice also that at Q_2 some persons were willing to pay a price as high as P_3 for the good, and yet they actually purchase the good for P_1. Thus, at quantities up to Q_1, there is a net positive value for both the producer and consumer.

Considering the market system as a whole, all the individual markets and factors are interrelated through the price mechanism. In other words, factor prices (i.e., land, labor, and capital) are determined across all industries, and product costs are directly dependent on factor prices. Thus, all factor prices are relative to productivity, and all product prices are relative to costs. All resources are allocated in accordance with marginal principles,[12] and each is utilized in the most productive way. The net benefit to society is maximum.

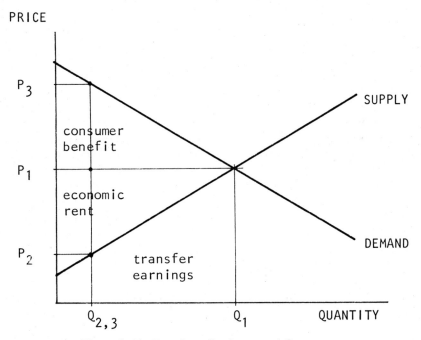

Figure 1-11. Benefit to Producers and Consumers

It is important here to remind the reader that all of the above is true in the theoretical perfect market that does not exist in reality. However, a market system, even with its imperfections, captures many of the inherent benefits of the perfect market, and thus forms the cornerstone of the U.S. economic system.

Cost

The term "cost" in an economic context refers to "opportunity cost." Opportunity cost is a measure of value foregone by not using a resource in its best alternate use. For example, the opportunity cost of using land for an airport is the benefit foregone by not using the land for its next best use—such as residential or industrial development. Of course, the measurement of such costs involves both objective and subjective factors, and will vary among individuals and groups (i.e., each will have different alternative uses). In a theoretical perfect market economy, the opportunity cost of utilizing a resource is measured by its price. The price of a factor of production reflects the "real" cost of utilizing the resource. For a variety of reasons actual markets are not perfect, and therefore, differences between "cash" costs and "opportunity" costs often exist. One dimension of difference involves who pays the costs—both private and social costs. Private costs accrue to the individual or firm involved in the transaction; social costs involve society as a whole. The differences between private and social costs and between cash and opportunity costs are extremely important to public sector management and planning; decisions at the local government level involve both cash costs (financial feasibility) and social costs (economic desirability).[13]

Firms exist to realize profit. Profit is the difference between total revenue and total cost. Cost to the firm involves the cost of all the factors of production—land, labor, and capital—all measured in a common unit of value—the dollar. The dollar cost, all things being equal, is the appropriate measure of "opportunity" cost for the firm. However, because markets are imperfect, the dollar cost may not reflect the "opportunity cost to society." For instance, a firm may treat clean air as a free factor in its manufacturing process. Using clean air and producing polluted air constitutes the use of a resource with an associated opportunity cost. However, in this case, the cost is borne by all those who have an alternate use for the clean air (that is, breathing). In this case, the loss of the clean air is part of the social cost.

Profits. The term "profit" has a different meaning to businessmen and economists. Both count profits as the difference between total revenues and total costs, but each counts costs in a different way. The businessman or accountant includes the costs of the factors of production, but excludes the cost of his own capital and risk-taking. The economist includes the cost of this capital and risk as a cost. That is, the return on investment is "profit" to the accountant, whereas "normal" return on investment is "cost of production" to the economist. "Normal" profits are returns required to obtain investors. This text generally uses the economist's terminology of normal profits as a cost. Thus, a firm with total revenues that equal economic costs receives a normal profit.

Costs and Production. There are three time frames for economic conditions: the short run, the long run, and the very long run. The short run refers to situations where most factors of production are fixed and labor might be variable. The long run refers to situations where all factors can be changed except the state of technology. The very long run refers to situations where changes of technology are included. Of course, these time frames vary among industries and firms and really represent a convenient way of stating a set of assumptions about factors for a particular economic situation.

Total cost is generally divided into two parts: fixed cost and variable cost. Fixed costs are sometimes called "overhead" costs and involve costs that do not vary with output. Variable costs are sometimes called "direct" costs and vary directly with output. Average cost is the total cost divided by the number of units of output. Marginal cost is the incremental cost associated with producing one more unit. Table 1-3 and Figures 1-12 and 1-13 show a typical short-run cost schedule and curves.

The cost schedule shows quantity produced, fixed cost, and variable cost as "given," as well as total cost, average fixed cost, average variable cost, average total cost, and marginal cost as "calculated figures."

Q = quantity produced in a given time period

FC = costs that do not vary with output

VC = direct costs that vary with output

TC = total cost = $FC + VC$

AFC = average fixed cost = $\dfrac{FC}{Q}$

AVC = average variable cost = $\dfrac{VC}{Q}$

$ATC = \dfrac{FC + VC}{Q}$

MC = marginal cost = $\dfrac{\Delta TC}{\Delta Q}$

where Δ indicates "the change in"

Table 1-3
Cost Schedule

Q	FC	VC	TC	AFC	AVC	ATC	MC
0	0	0	0	–	–	–	–
100	1,000	400	1,400	10.00	4.00	14.00	14.0
200	1,000	600	1,600	5.00	3.00	8.00	2.2
300	1,000	700	1,700	3.30	2.30	5.60	1.0
400	1,000	750	1,750	2.50	1.80	4.30	.5
500	1,000	800	1,800	2.00	1.60	3.60	.5
600	1,000	900	1,900	1.66	1.50	3.16	1.0
700	1,000	1,100	2,100	1.42	1.57	2.99	2.0
800	1,000	1,400	2,400	1.25	1.75	3.00	3.0

The marginal figure (14 for a quantity of 100) is the incremental cost per unit associated with an increase from 0 to 100 units, and the following marginal figure (2 for a quantity of 200) is associated with the increase from 100 to 200 units. The marginal figure occurs "between" the input increments, rather than at the input increments. This relationship is shown graphically in Figure 1-13. Figure 1-12 shows the relationship between total cost and quantity of output. Total cost increases with output; it is the sum of the fixed cost and the variable cost, and it takes the form of the variable cost curve. Figure 1-13 shows the relationship among average and marginal figures. Average fixed cost decreases with an increase in output, whereas the average variable cost curve takes the shape of a U. This U shape is based on the assumption of eventually diminishing

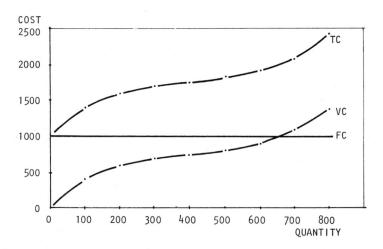

Figure 1-12. Total Cost, Variable Cost, Fixed Cost

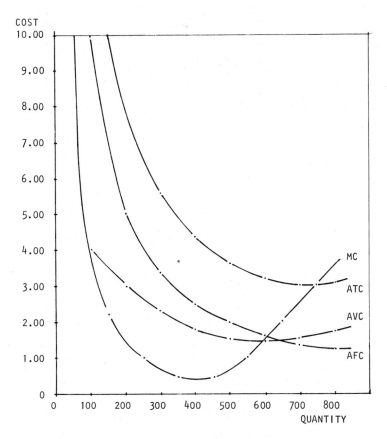

Figure 1-13. Average and Marginal Cost

productivity caused by constraints on the supply of resources. If the *AVC* rises faster than the *AFC* falls, then the *ATC* will rise (as with Figure 1-13). The *MC* curve exhibits an important relationship with the *ATC* curve. When the *MC* is less than the *ATC*, the *ATC* is falling, and when the *MC* is greater than the *ATC*, the *ATC* is rising. The *MC* curve crosses the *ATC* curve at the lowest point on the *ATC* curve; *ATC* is minimum where *MC* equals *ATC*.

Long-Run Cost Curves. In the long run, firms can alter their methods of production and mix of resources to exhibit a variety of cost curve shapes. Average cost curves may be downward sloping (economies of scale), horizontal (constant returns), or upward sloping (diseconomies of scale). However, even in the long run, the cost curve may typically be U shaped because of initial economies of scale

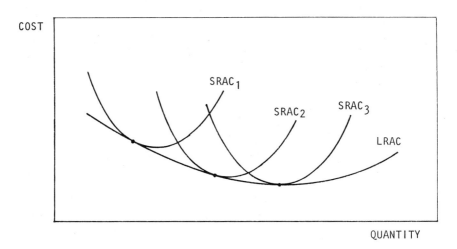

Figure 1-14. Long-Run Average Cost Curves

and eventually diminishing resources. Figure 1-14 shows the relationship between short-run and long-run curves. Here the short-run curves represent average cost pictures with land and capital fixed, and with labor the only variable (for example, a particular plant size). However, with long-run changes (such as a larger plant), the short-run cost curve shifts further along the long-run cost curve. The long-run curve is composed of a series of possible short-run curves. Therefore, a given firm could be operating at a low point of a short-run cost curve, as well as on the downward sloping portion of the long-run cost curve.

Market Structure

The structure of markets varies along dimensions that include the number of buyers and sellers, product characteristics, and ease of entry and exit of firms. Pure competition and pure monopoly are the extremes, with oligopoly and monopolistic competition in between.[14] The following sections briefly examine the extremes. The firm is assumed to be a "profit maximizer"; it will choose to produce if its total revenues exceed its total variable cost, and it will expand output so long as its marginal revenue exceeds its marginal cost, to a point where marginal revenue equals marginal cost (where profit is maximum).

Perfect Competition. Perfect competition in a market depends on two crucial factors. First, the individual firms must be "price takers" rather than "price setters." Second, the market must allow freedom of entry and exit of firms. The "price-taking" factor relates to the amount of power that an individual firm has in the market. If there are many buyers and sellers, if none have a large share of the market, and if products are identical, then each firm must sell its product at the prevailing market price. It must "take" the price. Entry and exit relate to the ease with which firms can enter into production of goods in markets where profits exist, and the ease with which they can cease production in markets where losses exist. Although perfect competition does not exist in reality, some of its characteristics exist to the extent that one refers to a "competitive market."

Consider the demand and supply curves for a particular product in a competitive market (Figures 1-15 and 1-16). The demand curve represents the relationship between the quantity demanded and the price for the entire market. The supply curve represents the relationship between quantity supplied and price for the entire market. The individual firm in the market has control over the quantity it will produce, but has no control over the price. It must sell at the prevailing market price—in this example, at P_1.

Therefore, the market demand curve is meaningless to the individual firm. The firm sees only a "horizontal' demand curve, where the prevailing market price equals the average revenue and the marginal revenue. That is, each and every unit must be sold at the market price, which is the average revenue to the firm, as well as the marginal revenue (price received for each additional unit sold).

The firm can not adjust price, but it can adjust the quantity of output in such a way as to maximize its profits. Profit maximization occurs where the marginal cost equals the marginal revenue. More specifically, the firm is doing as well as it can at this point. Whether or not the firm is actually making a profit depends on the position of the average cost curve. Figures 1-17, 1-18, and 1-19 show the position of the firm under three conditions: excess profits, loss, and

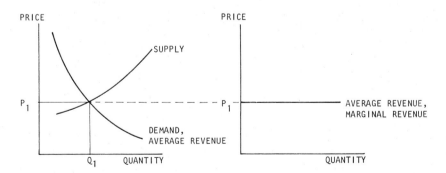

Figure 1-15. Market Supply and Demand

Figure 1-16. Demand for the Individual Firm

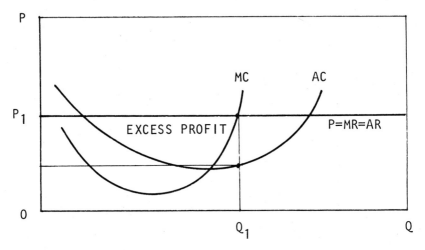

Figure 1-17. More than Normal Profits

normal profits (recall that normal profits are included in the computation of cost). In Figure 1-17, the firm has chosen to produce at a quantity (Q_1) that equates marginal revenue with marginal cost. Profit is maximized at this point. Up to the point where *MR* equals *MC*, the revenue from selling an additional unit exceeds the cost of producing the additional unit; therefore, profit is increased. Beyond that point the cost of producing an additional unit exceeds the revenue from that unit, and profits are diminished. It follows, then, that profits

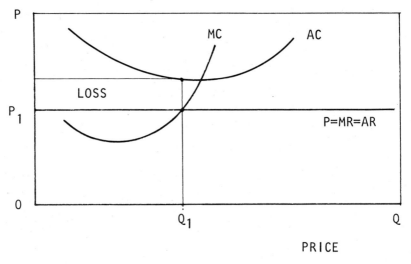

PRICE

Figure 1-18. Loss

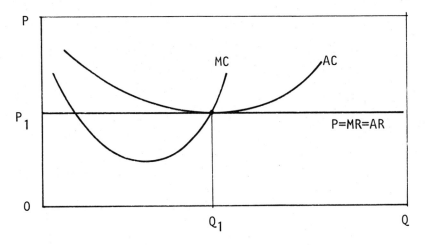

Figure 1-19. Normal Profits

are maximized at the point where *MR* equals *MC,* or where the net marginal contribution to profit is zero. In Figure 1-18, equating *MR* with *MC* minimizes losses. In the long run, the firm would either reduce costs or leave the market; in the short run, the firm would continue to produce if the price was greater than the average variable costs. In other words, producing and selling some quantity of goods at a given loss may be preferable to selling none and absorbing losses due to heavy fixed costs. In Figure 1-19 the firm is realizing only normal profits, and consumers are paying only the cost of the last unit produced and the lowest short-run average cost of production.

If firms are making excess profits (more than normal) in a market, then additional firms will enter the market, the supply will increase, and the price will fall (the law of supply). As the price falls, profits will fall, and an equilibrium of normal profits will be sought. If firms are operating at a loss, they will leave the market, the supply will fall, and the price will rise. As price rises, profits will rise, and again an equilibrium will be sought. The most efficient firms stay in the market; the least efficient firms leave the market.

Profits to an individual firm can be increased by lowering production costs. Where long-run economies of scale exist, the firm may expand output, and thus move to a lower part of the long-run cost curve. In a long-run equilibrium, the firm produces where prices equals marginal cost, short-run average cost, and long-run average cost (Figure 1-20). This equilibrium reflects a "social optimum" where consumers pay a price that equals only the cost of the last unit produced (price equals marginal cost) and the lowest possible average cost of production. There are only normal profits in the market. This "social optimum" is obtained automatically in a theoretically perfect and competitive market.

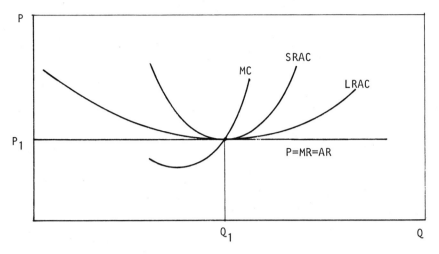

Figure 1-20. Long-Run Equilibrium for the Firm

Such markets do not exist, yet many of the characteristics of perfect markets do exist. Thus, the United States tends to rely heavily on a market system and the mechanism of competition. Where the market system fails, it depends on the public sector to regulate the market and to produce goods and services.

Monopoly. Monopoly is a market structure with only one producer and many buyers. Monopolies can develop in several ways. First, where significant economies of scale exist, the first firm to enter the market and expand the scale of production will realize the lowest costs of production. That firm can therefore sell its product at the lowest price and effectively drive less efficient firms out of the market. These are called "natural" monopolies. Second, monopolies can exist where there are barriers to the entry of additional firms to a market. For example, a local government may charter a utility as a monopoly, effectively prohibiting competition.

The demand curve for the entire market is the effective demand curve for the monopolistic firm. The monopolist is not a price taker (as in a competitive situation) but rather a "price setter." Given the demand curve, it can operate at any quantity-price combination. To maximize profits, it will follow the same rule of equating marginal cost with marginal revenue. Consider the situation in Figure 1-21.

Given these curves and a "single price" structure, the monopolist will produce at Q_1 quantity and P_1 price. At this point ($MR = MC$), the monopolist is doing as well as can be done. As with the competitive situation, nothing ensures that profits will be realized. That situation depends on the position of the average cost curve. However, if profits are not realized, then the monopolist will cease production. Therefore, functioning monopolists are assumed to be making profits. In Figure 1-21 profits are obtained. Because the monopolistic firm can select price-quantity combinations, it can effectively restrict quantity to increase price and profits. If in addition the monopolist can use "price discrimination" (charge different prices to different consumers), then profits can be further increased. That is, every purchaser can be charged the maximum amount that he or she is willing to pay. In addition, the price-discriminating monopolist will produce a higher quantity—up to the point where the price equals the marginal cost.

Monopoly versus Competition. The classical argument against monopoly is that the theoretical effects of monopoly are at variance with the "social optimum" of the competitive situation. The social optimum allows the consumer to purchase a good at the cost of producing the last unit and the lowest possible average cost, with only normal profits in the market. The monopoly can be expected to restrict output to increase price. There is less consumer benefit and more producer profit. However, there are some strong arguments in favor of monopolies. The previous arguments assume that the monopolizing of a competitive

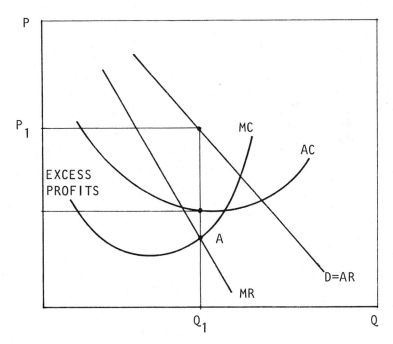

Figure 1-21. Monopoly Pricing

industry would leave the cost curves unchanged. However, some industries may exhibit economies of scale whereby a single producer or even a few large producers can function with lower average costs than a larger number of small firms. This is often the case with capital-heavy enterprises such as space travel, automobile manufacturing, electric power, and water supply. For example, it is usually more efficient to operate a single water supply system in a given area than to have competing, overlapping systems. In such cases, cost savings can lead to lower prices and more consumer benefit than would be generated by a competitive situation. Another argument for monopolies involves excess profits and the rate of innovation. It may be that the availability of excess profits allows for higher research expenditures, and thus for an increase level of technology and lower long-run costs.

Summary

An understanding of basic microeconomic structure is prerequisite to the study of public sector economics and financial management and planning in local government.

Basic economic goals include the maximization of wealth and an equitable distribution of wealth. Basic economic system functions include the allocation of scarce resources among activities, the selection of methods of production, the distribution of wealth, and the provision of stabilization and growth. The United States relies on a mixed private-public economic system to perform these functions, with an emphasis on private production of private goods and services and on the public production of public goods and services.

The private sector operates through a series of markets where households sell the factors of production (land, labor, and capital) to firms in exchange for wages, rents, profits, and interest. The firms transform these factors into goods and services that are sold to households. Money is the medium of exchange that allows for the measurement and holding of value.

The demand for goods and services is a function of population preferences, population size, the level and distribution of income, and the prices of goods and services. The supply of goods and services is a function of the goals of firms, the state of technology, the costs of factors of production, and the prices of goods and services. Price is the common element in supply and demand; it is the mechanism for agreement to exchange. Buyers purchase if the value received exceeds price, and producers sell if the price exceeds cost. Thus, there is a net increase in value for every transaction. A theoretically perfect market system is characterized by pure competition: many buyers and sellers, freedom of entry and exit of firms, perfect information, complete mobility of resources, maximization goals for all households and firms, and the absence of public goods. Under such conditions, the market system performs all the required economic functions. Scarce resources are allocated among competing demands in such a way that the total wealth is maximized; the most efficient methods of production are selected; wealth is distributed to the owners of factors of production relative to the productivity of factors; and stabilization and growth are facilitated through the mechanism of money (for savings and investment) and because consumption is limited to production. Supply equals demand in an equilibrium that is automatically created by the independent actions of households and firms. In addition, the long-run equilibrium creates a "social optimum" whereby consumers purchase products at the lowest average cost, and firms realize only normal profits.

Such perfect markets do not exist in reality. Upon scrutiny, every condition for such a market is violated. However, much of the United States economy is characterized by markets with many buyers and sellers, easy entry and exit of firms, and other conditions that approximate competition. Therefore, the theoretical structure does hold significant value in terms of understanding economic behavior.

The theoretical monopoly construct is of interest because it illustrates the differences in economic behavior under varying conditions. For example, the monopolizing of a competitive industry might be expected to lead to restricted output and higher prices, with less benefit to consumers and more profit to the monopolist.

An understanding of microeconomic behavior is necessary to the further consideration of the role of the public sector of the economy and to fiscal management and planning. In many ways, governmental units are monopolists attempting to create the beneficial attributes of a perfect competitive market. That is the subject of Chapter 2.

Notes

1. There is always a danger in providing such a brief presentation of such an extensive subject area; many readers will want to refer to additional materials to fill in the voids. Any number of basic economic texts are currently available; one which I have found to be particularly readable and useful is Richard G. Lipsey and Peter O. Steiner, *Economics* (New York: Harper and Row, 1966).

2. Economists vary on the classification of resources or factors of production; some include a fourth term of "management" or "enterprise" as a factor which coordinates land, labor, and capital.

3. The task of evaluation is addressed specifically in Chapter 11, Program Evaluation.

4. Several excellent texts cover this area, for example, Wilbur Thompson, *A Preface to Urban Economics* (Baltimore: The Johns Hopkins Press, 1965);

James Heilbrun, *Urban Economics and Public Policy* (New York: St. Martin's Press, 1974); and Werner Z. Hirsch, *Urban Economic Analysis* (New York: McGraw-Hill, 1973).

5. Private goods are purchased and consumed by individuals, with most of the benefit accruing to the individuals; public goods are collectively purchased with most of the benefit being indivisible and collectively consumed. Once a "public good" is provided no one can be excluded from its use. For example, an automobile is a private good; public safety is a public good. Public goods are specifically addressed in Chapter 2, The Public Sector.

6. The reader must temporarily take this on faith; a more complete explanation is forthcoming.

7. Lipsey and Steiner, *Economics.*

8. The actual estimation and projection of demand can involve rather complex multivariate statistical analysis; estimation and projection in the context of this text are covered in Chapter 4, Fiscal Management and Planning.

9. The upward slope of the supply curve is based on the assumption of increasing per unit costs in the short run. That is, the entire market supply is the summation of the quantities supplied by individual firms, and the supply curve for an individual firm is identical to its marginal cost curve. The firm, in attempting to maximize profits, equates marginal cost with market price (marginal revenue) and in so doing, exhibits an upward sloping supply curve. Most short-run cost curves are thought to be eventually upward sloping, where increases in demand may bid up the costs of factors and/or where land and capital are fixed. Long-run cost curves may take any shape, including a downward slope, because of economies of scale, new technology, and the like.

10. Elasticity can be calculated as "point" or "arc" elasticity. The point method uses the first derivative of calculus to determine the slope of the demand curve at a single point. The arc method uses the slope between two points on the curve; percentage change is calculated as the difference between the figures, divided by the average of the figures. For example, if a price change of 60 cents to 40 cents per unit yielded an increase in quantity demanded of 100 to 130 units per day, the price elasticity would be calculated as:

$$\frac{\dfrac{130 - 100}{115}}{\dfrac{60 - 40}{50}} = \frac{0.26}{0.4} = 0.65$$

Arc elasticities are relatively convenient to use because only two points on the demand curve, rather than the entire curve, are needed.

11. A stable equilibrium may be the typical case, yet conditions can exist whereby an unstable equilibrium exists and/or where there is no automatic correction.

12. Marginal principles are covered in detail in Chapter 12, Marginal Analysis.

13. Cost concepts are discussed later in this chapter and in Chapter 10, Structuring the Analysis.

14. Oligopoly is a situation with a few powerful firms, each with market power over price, but without monopoly power, such as with the automobile industry. Monopolistic competition is a situation with many firms, but with some product differentiation, leading to some control of market prices.

2

The Public Sector

Chapter 1 presented the basic economic goals and functions of society, as well as the mechanics of the classic market system on which the United States places heavy reliance. It demonstrated that a theoretically perfect market would satisfy economic goals and functions and would additionally create a "social" optimum whereby resources would be optimally allocated and the level of economic welfare would be maximized.[1] However, such a perfect market does not actually exist, and therefore society cannot rely exclusively on a market mechanism.

Where the market system fails to provide a mechanism for achieving certain economic goals, or where the market performance is unacceptable, society turns to government—the public sector of the economy. The reliance on a public-private economy has its roots in early economic history. Adam Smith, who was generally considered to be an advocate of minimal government activity, identified justifiable categories of government allocational activity in his *Wealth of Nations* (1776), including the provision of national defense and "desirable public institutions and public works that are of a nature that they fail to return a profit, and would therefore be undersupplied."[2] Economic thought and practice have developed from that minimum but positive public involvement in allocational activity to today's vastly expanded scope of public economic activity. The question is not one of justifying public economic activity, but rather is one of determining the appropriate mix of private and public activity. When should the public sector get involved? How should it behave when involved? An understanding of the rationale for public sector economic activity is important to the process of financial management and planning.

Collective Consumption and Public Goods

A perfect market requires that all the benefits of an economic transaction accrue to the buyer and seller, with everyone else being excluded (the "exclusion principle"). Goods that are so produced and consumed are "divisible" in that the supply can be subdivided into increments that can be sold to individuals. They are "private goods." However, some goods and services are not divisible, and therefore must be consumed collectively. That is, once a collective consumption good is supplied, it is consumed equally by more than one person. If, in addition, no one can be excluded from consuming a collective consumption good, it is termed a "public good." For example, an ice cream cone is primarily a

35

private good, with the benefit accruing to the individual consumer. A music concert is a collective consumption good, but one for which exclusion can be enforced. National defense is primarily a public good, collectively consumed, from which no one can be excluded. The fact that a good or service is "public" does not imply that everyone wants or values the good at the same level, but that no one can be excluded from its effects, positive or negative. One person may view an effect as a public good, while another person views it as a public evil (for example, the smoker of fine cigars).

Actually, few if any goods are purely public or private; most lie on a continuum between the extremes, with some benefit accruing to the buyer and some to a larger group or to society as a whole. For example, emergency medical care provides direct benefits for those individuals who must utilize it, but it also provides benefits to nonusers in such terms as peace of mind, lower insurance costs, or fewer productivity losses. Likewise, education benefits the individual in terms of self-satisfaction, higher potential earnings, and better working conditions, while benefiting society in terms of having a more educated voting population and a more productive labor force. These mixed goods are generally termed "quasi-public goods" if they are supplied primarily by the public sector, and "quasi-private goods" if provided by the private sector. Goods for which private consumption yields substantial public benefits are called "merit goods" (such as higher education).

The market cannot effectively supply public goods because firms cannot exact a price for each unit of benefit. Once supplied, no one can be excluded from the benefits. Payment would have to be voluntary; some consumers would be "free riders." That is, some individuals would find it advantageous to conceal their demand for a particular public good, knowing that they cannot be excluded from the benefits of the good when it is supplied. Because of the necessity of voluntary payment and free riders, the revenue to producing firms would be artificially low. Thus, the good would be undersupplied or unsupplied. In such situations, the public sector assumes production of the public good or service and exacts a price from consumers in the form of taxation. Government may actually produce and supply the good or service, or it may otherwise affect the private production of the good via techniques covered later in this chapter. In the case of merit goods (such as public health and education), the government may force certain levels of individual consumption.

Distribution

The public sector is involved with the distribution, as well as the supply, of public and quasi-public goods and services. It is also involved with the distribution of private goods and services. Society has a goal of an equitable distribution of wealth, but it is not assured that a market economy would yield an equitable situation. The market system rewards factors of production relative to their levels of productivity. Units of land, labor, and capital receive rent, wages, interest, and profit in amounts that reflect the relative contribution of each unit to the total wealth. However, the object of equity is not the units of a resource but rather the persons in society. Therefore, the market distribution of wealth to persons depends on the pattern of ownership of resources. For example, an equal distribution to persons can result only from an equal ownership of resources of equal productivity. In reality, resources are not equally held, and productivity varies among units of a resource. One's view of equity must start with a value judgment of the existing pattern of ownership of resources. Resolution of conflicting values must be accomplished in the political system; once a determination is made, the desired state of equity can be affected by public sector economic activity.[3]

Although the question of equity cannot be settled here, some areas where the market mechanism appears unsatisfactory can be identified. Some persons may control so few resources that total market rewards fall below a subsistence level. For example, a person may own no land or capital and possess only marginal, unskilled labor. Wages may be less than that required to survive. The society that guarantees adequate necessities of life can redistribute wealth through various public sector techniques to achieve some equity goal. Redistributive techniques may involve direct transfers from some groups to others (various welfare programs) or may be affected by differential incidences in public program benefits and costs. That is, a program may provide substantial benefits only to disadvantaged persons while being financed through general tax revenues. Because the incidences of benefits and costs are rarely identical, public sector programs will have some net distributional impact.

The estimation of the distributional impact of public programs is important to the planner and manager because implicit and explicit distributional goals and/or constraints will always exist in local government. The estimation of impact for particular fiscal actions must include the existing state of distribution, the probable impact of the particular action, and the desired state of distribution. Normally, the task of program evaluation will include a distributional impact component.[4] The objects of impact are generally groups of persons identified by geographic area, sex, age, race, or family income level.

Market Failure

The previously discussed rationale for public sector activity (public goods, distribution) are primarily derived from the inability of the market system to affect certain economic functions. Additional rationales exist because of imperfections in real world market systems. All the conditions for a perfect market are violated to some extent, including:

1. fewer than "many" buyers and sellers
2. restrictions to the entry and exit of firms
3. imperfect information for producers and consumers
4. constraints on the mobility of resources
5. nonmaximizing behavior
6. the existence of "public goods" and externalities

These conditions can lead to a suboptional market performance. Two important factors, natural monopolies and externalities, are discussed in the following sections.

Natural Monopolies

In industrialized economies, technology and specialization often lead to significant economies of scale, where average costs of production decrease as the scale of production increases. In these cases, large firms are more efficient than small firms, and with limited demand the small firms are priced out of the market. The market then relies on one or a few large firms with decreasing average cost curves. It is not essential that the long-run average cost curve be forever decreasing in these situations, but only that the relevant range of production falls within the downward sloping part of the cost curve.

These "natural monopolies" violate the conditions for a perfect market, and therefore the social optimum is not assured. However, this is not necessarily an undesirable condition. If the gains to society from the economies of scale (lower costs, greater efficiency) exceed the higher prices normally associated with monopolies, then society is better off. When such conditions exist, society can respond by allowing the monopoly production to exist (to capture the economies of scale) and by assuming public ownership or regulation of price. For example, the production of electric power, water, and many other capital-heavy products clearly exhibit economies of scale. Government generally assumes ownership (the public utility) and/or regulates service prices via a public service commission. The benefits of lower costs are obtained without the problems of higher prices.

However, there is a problem with the achievement of the social optimum where average costs are decreasing. There can be no profit at this point (price equals marginal cost). Consider Figure 2-1. Point A identifies the "social optimum" ($MC = AR$), where the price paid equals the marginal cost of producing the last unit of the good. However, at this point, the average cost exceeds the average revenue and the producer, whether public or private, will show a loss. Competitive firms would not enter production. A profit-maximizing monopolist would produce at point B, where marginal cost equals marginal revenue, with price P_2, and with more than normal profits. The government can allow the

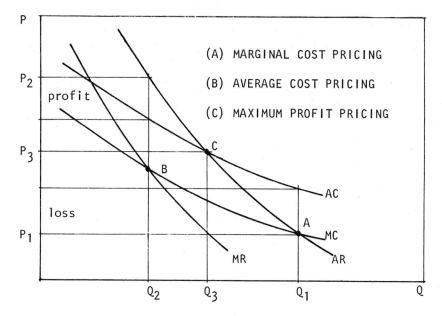

Figure 2-1. Decreasing Average Total Costs

monopoly to exist publicly or privately by setting the price at point *C*, where the price equals the average cost. Here, only normal profits are obtained. Although the situation is not the classic "social optimum," it is closer to that point than might be expected with an unconstrained monopolist, and some of the economies of scale are captured. This is the rationale for "average cost pricing" in many publicly operated enterprises. Price regulation also provides a mechanism for achieving other policies relative to consumption. For example, consumption can be encouraged or discouraged by adjusting the prices of goods and services. If a local government wanted to discourage consumption of a particular good (such as energy), the price could be artificially increased over average cost. As the price rises, consumption decreases. In addition, more than normal profits are obtained for possible use in increasing energy production. Likewise, an artificial decrease in price will encourage consumption, but a "subsidy" will then be required (such as for education). The strategic control of price can thus be used as an effective instrument of public policy. Such price control can additionally be applied to privately produced goods and services through the use of excise taxes (such as on gasoline) and subsidies.

The extreme case of decreasing costs exists where the marginal cost of production equals zero.[5] Consider Figure 2-2. A profit-maximizing monopolist would produce at point *C*, with price at P_1, and with the resultant excess profits.

However, the social optimum is at point *A,* with a price at zero. At this point, everyone is able to obtain the good without cost; the benefit is maximum. That is, increasing consumption to this point requires no additional utilization of resources; the cost of additional units is zero; the action is a net benefit to society. However, production at this level yields a loss which must be covered by a subsidy from other revenue sources. Optionally, a governmental unit can operate at point *B,* where price equals average cost (break even). For example, consider a public road bridge. Once the bridge is constructed, the marginal cost of additional users is essentially zero (up to the point of congestion). The maximum benefit is obtained by letting everyone use the bridge. Therefore, a zero price is set and construction costs are financed from other revenue sources. At the point of congestion, marginal costs begin to exceed zero (waiting time), and a price (toll) might be introduced to decrease the quantity demanded (below congestion) and to generate revenue for enlarging the bridge.

Externalities

"Externalities," "spillover effects," or "third-party effects" refer to economic effects that accrue to entities outside those units directly involved in an activity or transaction. Externalities can involve gains or losses, and are referred to as "positive externalities" and "negative externalities." Because there are few, if any, "pure private" goods, most goods will have some of the characteristics of

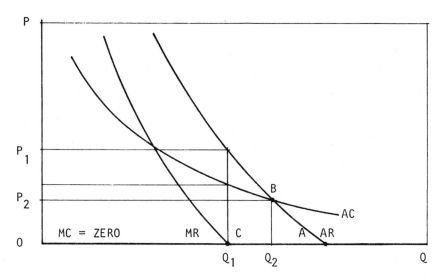

Figure 2-2. Marginal Cost Equals Zero

collective consumption, and will therefore yield "spillovers." Costs or benefits that accrue to those directly involved in an economic activity are called "private" or "internal' costs or benefits. Private costs (benefits), summed with external costs (benefits), constitute the "total," "social," or "real" costs (benefits). Examples are numerous:

1. A power plant chooses to treat air as a free factor of production and discharges polluted air rather than buy antipollution equipment. The polluted air drifts to a neighboring district where residents experience increased levels of soot and breathing difficulty. The production economy to the power plant produces a consumption diseconomy. Part of the total cost of producing power is the cost of utilizing the resource of clean air; the opportunity cost of the air is the benefit foregone by not using the air in an alternate use such as breathing. This particular cost of power is being passed on to the residents of the next district in the form of polluted air.

2. A person utilizes his backyard to store trash and junk automobiles as an alternative to paying for trash removal. His neighbors object to looking at the trash, and property values decline as the neighborhood appears less desirable. The person's consumption economy produces the neighbors' consumption diseconomy.

3. A city provides a large recreational park without admission fees for the use of its residents. The attractiveness of the park is such that residents from surrounding jurisdictions come to use the park. Some of the benefits of the park spill over to nonresidents.

Economic theory predicts the consequences of externalities on the allocation of resources. In a classic market equilibrium, the optimum quantity of a good produced and consumed is determined by the interacting forces of supply and demand. However, when externalities or spillovers exist, not all the costs and benefits are reflected in the supply and demand curves. Therefore, the quantity produced and consumed may be suboptimal. Where external costs exist (social costs exceeding private costs), the market output will exceed the social optimum. For example, the factory that passes along part of its production cost to neighboring residents in the form of polluted air realizes artificially low private costs (private cost below social cost). Because the perceived production costs are lower, the quantity produced will be higher. If, however, external benefits exist (social benefits exceed private benefits), the market output will fall short of the social optimum. For example, consider the city that provides a park that is highly utilized by nonresidents. Part of the benefit goes to the nonresidents, with relatively less benefit going to the residents. Thus, the internal benefit per dollar spent on parks is artificially low. An investment in parks is relatively less attractive than alternative investments; consequently, fewer parks are provided. The fact that most of our urban areas have a multiplicity of governmental units leads to major externalities among units and therefore to arguments that public resources are often misallocated and undersupplied.

Several public policy questions arise relative to externalities. First, governmental units must determine the optimum production level for public goods and services. Second, they must determine whether or not the benefits of an externality exceed the costs. For example, a city incinerator may externalize part of its cost by polluting the air. The air drifts over a portion of the city. The city's internal costs are less than the social cost—the difference being borne by residents of the downwind area. However, the city can charge artificially low solid-waste collection rates because of its lower costs. The question is whether the benefits to the city residents (in terms of lower charges) exceed the costs to the residents of the downwind areas. If they do, the city maximizes net benefits by continuing to pollute. However, the question of equity arises. The whole city benefits at the expense of a few. Two mechanisms are available to resolve the issue: *compensation* and *internalization of costs.* The downwind area could be compensated (for example, with lower service charges or taxes) at a level that would equalize total costs and benefits in all areas. However, the practical problem with this approach is that few mechanisms for compensation exist between or within jurisdictions. One local government cannot exact compensation from another without legal authority. For example, in the central city-suburb argument, the city is held to suffer from a net outflow of benefits to the suburbs, but has no authority to levy taxes against the suburbs. However, partial compensation can sometimes be affected by internal user charges, local payroll taxes, and intergovernmental contracts. Another problem with the compensation approach is that the level of compensation and the desires of those affected are often difficult to measure.

The second mechanism involves the "internalization" of all external costs and benefits. For example, an offending incinerator could buy pollution equipment, leave the air unaffected, and pass the cost along to the consumers in the form of higher prices. This has the advantage that the residents are then paying the "real" cost of the solid-waste disposal. Again, the costs of internalizing must be compared with the costs in terms of higher prices and distributional-equity effects.

The public sector responds to the existence of externalities through both mechanisms. Inequities are resolved via the legal system and through the purposive adjustment of the incidence of public goods, services, taxes, and transfer payments. Internalization of social costs are affected via direct regulation, tax incentives, and cooperative agreements. However, the fragmentation of local governmental jurisdictions yields extremely complex spillovers that can be difficult to resolve. The recognition of complex spillovers and their effects at the local level are important; mechanisms for area-wide resolution include regional or metropolitan planning and management, area-wide authorities, and intergovernmental contracts. For example, if major spillover benefits exist from recreational facilities in a metropolitan area, those spillovers can be internalized by enlarging the production and consumption jurisdiction to a regional scale, with local government responsibilities articulated via contracts between local governments and a regional authority. Likewise, adjacent units of government with similar needs for particular spillover services can cooperatively agree (via contract) to provide the joint service (such as a multiunit emergency medical care service).

Collective Risk and Other Considerations

There are some additional conditions under which the public sector becomes involved in the economy. One such condition is when a project is so large or risky that the private sector cannot or will not undertake production. The space program and the interstate highway system are examples of this at the federal level. Civic centers, sports arenas, and other large public works are possible examples at the state and local level.

Another case involves "collection cost." Sometimes a service is such that the cost of collecting the appropriate price exceeds the benefits to consumers (such as a neighborhood park). Private enterprise would not undertake such an activity. Therefore, government supplies the good or service "free," via financing from a general tax source.

Public Sector Policy and Techniques

The public sector explicitly and implicitly affects economic policy. Explicit policy affects the allocation of resources, the distribution of wealth, economic stabilization, and growth. Because these functions are interrelated, fiscal policy directed towards one usually affects all. Likewise, almost any general public policy will have some implicit economic effects. Therefore, existing and proposed general public policy, as well as specific economic policy, should be evaluated in terms of probable economic effects.

Because local governments are general-purpose governments with responsibilities for providing basic services, the major economic concern is "allocation." Scarce resources must be allocated among competing demands in such a way as to yield the highest net benefit consistent with economic goals. Explicit allocational policies at the local level involve legislative or administrative assignment of public resources to the production of goods and services, and the legislative levy of taxes and user charges to finance those goods and services. This process surfaces most dramatically in the formulation and adoption of the governmental budget, and in other laws, codes, and administrative regulations that affect economic behavior. The allocational decision is complicated by the problems associated with the absence of a price mechanism (as exists within the private sector), the determination of levels of demand for public goods, and the differences between individual and collective decision mechanisms.

Distributional policy is also a concern at the local level. Although federal and state governments generally take the major responsibility for the distribution of wealth, every local government activity necessarily affects distribution in the incidence of public program benefits and costs and in the incidence of local taxes and charges. Local politics always involve the questions of "who gets what" and "who pays for it."

Growth and stabilization are concerns for local government in terms of encouraging growth in industry and commerce towards the goal of an increased standard of living and in maintaining adequate levels of public service in difficult economic times. These issues relate to the maintenance of a sound financial condition and an appropriate level of capital investment. All these functions relate to the maintenance of a sound fiscal management and planning mechanism within local government.

Size and Scope of the Public Sector

A comprehensive review of the financial composition of the public sector is clearly beyond the scope of this text. However, an understanding of the magnitude and distribution of fiscal responsibilities is useful to the local government manager-planner. Therefore, the briefest coverage is provided here; more specific information can be found in typical public finance texts and numerous U.S. government publications.[6]

Basically, the federal government is dominant in fiscal responsibilities, with heavy reliance on individual and corporate income taxes for revenues, and with major expenditures in the areas of national defense, income security, health, and transportation. In addition, the federal government transfers substantial resources to states and local governments (grants and aids), and assumes substantial regulation of both the public and private sectors of the economy. The states rely heavily on sales taxes, and to some extent on income taxes, for revenues and assume major expenditure responsibilities in the areas of education, highways, and public welfare. Local governments are the general-purpose units closest to the people; they rely heavily on the property tax for revenues and assume responsibility for education, police and fire protection, public welfare, streets, hospitals, sewage, sanitation, recreation, and other general service areas.

However, the distribution of fiscal responsibilities among governments is not clearly drawn. An idea of the complexity of the public sector is exhibited in the federal structure of a national government, 50 state governments, and over 78,000 units of local government, each providing a set of public and quasi-public goods and services, most with taxing authority, and often with functionally and/or geographically overlapping responsibilities (Table 2-1). Forty years ago there were approximately 180,000 units of government; the reduction is primarily attributed to a dramatic decrease in the number of school districts, with a

Table 2-1
Local Governments by Type, 1972

Type	Number
Counties	3,044
Municipalities	18,517
Townships	16,991
Special Districts	23,885
School Districts	15,781
With Property Tax Power	65,914
Without Property Tax Power	12,304
Total	78,218

Source: U.S. Bureau of the Census, *Statistical Abstract of the United States: 1974,* 95th edition (Washington: Government Printing Office, 1974), Table 399, p. 244.

smaller but significant increase in the numbers of municipalities and special districts. This multiplicity of governmental units and the resultant fragmentation of public responsibilities understandably leads to complications for fiscal planning and management (see Chapter 7, Intergovernmental Relations). Problems are generally most severe in metropolitan areas where a particular geographic area may be covered by six or more overlapping local governments (county, municipality, school board, special districts), each with its own function, revenue authority, and management and little or no overall coordination among units or services. Table 2-2 shows the extent of fragmentation in some typical metropolitan areas.

Table 2-2
Political Fragmentation in Metropolitan Areas,[a] 1972

Area	Population	Number of Governments
New York, N.Y.–N.J.	9,943,800	349
Chicago, Ill.	7,084,700	1,172
Boston, Mass.	3,417,000	231
San Francisco–Oakland, Calif.	3,131,800	302
Atlanta, Georgia	1,683,600	163
Denver–Boulder, Colo.	1,309,200	277
Portland, Oreg.–Wash.	1,036,300	298
Louisville, Ky.–Ind.	887,700	202
Flint, Mich.	521,200	91

Source: U.S. Bureau of the Census, *Local Government Employment in Selected Metropolitan Areas and Large Counties, 1973,* Series GE 73-3 (Washington: Government Printing Office, 1974), Table C, p. 3.
[a]Standard Metropolitan Statistical Areas (SMSA)

The historical growth of the economy and the aggregate public sector is well documented.[7] Total public expenditures have grown in the United States in absolute terms, in per capita terms, and as a percentage of the gross national product (GNP). That growth has been somewhat uneven and has shifted among federal, state, and local components. Since the great depression of the early 1930's, public expenditures have more than doubled as a percentage of the gross national product to 31 percent in 1973, and reaching nearly 50 percent during World War II (Table 2–3).

During that period, the federal government's share of public economic activity increased dramatically from 34 percent of total government expenditures in 1932 to over 60 percent in the 1960's. State governments' share has remained relatively stable, while local governments' expenditures exhibited a dramatic decrease from 45 percent in 1932 to less than 20 percent in 1974. The relative growth of the federal share is largely caused by increases in expenditures for national defense, interest on the national debt, social trust funds, and international affairs. Inspection of tax receipts reveals a similar pattern (Table 2–4).

Summary statistics of this kind are necessarily oversimplifications of a more complex public sector situation. "Expenditures" and "revenues" are only two measures from a number of important indicators. Percentage figures often vary among sources, depending on the definitions and assumptions used, and statistics say little about the extent and the effects of federal, state, and local "regulation" of private sector activities. Intergovernmental fiscal relations (grants and aids among levels and units of government) add a further complication. Never-

Table 2–3
Government Expenditures and Gross National Product

Year	GNP (Billions)	Government Expenditures (Billions)	Percentage of GNP		
			Total	Federal	State-Local
1930	90.4	11.1	12.3	3.1	9.2
1935	72.2	13.4	18.5	9.0	9.4
1940	99.7	18.4	18.5	10.0	8.5
1945	211.9	92.7	43.7	39.9	3.8
1950	284.8	60.8	21.3	14.3	7.0
1955	398.0	97.6	24.5	17.1	7.4
1960	503.7	136.1	27.0	18.4	8.6
1965	681.2	185.8	27.3	18.1	9.2
1970	997.1	312.7	32.0	20.9	11.1
1971	1,054.9	340.1	32.2	20.9	11.4
1972	1,158.0	372.1	32.1	21.1	11.0
1973	1,294.9	408.1	31.5	20.4	11.1

Source: Tax Foundation, Inc., *Facts and Figures on Government Finance,* 18th edition (New York: Tax Foundation, 1975), Table 20, p. 33.

Table 2-4
Tax Receipts and Expenditures by Level of Government

Year	Total Government (Billions)	Total Per Capita ($)	Percentages Federal	State	Local
Tax Receipts					
1932	8	64	22.7	23.7	53.6
1940	14	108	39.2	29.2	31.6
1950	55	365	69.1	16.3	14.6
1960	127	709	69.8	15.9	14.3
1970	275	1,357	67.5	18.4	14.1
1974	394	1,869	64.1	20.9	15.0
Expenditures					
1932	12	100	34.3	20.6	45.1
1940	20	155	49.3	22.3	28.5
1950	70	468	63.7	18.2	18.1
1960	151	846	64.3	16.5	19.1
1970	333	1,643	62.5	19.4	18.1
1974	465	2,210	61.1	21.0	17.9

Source: Tax Foundation, Inc., *Facts and Figures on Government Finance,* 18th ed. (New York: Tax Foundation, 1975), Tables 5, 6, 8, 9, pp. 18–21.

theless, inspection of nearly every source points to the same general conclusion: the public component of the economy exhibits a long-run growth relative to the private sector. What is uncertain is the "appropriate" mixture of public and private activity and the future of the total U.S. economy. The historic preference seems to lie toward a major reliance on the private sector, yet the trend toward larger government is clear; there appears to be no universally accepted practical or theoretical limit to the size of the public sector.

There are several formal explanations for the growth of the public sector. The "Wagner hypothesis" holds that the growth of an industrialized economy and the absolute and relative growth of the public sector are functionally related.[8] That is, economic/industrial growth requires increasing levels of centralized administration, which leads to increased specialization and complex economic interdependencies, which in turn require increased levels of governmental service. Social progress leads to an increased need for governmental maintenance of an environment for industrial growth, including the provision of large fixed investment and collective risk. A second explanation has been forwarded by Peacock and Wiseman.[9] The growth process is here related to three concepts: displacement, inspection, and concentration. Displacement involves the rapid increase of public fiscal activity in times of crisis such as war. After the crisis, levels do not return to original positions. Rather, society directs attention to areas that were otherwise neglected during the crisis (inspection); society has become accustomed to carrying the greater tax burden. In addition, there is a tendency for public activity to become increasingly centralized in times of economic growth (concentration). Thus, the public sector tends to grow in a step-like fashion, with major increases during crises and with increasing centralization at the federal level. Both of these explanations are useful in terms of what has occurred in industrialized societies, but again, neither address what "ought to be."

Local governments, particularly city governments, remain as the general-purpose units closest to the people. The most recent decade has been characterized by absolute and per capita increases in levels of city revenues and expenditures, with per capita increases of more than double the rate of general price inflation. The most recent (1974–1976) dramatic increases in absolute levels have been largely caused by high rates of overall price inflation, especially the inflation of public worker wages (public worker unionization).

The overall distribution of resources within local governments is difficult to ascertain; accounting conventions and the division of state and local responsibilities varies among states and cities. However, Table 2–5 shows per capita figures for all municipalities and for the largest and smallest cities. Per capita figures tend to increase with city size, yet intercity comparisons are difficult to make because of the high level of variation within categories.

Summary

The United States has historically relied on a mixed private-public economic system. Although the tradition has been one of general reliance on the private sector, the public sector is utilized where the market system fails to satisfy social goals. More specifically, the rationale for public sector economic activity includes:

1. the provision of public goods
2. the affectation of states of distribution
3. the correction of market imperfections, including natural monopolies, externalities, and others
4. the provision of collective risk

Public sector policies address the allocation of resources—the distribution of wealth, stabilization, and growth. Governments directly produce and supply public goods and services and may encourage or discourage the production and consumption of other goods and services via the regulation of economic behavior.

At the local government level, allocational policy is affected via the "budget" and other legislative or administrative constraints on economic behavior. Distributional policy is primarily the responsibility of higher units of govern-

Table 2-5
Per Capita Revenue and Expenditure, City Governments[a]

Item	All Municipalities	Municipalities, Population	
		1 million +	Less than 50,000
General Revenue	264.67	620.48	138.14
Intergovernmental Revenue	86.62	256.73	31.03
General Revenue, Own Sources	178.04	263.74	106.76
Taxes	129.22	292.26	69.64
Property	83.24	158.14	50.06
General sales	14.14	36.83	6.80
Selective sales	9.99	23.43	4.73
Other	21.86	73.85	8.07
Current charges	29.88	45.31	20.71
Miscellaneous	18.94	26.18	16.75
General Expenditure	270.42	636.36	138.11
Capital outlay	49.52	86.65	27.35
Other	220.90	549.71	110.77
Personal services	137.05	322.10	66.93
Education	44.14	125.14	13.50
Highways	20.97	19.10	19.65
Public welfare	22.96	120.43	.86
Hospitals	15.82	56.48	6.47
Health	5.18	19.60	.74
Police protection	29.68	64.57	18.02
Fire protection	16.73	27.00	9.43
Sewage	14.88	16.03	12.85
Sanitation	10.11	19.47	6.38
Parks and recreation	11.90	13.21	6.58
Housing and urban renewal	11.17	31.81	2.02
Libraries	3.52	6.06	1.90
Financial administration	4.28	5.82	3.11
General control	7.44	11.74	6.16
General public buildings	4.02	6.94	2.58
Interest on general debt	11.57	24.73	6.75
All other	35.86	68.25	21.08

Source: U.S. Bureau of the Census, *City Government Finances in 1971-72,* Series GF 72-No. 4 (Washington: Government Printing Office, 1973), Table 4, p. 8.
[a]Figures in dollars.

ment, but is necessarily affected by the incidence of local program costs and benefits and the incidence of the tax burden. Stabilization and growth are concerns of local governments in terms of maintaining an adequate economic base, an adequate level of public service, an appropriate level of capital investment, and reasonable stability of public revenue.

Fiscal management and planning in the public sector is complicated by the complexity of economic interrelationships produced by over 78,000 units of local government, often with the functional and/or geographic overlapping of responsibilities.

The history of the public sector is one of relatively continuous but uneven growth. Total public expenditures have increased in the United States in absolute and per capita terms and as a percentage of the gross national product. Although the relative size of the federal government has dramatically increased in the last 30 years, recent trends involve a significant increase in local government fiscal activity. The overall long run trend for the relative growth of the public sector of the economy is clear. However, there is little agreement as to what the private-public mix should be.

Notes

1. This condition is termed "Pareto optimality," and refers to a situation where there is no action that will make one person better off without making another person worse off. A "Pareto-optimal" action is one that makes at least one person better off without making anyone worse off and, therefore, increases the total welfare.

2. A short review of this history can be found in Bernard P. Herber, *Modern Public Finance: The Study of the Public Sector* (Homewood, Ill.: Richard D. Irwin, 1971), pp. 21-24.

3. There has been much recent interest in the changing views of equality in the literature; see Daniel Bell, "The Revolution of Rising Entitlements," *Fortune* (April 1975), pp. 98-103, and Herbert J. Gans, *More Equality* (New York: Pantheon Books, 1968), passim.

4. The mechanics of estimating the incidence of costs and benefits are covered in Chapter 11, Program Evaluation.

5. Herber, *Modern Public Finance,* p. 31.

6. Historical aspects of government finance can be found in U.S. Bureau of the Census, *Historical Statistics on Government Finances and Employment,* Volume 6, No. 4, 1972 Census of Governments (Washington, D.C.: Government Printing Office, 1973), and Herber, *Modern Public Finance,* p. 352. Other useful statistics can be found in U.S. Bureau of the Census, *Statistical Abstract of the United States,* 95th edition (Washington: Government Printing Office, 1974), Sections 8, 9; U.S. Bureau of the Census, *City Government Finances in 1971-72,* Series GF 72-4 (Washington: Government Printing Office, 1973); U.S. Bureau of the Census, *Government Finances in 1971-72,* Series GF 72-5 (Washington: Government Printing Office, 1973); U.S. Bureau of the Census, *Local Government Employment in Selected Metropolitan Areas and Large Counties, 1973,* Series GE 73-3 (Washington: Government Printing Office, 1974); Advisory Commission on Intergovernmental Relations, *State-Local Finances: Significant Features and Suggested Legislation,* 1972 edition (Washington: Government Printing Office, 1974), passim; and Tax Foundation, *Facts and Figures on Government Finance,* 18th edition (New York: Tax Foundation, 1975), passim.

7. U.S. Bureau of the Census, *Historical Statistics of the United States, Colonial Times to 1957* (Washington: Government Printing Office, 1960).

8. See Herber, *Modern Public Finance,* p. 371.

9. Ibid., p. 378, citing Alan T. Peacock and Jack Wiseman, *The Growth of Expenditures in the United Kingdom* (Princeton, N.J.: Princeton University Press, 1961), p. xxiii.

3

Public Management and Planning

This chapter covers public management and planning in a broad context to provide the basic conceptual background and structure for the more detailed treatment of fiscal management and planning disucssed in later chapters. Major sections describe the basic structure of local government and the organizational location of financial and planning components, the management process, and planning as an integral part of that process.

Local Government

The government of the United States is a constitutional and federal entity. It is "constitutional" in the sense that it is established and controlled by a written constitution. The term "federal" is applicable because that constitution establishes two levels of government: the national level and the state level. Each state, in turn, exists under a state constitution that establishes the state government and all the levels of government below the state level. Local governments are created by the state governments (that is, their constitutions and legislatures); they are limited to those powers and responsibilities specifically granted to them.

Local governments are the structural units closest to the people and are usually "general purpose" in nature. Cities, or incorporated municipalities, provide services to urban areas, while counties and townships provide services to rural areas. Special districts are responsible for limited services to particular functional areas. Of course, there is always an overlapping of geographical areas (cities exist in counties) and services, the latter being affected by intergovernmental arrangements.

Although much of what is reviewed in this section applies to most local governments and to some aspects of state governments, the focus is primarily on city governments. By way of definition, cities are "distinct legal entities individually incorporated under the laws of their respective states and expected to perform certain basic governmental and nongovernmental functions. Cities are thus units of government with established boundaries, elected leaders, defined and limited authority, and taxing and regulatory powers."[1] The organizational structure of a typical local government is shown in Figure 3-1.

Because there is a great deal of variation among local governments, only the most general conceptual structure is presented here. The voters elect a mayor,

53

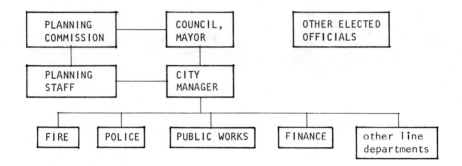

Figure 3-1. Typical Administrative Structure, City Government

city council, and other elected officials (such as the clerk, treasurer, and assessor). The city council serves as the legislative body. The mayor can serve in several different positions. He may serve as the presiding officer of the council (that is, a "weak" mayor), or he may serve as the chief executive officer (that is, a "strong" mayor). A council-manager structure (Figure 3-1) utilizes a city manager who is appointed by the council and/or mayor. The council and mayor are responsible for all city policy, while the city manager is responsible for administration. City operations are distributed among functional "line" departments; each line department has a department head who is responsible to the city manager.

Finance and Planning in Local Government

Both financial and planning operations have "line" and "staff" functions. "Line functions" are those tasks related to the actual production and delivery of service, whereas "staff functions" are the tasks of formulating policy and advising the manager, mayor, and city council. For example, the finance department must distribute bills and collect payments as a line function and formulate alternative fiscal policies as a staff function. Likewise, the planning department must review subdivision proposals as a line function and develop alternative land use policies as a staff function. Also, there is a particularly strong and functional relationship between the policy components of finance and planning. Most decisions with future consequences will have financial implications. For example, the implementation of a land use plan requires large capital investments that must be programmed by the finance department. However similar planning and finance functions may be, they have developed quite differently in the structure of local government.

In the early 1900's there was little, if any, actual financial management. Rather, the concern was only to prohibit "illegal" spending.[2] Financial functions were distributed among several independent officials: the treasurer, the tax collector, and the controller. Each was a check on the other's operations. Centralization of these financial functions came with the emergence of the strong mayor and city manager forms of government in the 1920's and 1930's. Financial functions were placed in a single department that reported directly to the mayor or manager. This comprehensiveness and centralization of power allowed for the development of the "management" of financial matters. Today, financial operations are generally found in a distinct department under the mayor or manager. (The "process" of financial management, however, involves actors from various other units within local government—as discussed in Chapter 4).

Planning developed along different lines.[3] Before World War Two, planning responsibilities resided in an "independent commission of citizens," which was presumably free from political influence. The commissions were usually established by ordinance and were composed of five to nine members appointed by the mayor and council. The members were responsible to the "community at large" rather than to the mayor and council. The commission usually hired a professional staff of its own, and was expected to ascertain the "public interest," to make plans for the future based on that interest, and to recommend its plans to the legislative body. Plans focused on the physical elements of land use, transportation, and certain public facilities, combined in a long-range "master plan." There was no direct relationship between the planning commission/staff and the rest of local government. Thus, the master plans were usually "advisory." Because short-range opportunities often take precedence over long-range uncertainties, these plans were seldom as influential or effective as planners would have liked.

Thus, planning of this type was subjected to heavy criticism—because the structural remoteness of planning from the rest of local government yielded little effectiveness, and because the "physical" emphasis was too narrow. In the 1940's a new concept of planning emerged that identified planning as a staff function to the mayor, manager, or city council. The acceptance of this concept has facilitated an integration of planning into the overall management system of local government and encouraged closer ties between planning and other departments such as finance. Some states and cities have combined certain planning and finance activities into single organizational units such as an "office of planning and budget." Another change that has occurred involves an expansion of context from "physical" to "comprehensive." That is, emphasis has shifted from the static land use–transportation plans to policy and program formulation for physical, economic, and social functions.

All this means that planning may be located in any number of organizational positions, with any scope of function. Many communities maintain an independent planning commission with an emphasis on physical planning. Others may have reduced or eliminated the role of the commission and utilize a professional planning staff as a line department or staff entity, with a functional context as wide as government itself. The process of planning, and indeed public management, is evolving. Organizational structure is changing to accommodate new processes, with a characteristic time lag. However, some trends are relatively clear. Planning is increasingly becoming a staff function, responsible to the chief executive or manager. It is expanding in context to include all aspects of local government, and as such it is becoming an integral part of the overall management system. Particularly strong ties are emerging between planning and financial functions.

Management and Planning

Management is such a broad and general concept that precise definitions are nonexistent. Steiss refers to management as "the art of getting things done" involving "the direction, coordination, and control of resources to achieve some purpose or objective."[4] Munson describes management as that "which keeps the various activities of the organization coordinated and continuously striving towards fulfillment of the organization's internal and external purposes."[5] Management can also be looked at as a decision process. Munson states that "the management function will consist of decisions determining what the organization's purposes are, what the organization is going to do to fulfill those purposes, how the organization is going to do these things, and who in the organization is going to do them."[6]

Management as a Decision Process

A "decision" is a choice among alternatives; a decisionmaker must always make a choice among alternative courses of action where one alternative is to do nothing. A city council selects a public policy as a subset of all the possible public policies; planners select programs from a larger set of possible programs. The quality of the management process then depends on the quality of the management decisions. A "good" decision is a "rational" decision. Decisions should be rational in that they are reasonable and follow from the premises. Four types of nonrational decisions can be identified:

1. Illogical decision—when the decisionmaker commits "errors of logic" by confusing possible consequences of his actions with necessary consequences
2. Blind decision—when certain consequences important to the decision are not considered
3. Rash decision—when a decision is made after an incomplete or hasty review of the alternatives

4. Ignorant decision—when there are mistakes about the facts, or available relevant facts are omitted from consideration.[7]

Rational decisions depend on the availability of information and an efficiency of decision-making mechanisms.

Decisionmakers base decisions on both subjective (values) and objective (facts) information. For example, a mayor may decide on a particular issue by drawing on his or her years of previous political experience and on the facts presented on the particular issue. Both provide estimates of the potential consequences of the alternative courses of action. Better information allows for a better decision. The role of the professional (such as an administrator, planner, or analyst) is to provide the decisionmaker with the appropriate "factual" information. Although both subjective and objective arguments surround any issue, the professional analyst, by definition, claims expertise relative to the factual component. Appropriate factual information includes:

1. Identification of the feasible alternative courses of action
2. Identification of the probable consequences of alternatives in such terms as cost, benefits, risks, or intangible factors
3. Identification of appropriate criteria for the decision, and the subsequent ranking of alternatives in terms of potential for goal satisfaction

The array of factual information should aid the decisionmaker in ordering both objective and subjective inputs to make a choice among the relevant alternatives. There is, however, a cost associated with conducting analysis and generating information. A trade-off exists between the cost of information and the benefits of making a better decision. Most theories of optimal decision-making assume a state of perfect information that is impossible in real world situations. However, applied decision theory has made significant progress in recent years in providing for decision techniques under conditions of risk and uncertainty through the use of certain statistical approaches.[8] Thus, good management decisions depend, in part, on using analysis techniques to generate an appropriate level of factual information.

A realistic decision process is revealed in Simon's concept of "satisficing."[9] Satisficing is the process whereby a decisionmaker scans only a limited set of feasible alternatives, selecting the first one that "satisfies" some basic criteria. He stops searching when he finds an alternative course of action that works. He "satisfices" rather than maximizes. This means that the appropriate array of factual information, and thus the format of the analysis, depends on the extent to which the decisionmaker is a satisficer. Another aspect of good decisions involves the decision-making mechanism itself. Group decisions are relatively more complex than individual decisions, in that group decisions rely on the mechanisms of majority voting or concensus. These mechanisms are discussed later in this chapter, under Articulation of the Public Interest.

Management Systems

A management system is an interrelated group of decision processes; the planning function is an integral part of the management system rather than a separate element. The elements of the system can be described as broad categories of tasks. Munson uses the following categories:

1. *Strategic Planning* involves the formulation of overall goals and objectives and the selection of policies that apply to the acquisition and expenditure of resources.
2. *Management Planning* involves the formulation of programs of activities that are designed to accomplish goals and objectives within policy constraints.
3. *Operational Control* involves the conduct of specific program tasks in order to affect objectives.[10]

Figure 3-2 shows these three categories grouped into a conceptual functional hierarchy (not an organizational chart).

Strategic planning involves the tasks of determining goals, objectives, and policies for the organization. These are passed on to the management planning unit. This is not to say that management planning has no effect on the formulation of goals and policies. Alternate goals and policies may originate at any level, but the decisions are made at the strategic planning level. Also, specific individuals in the organization may have responsibilities in several of the functional categories. For example, a city mayor might sit with the city council for strategic decisions while serving as chief administrative officer for management planning decisions.

Management planning involves the tasks of selecting the operations that will be required to satisfy the objectives and policies of the organization. This planning process is discussed in detail later in this chapter under Selection of Operations—Planning. The output of management planning is essentially a plan of programs to be implemented. The operational control function transforms the programs into a series of tasks and then implements the tasks. Ideally, these tasks affect the environment in a way that satisfies the goals and objectives of the organization.

It is important to note that the process of management is *continuous*. Changes occur in the environment because of the effects of the organization's activities as well as other external factors. Therefore, the organization must continuously assess the state of the environment to alter its goals, objectives, policies, programs, and tasks. For example, assume that a city is organized in such a way that the strategic planning function is the responsibility of the city council, the management planning function falls to the city manager and his planning staff, and operational control rests with the line departments. The city

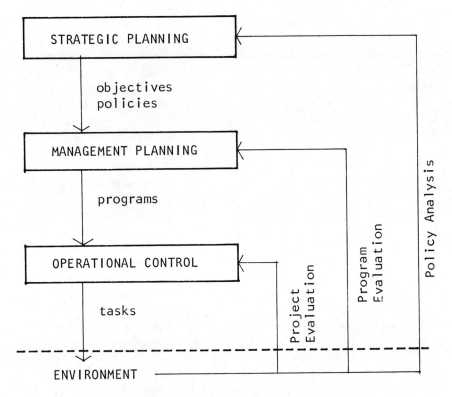

Figure 3-2. Management System

council continually assesses the city environment to identify problems that may exist. Often these problems surface as issues, brought to light by individuals or groups in the environment, or internally from within the management system. In this case, assume that the issue is one of traffic congestion in the central business district. The city council recognizes the problem and adopts the strategic goal of "solving the CBD traffic problem." The manager and his planning staff are directed to analyze the problem. The planning staff conducts the appropriate analysis and articulates the problem as one of insufficient traffic control and insufficient parking space. Further, they explore some alternative ways of providing better traffic control and more parking space, including the provision of additional off-street parking, improved traffic signals, and enforcement of existing parking regulations. The council reviews and accepts (or rejects) these alternatives and actuates the relevant policies with legislation and administrative directives to the city manager. For example, the council might alter the budget (by a legislative amendment) to allocate resources to programs for acquiring land, constructing parking lots, designing traffic signal systems, and the like. The manager and his or her staff then select the operations and sequence of operations that are required to implement these policies. Each set of activities constitutes a program design. The programs are then directed to the relevant line departments (such as public works, streets, and police) to carry out the tasks identified in the programs. As the various tasks are carried out over some period of time, the traffic problem is presumably affected. An evaluation takes place at each management level. The city council evaluates the effectiveness of its policies, the manager evaluates the effectiveness of the programs, and the line departments evaluate the effectiveness of program tasks, all relative to the effects on the environment, or in this case, on the CBD traffic problem.

Evaluation is essential to the continuous process of management. The results of the evaluation of policies, programs, and operational tasks allow for a new round of decision-making. Has the problem been solved? If not, how has the problem been affected? Should policies, programs, and/or tasks be altered? Are more resources required? This process of incremental, continuous readjustment of the organization is "management."

The value of this type of conceptualization is that it separates organizational structure from the process of management. Efforts to improve public management and planning must focus on the process and on the output of process. Organizational structure should be designed to accommodate a rational process, rather than the reverse. The model represents management as a system of sequential, interrelated functions. Each function is critical to the "whole"; a weakness in any part reduces the effectiveness of the system. Planning is an integral part of management rather than a simple supportive element.

Management Tasks

Given the general management model previously described, this section turns to a more detailed discussion of the major management tasks:

1. Selection of goals, objectives, and policies
2. Selection of operations, planning
3. Control

Selection of Goals, Objectives, and Policies

The current literature and practice produce no agreement or concensus on the definitions of the terms "goals," "objectives," and "policies." Therefore, for purposes of this text, it is appropriate to select some definitions in order of their implied specificity:

1. Value—a broad, individually and socially internalized guide to decision-making; a set of subjective personal preferences and beliefs that guide behavior
2. Goal—a general statement of desired conditions or ends, often related to perceived problems, and related to explicit or implicit value assumptions
3. Objective—statement of goals or components of goals in measurable terms (a quantity implication)
4. Policy—a general guide for decision-making relative to a specific goal and/or objective, that includes the means for achieving them; usually stated as legislation or administrative procedure
5. Plan—a statement of a set of decisions for action in the future
6. Program—a statement of a set of interrelated resources and activities, ordered in sequence, and required to carry out some part of a plan consistent with policy to achieve objectives and goals

For example, the citizens of a community with some substandard housing may hold beliefs or values that involve a "decent" living environment for all persons. Assuming that these values are translated into government action, the following elements might be formulated:

1. Goal—the provision of standard quality housing for every resident
2. Objective—the reduction of the number of substandard housing units by 10 percent per year
3. Policy—to reduce the percentage of substandard housing units through the use of condemnation, code enforcement, and the construction of public housing, financed from community development funds
4. Plan—the identification of substandard housing units, with specific actions to be taken for each unit or class of units
5. Program—the identification of the detailed resources, participants, and sequence of activities required for implementing the code enforcement and other plans

Formulating goals, objectives, and policies is one of the more difficult tasks of public sector management. The existing theory fails to provide a completely satisfactory explanation of the process. The task is less complicated in the private sector where firms undertake a variety of activities towards relatively few goals such as the maximization of profits or sales; goals and objectives are more clearly and easily measured. Policies are formulated and evaluated relative to their ability to satisfy objectives. However, this process is more complicated in the public sector for a variety of reasons. The public sector must select "collective" or "social" goals that may be different from individual goals. These goals are multiple, often conflicting, difficult to measure, and indirectly articulated. Society has preferences for means as well as ends; therefore, the same difficulties arise in the formulation of public policy.

Articulation of the Public Interest. The formation and selection of public goals relates directly to the concept of the "public interest"—the public good or general welfare. Public interest involves the welfare of the "whole" community rather than the welfare of any individual or group. Two questions arise: What is the public interest? How is it articulated?

There are two basic concepts of the public interest. One views the public interest as a collection or aggregation of "individual" interests, and the other views it as an aggregate "social" interest. The individual view holds that collective action is required to satisfy individual wants. Public interest decisions can be made by comparing the total benefits of a collective good with the total costs, where total measures are summations of individual measures. In reality, simple summations of individual rational decisions do not always equal a collective rational decision. For example, each individual's decision to use his or her land in its most profitable use can lead to a suboptimal overall land use pattern. This leads, in turn to other inefficiencies and lower overall levels of welfare.

The articulation of individual interests depends on whether each individual's interest is assigned equal weight or varying weight (that is, intensity of interest). If one assumes varying weights of interest (for example, as does the private market via dollars), then interpersonal utility comparisons are necessary. However, it is difficult if not impossible to make those comparisons for collective goods. If, on the other hand, one assumes a "unitary" weight to each person's interest, then the public interest is articulated through the simple grouping of individual preferences in families, clubs, unions, political parties, and other organizations to the extent that political power or majority voting power is created. Competing wants are compromised by the group decision mechanism. However, several problems arise with this view. A decision is in the public interest only if it satisfies the largest possible number of persons (i.e., the majority). There is no protection of the minority. Minority preferences can not be satisfied on particular issues even if the minority is willing to bear the entire cost associated with the issue. Still another problem relates to the distributional impacts of public activity. Most programs leave some individuals better off while leaving others worse off. Over the long run, the "win some, lose some" ethic keeps individuals in the system. A particular activity however, might provide large benefits to 49 percent of the population, while assigning small costs to the other 51 percent with a net increase in the total level of welfare. A simple summation of preferences would result in the rejection of the proposed activity. A system of compensation of losers by winners might neutralize the distributional effects, but that has obvious practical difficulties. Therefore, total reliance on the individual concept of public interest leads to some practical problems, and requires a high level of faith in the political system as an articulator of the plural interest.

The other major view of the public interest has as a basis an aggregate social interest that may be different from a simple summation of individual interests. This view holds that individuals voluntarily release power to the government.

The government determines the public interest. This implicit weighting assumes that commonly shared goals are more important than individual goals. The acceptance of this view is more a release from adherence to the "individual" view than it is a specific guide to determining the public interest. It allows, for example, distributional impacts and benefits to minorities to be treated as explicit public goals. The substance of the public interest is derived from perceptions of the general values of society as revealed socially and historically by the actions of society and bounded by the pattern of political power and tolerance.

Neither the individual nor the social view of the public interest leads to a satisfactory operational guide for goal formulation. As Steiner has concluded: "Obviously the question 'What is the public interest?' has no simple answer. Indeed, asking the question invites the sort of smile reserved for small children and benign idiots."[11] However, there is a public interest and it exists in a way that reflects both the above views. It is an explicit or implicit part of public goals, objectives, and policies. The operational question is How should public goals be formulated?

Goal Formulation. In a broad sense, the question is answered by the political system. The community (power elite or plural) identifies perceived problems and introduces them into the political system as issues. The issues are resolved by the political mechanisms of negotiation, argument, persuasion, and voting. Implicit goals are products of settled issues. Alternately, the government may formulate explicit goals in anticipation of future problems. Implicit and explicit goals are translated into policy that is usually legislative or administrative which is accompanied by an allocation of resources. These policies are directives to action.

Both elected officials and professional managers have a role in this process. However, this idea would have been public administration heresy in the 1920's and 1930's. Early public administration doctrine of "separation of functions" separated policy (that is, politics) from administration. Politicians were not to be involved in administration; administrators were not to be involved with politics. Thus, professional managers were to have no influence on the formulation of public policy. This normative or ideal view of public management was replaced in the 1940's by empirical views of the actual workings of organizations. Max Weber and others found that bureaucratic organizations had "inner" workings that varied from the formal organizational structures.[12] Organizations did not function like scientific machines, but rather as sets of complex, informal, personal, and political interactions.

The study of organizations shifted to a focus on decision-making within organizations. Simon (1947) introduced the concept of "logical positivism," which identified two components of all decisions: factual premises and value premises.[13] This concept holds that all decisions include both value components (what ought to be) that do not appeal to facts and factual components that do appeal to scientific verification. Organizations are articulated in terms of a vertical hierarchy of levels of authority to make decisions. Decisions at the top of the hierarchy (goals, objectives, policies) are based heavily on value premises, and those at the lower end (programs, activities) are based more on factual premises. Individuals at the top are more involved with policy decisions, while those at the bottom are more involved with carrying out activities. However, decisions within an organization are passed down through the hierarchical structure. At each step, policies are broken down into simpler, more specific decisions. Thus, decisions are made at every level and are based on the values and facts that exist at each level. Therefore, the "separation of functions" doctrine has been generally rejected; administrators do affect public policy via decisions that are made as part of the management function.

For example, a city council may initially set policies relative to public safety by authorizing and funding a set of crime prevention programs. The city manager must administer these programs. The manager interprets the enacted legislation, breaking it down into a set of decisions (administrative policies) to be passed down to functional departments (such as police department or streets department). The manager's decisions will involve the application of the facts of the situation as the manager sees them (including the existence of the legislation and additional facts) and the manager's personal values. Administrative directives will be issued to department heads, indicating the decisions that have been made. The department heads then break down the directives into more detailed decisions and so on. The policy becomes more articulated at each decision level. Of course, the flow of information is not only in a downward direction, but rather is (vertically and horizontally) in all directions.

The professional administrator has a very definite role in the formulation of public policy, in the creation and communication of factual information within the organization, and in the management decisions that must be made. Although formal decision authority may rest solely with elected officials, everyone within an organization has some effect on public policy. Planners and other experts with less decision-making authority and more interest in factual information influence public policy primarily by creating the relevant information on which decisions are made.

In summary, goal and policy formulation relates to the public interest, a concept that is difficult to define and articulate. However, goals and policies are formulated implicitly and explicitly through the political and bureaucratic systems. Perceived problems become issues that, when settled, reveal implicit goals and objectives; explicit goals are formulated in anticipation of problems. Policies are formulated to identify acceptable means for the pursuit of goals and objectives. Although authority for policy decisions rest formally with elected officials, administrators, planners, and other staff influence public policy by creating factual information and management decisions. The factual inputs can take a variety of forms including the identification and ordering of alternatives, the estimation of the probable consequences of alternatives, and the selection of appropriate decision criteria.

Techniques of Goal Formulation. The urban planner is often assigned the task of formulating alternative goal and policy statements. This role is based, at least traditionally, on the planner's claim to a comprehensiveness of interests and an expertise with certain techniques.[14] Techniques often used for goal formulation include:

1. *Interviews with experts.* Often a number of persons have particular knowledge about some subject or problem area. These persons can be interviewed or placed on ad hoc advisory groups to identify problems, issues, alternative solutions, and so on. Advantages include low cost; disadvantages include lack of population representation.
2. *Group inputs.* A variety of groups (such as churches, civic clubs, or unions) contribute to the formulation of goals through their activities and reports. Group leaders can be interviewed and reports reviewed for the purpose of identifying goals. Advantages and disadvantages are the same as above.
3. *Content analysis.* Printed sources (such as books, magazines, or newspapers) often identify problems and reveal issues. Systematic review of these sources can be helpful.
4. *Survey research.* Survey research is perhaps the most sophisticated technique for gathering information about attitudes. Personal, mail, and telephone interviews with a random sample of the population can produce a representative view of perceived problems and goals. It is a highly technical activity, capable of producing high-quality information, and is more expensive than other methods.

Selection of Operations—Planning

The second major task of the management system, given a set of goals, objectives, and policies, is the selection of the operations required to carry out the policies. This task is commonly called "planning." Yehezkel Dror defines planning as "the process of preparing a set of decisions for actions in the future, directed at achieving goals by optimal means."[15] There are, however, a variety of kinds of planning, planners, and plans. One can differentiate on "context" (such as corporate or public) and on "level" (such as national, state, city, or streets). This section covers three types of planning relevant to this text: policy planning, comprehensive planning, and program planning.

Policy Planning. "Policy planning" refers to the identification and evaluation of alternative public policies, as opposed to the more detailed comprehensive or program planning. It includes the systematic articulation of public goals and objectives and the means for achieving those goals and objectives. Such planning is usually carried out by a staff that is directly responsible to the legislative body, mayor, or city manager. In many cities policy planning is conducted by the planning department staff as part of the comprehensive planning effort. The output of such planning generally includes an identification of public problems, goals, and objectives and a set of policies directed towards those problems. The legislative body then adopts the goals and some subset of policies in the form of legislation, appropriation, or resolution. These policies then become general guides to the further formulation of plans and programs. Policy outputs are not always explicit; they may simply involve a consensus among legislative and management entities relative to "the direction to go."

Comprehensive Planning. Comprehensive urban planning has historically been the dominant form of planning local government. Until recent times, the context has been primarily "physical' in nature, including those elements that could be represented on a graphic map. Land use, streets, and public facilities were the major elements; the emphasis was placed on orderly spatial and functional relationships among the elements. More recently, however, the context has been extended to include public services and other nonphysical elements. The traditional planning process included and, to a significant degree, still includes the following general sequential tasks:

1. *Selection of a time frame.* The future orientation of planning requires that a time frame be adopted. Typical plans utilize a 10- to 25-year period (long range) divided into 5-year segments (short range).
2. *Assignment of goals and objectives.* Explicit general goals are identified and objectives assigned to each of the future dates (such as economic growth).
3. *Inventory.* An inventory of all elements of the plan is assembled, including population, employment, income, economic growth, land use, transportation, public facilities, and services.
4. *Projection of basic parameters and future requirements.* The basic elements (variables beyond control) of population, employment, income, and economic growth are projected to each future date. These are translated into requirements for land use, transportation, public facilities, and services. Together, they form a quantitative picture of each future state. The projection process can vary from a simple additive procedure to the construction of a complex, dynamic urban growth model.
5. *Model manipulation.* Once a picture of each future state is constructed, whether simple or complex, variables that are subject to control (such as land use pattern or transportation facilities pattern) can be varied in such a way as to produce alternative arrangements or plans.

6. *Plan selection.* Alternate plans are evaluated in terms of their potential for achieving stated goals and objectives, and the "best" plan selected.
7. *Selection of short-range policies and programs.* Each segment of the time frame becomes an increment in the process of plan achievement. The first five-year increment becomes the short-range period for which policies and programs must be formulated.
8. *Plan reevaluation.* The above process is repeated at regular intervals (five years), and revised plans are formulated.

Planning is then a continuous process of assessing existing problems, formulating desirable long-range states, and formulating short-range programs.

The comprehensive planning process generally includes, but is not limited to, the previous sequence of tasks. The resulting plans are generally presented in graphic and text form and include policy and general program recommendations. The plan is often adopted by local government legislation and is utilized as a general guide to capital improvements and public services. There are, however, some recent trends in the comprehensive planning process. First, the context is becoming broader. Heavy reliance on physical or capital elements is waning as additional elements are being included. More emphasis is being placed on the planning of such public services as criminal justice, public health, education, social and welfare services, and economic development, and on variables previously considered beyond control such as environmental quality and population size. A second trend involves an emphasis on "process" rather than on static "plans." For instance, more effort is being directed at improving the public decision-making process relative to the future, and less effort is directed toward formulating a picture of the ideal future. The basis for this is the belief that current rational decisions will lead to a rational future state. The two views are not exclusive but are rather an extension of planning activity.

These two trends lead to a third trend that involves the integration of the planning process into the overall management process. Increasingly, planning appears as a staff function directly under the chief executive or administrator. Planning is being treated as part of the management process, and it is not limited to physical development. Frequently planning and certain financial functions are integrated into a single department or other functional unit.

Program Planning. A "program" has been defined as the identification of the detailed resources, participants, and sequence of activities required for the implementation of a plan (or part of a plan). Program planning or analysis is the process of formulating alternative programs and selecting the best programs. Programs are functional classifications of activities that are tied directly to specific goals, objectives, and policies. They are functionally rather than organizationally defined. For example, a public program might address the functional area of public safety as a unit, although the many tasks might fall to a variety of organizational units such as the police and fire departments. In effect, programs provide the critical link between planning and implementation, thereby facilitating the analysis and evaluation of sets of activities relative to their ability to satisfy goals and objectives.

Programs have two primary components: structure and measurement. Structural elements include program categories, program subcategories, and program elements. *Program categories* are the broadest classifications of activities dealing with organization at the executive and legislative levels. Local government program categories might include general administration, public safety, human resources, and natural resources. *Program subcategories* are substantive breakdowns of program categories. For example, public safety might be broken down into such subcategories as crime prevention, fire prevention, fire fighting, law enforcement, offender retention, and rehabilitation. *Program elements,* the basic units of a program, are groups of similar activities that directly affect the defined program outputs. For example, law enforcement might be broken down into the elements of traffic enforcement, general enforcement, apprehension, and investigation. All elements are related to functions and are "cross-walked" to organizational units.[16]

"Measurement" is the second component of programs. Once program categories, subcategories, and elements have been identified, measurements are developed for program inputs and outputs. These measurements allow for the identification of the relationships between inputs and outputs and thus for the evaluation of programs. The costs and accomplishments of one program can be compared with other programs, thereby aiding the decisionmaker in selecting programs from among alternatives and allocating resources among programs to achieve the maximum progress towards satisfying goals. Program analysis includes the following elements:

1. identification of existing goals and objectives
2. selection of an appropriate evaluation criterion
3. identification and/or design of alternative means (programs) for accomplishing objectives
4. estimation of program costs and benefits for each alternative
5. application of evaluation criterion
6. presentation of findings (with uncertainties) to the decision makers
7. selection of the "best" program design.[17]

The first step (identification of objectives) is typically assumed as given. Often, however, only general goals are available and additional efforts must be assigned to the translation of goals into more specific measurable objectives. For example, the general goal of "elimination of substandard housing" is of little use in program formulation. Rather, a specific objective such as "the reduction of the number of substandard housing units by 10 percent per year" must be formulated. Setting objectives is part of the goal formulation process, because measurable objectives carry an implicit weighting or priority. Steps 2 through 7 involve the technical tasks of program analysis that are covered in considerable detail in the last four chapters of this text.

Operational Control

The function of operational control involves the planning, management, and implementation of activities that are included in the organization's programs. This integral part of the management system is responsible for carrying out the tasks that have been identified at the strategic and management planning levels. The general operational control process includes:

1. identification of program tasks
2. identification of organizational assignments
3. identification of resources to be utilized (budget)
4. identification of applicable policies and other constraints (legal, administrative)
5. selection of methods of production, with time and cost
6. selection of a sequence of tasks
7. assignment of resources (land, labor, capital)
8. monitoring of activities and adjustment

Operations in local government are usually housed in line departments, such as police, fire, public works, or water. Programs are typically formulated at the management planning level (execuive, staff planning), but normally include a high level of input from the departments. In some cases, the departments may initiate program designs for the consideration of higher level units. Program plans identify required activities or tasks that are then assigned to the various participating departments. Each department receives assignments from a number of programs. (Modern government organizational structures attempt to maintain "functional" departments such as the department of public safety or the department of human resources.) Each task assignment is accompanied by a budget allocation of resources.

Once the tasks and resources are identified, other constraints such as completion dates and timing requirements among projects must be identified. Production and delivery methods must be selected for each task along with the associated time and cost. Next, the entire set of tasks must be scheduled. Optimal scheduling is a technical task, involving some quantitative expertise. Network designs, PERT (Program Evaluation and Review Technique), CPM (Critical Path Method), and variations of these techniques are useful in formulating optimal schedules and resource assignments. Finally, the activities must be monitored to ensure that the actual conduct of tasks conforms to the constraints and schedule. Continuous evaluation allows for the real time adjustment of elements of the operational control function.

Summary

Financial functions in local government have generally evolved from the responsibility of several independent officials (for example, the treasurer or comptroller) to a centralized line department responsible to the chief executive or city manager. Planning functions have generally evolved from an independent advisory planning commission with a professional staff to a variety of organizational arrangements, including line departments under the chief executive and staff to commissions. Both finance and planning involve staff and line tasks; finance pays bills as a line function and formulates fiscal policy as a staff function, and planning reviews subdivision proposals as a line function and prepares comprehensive plans as a staff function. Because the staff functions of planning and finance are so closely interrelated there is a strong trend to combine some of these activities into a single staff (such as an office of planning and budget) under the direction of the chief executive or city manager.

An understanding of the role of planning in local government is perhaps facilitated by reviewing the overall process of management. Management is essentially a decision process whereby decision-makers choose courses of action from among alternatives. Effective management then depends on the rationality of the decisions (such as the availability of information or adherence to logic) and on the decision-making mechanism (such as an individual or group).

Management systems are composed of the interrelated continuous processes of strategic planning, management planning, operational control, and evaluation. Strategic planning involves interpretation of the public interest, the selection of goals and objectives, and the formulation of policies. Management planning involves the formulation of plans and programs directed toward satisfying the goals and objectives within the guidelines of policy. Operational control involves the scheduling and implementation of program tasks. Evaluation takes place at each of the previous levels to provide the feedback that facilitates incremental adjustments to components of the system.

Of course, this model of management process is not always obvious, or even existent, in local government situations. Certainly, organizational structure may not coincide with process components, except that city legislative entities may perform much of the strategic planning function, the city manager and his or her planning staff may perform much of the management planning function, and line departments probably perform most of the operational control. Yet, effective management depends on the existence of a rational planning process. Planning is an integral part of the management system, rather than a simple supportive element.

Notes

1. James M. Banovetz, "The Developing City," in *Managing the Modern City* (Washington: International City Management Association, 1971), p. 3.

2. International City Manager's Association, *Municipal Finance Administration* (Chicago: International City Manager's Association, 1962), p. 20.

3. Clyde J. Wingfield, "City Planning," in James M. Banovetz, ed., *Managing the Modern City* (Washington, D.C.: International City Manager's Association, 1971).

4. Alan W. Steiss, *Public Budgeting and Management* (Lexington, Mass.: D.C. Heath, 1972), p. 1.

5. Michael J. Munson, "How to Keep Plans off the Shelf: An Organizational View of Planning, Management, and Implementation" (Ph.D. dissertation, University of Michigan, 1972), p. 14.

6. Ibid., p. 24.

7. Steiss, *Public Budgeting and Management*, p. 24.

8. See Part III, Techniques of Analysis, this book.

9. James G. March and Herbert A. Simon, *Organizations* (New York: Wiley, 1958).

10. The categories are taken from Munson, "How to Keep Plans Off the Shelf," p. 15, which in turn were derived from Robert Anthony, *Planning and Control Systems: A Framework for Analysis* (Cambridge: Harvard University Press, 1965).

11. Peter O. Steiner, "The Public Sector and the Public Interest," in Robert H. Haveman and Julius Margolis, eds., *Public Expenditures and Policy Analysis* (Chicago: Markham, 1970), p. 54.

12. See Steiss, *Public Budgeting,* Chapter 3, for a more detailed treatment of the contribution of Max Weber and others.

13. Herbert Simon, *Administrative Behavior: A Study of Decision-Making in Administrative Organization* (New York: The Free Press, 1957).

14. This is not to say that the planner has any special influence over the public interest, but rather that he should have the skills required for assessing the public interest.

15. Yehezkel Dror, "The Planning Process: A Facet Design," in Fremont J. Lyden and Ernest G. Miller, eds., *Planning Programming Budgeting* (Chicago: Markham, 1968).

16. See Chapters 10 and 11 for a more detailed treatment of program analysis.

17. Harry P. Hatry, "Overview of Modern Program Analysis Characteristics and Techniques" (Washington: Urban Institute, 1970), p. 39.

Part II:
Practice

4

Fiscal Management and Planning

Local Government Finance

Finance is an integral part of every activity of local government in that the production of public and quasi-public goods and services requires the acquisition and allocation of resources, the values of which are measured in the common units of dollars. Thus, every unit of a local government is involved in some aspect of the public financial system. Because of this "integral" nature, finance is a central element in the overall management and planning system, including specific fiscal policies, plans, and programs and financial components of virtually every overall policy, plan, and program. This chapter addresses financial management and planning as a subsystem of the overall management process (as described in Chapter 3). More specifically, it examines the strategic planning and management planning components of the financial system, including basic economic research, fiscal policy analysis, long-range financial planning, capital programming, services programming, revenue programming, and operating and capital budgets. The management objective for the financial system is the direction, coordination, and control of "financial" resources to achieve organizational goals and objectives.

Organization

The distribution of financial activities within a local government may vary considerably depending on the form of government, the existing legal constraints, the size of the governmental unit, and the structure of the management system. The general emergence of the chief executive form of governmental structure (for example, city manager, strong mayor) has led to an increased centralization of management responsibility and to a concentration of financial staff functions in a single organizational unit under the chief executive. However, because any number of particular organizational variations can be satisfactory, only general guidelines can be forwarded here.

The organizational arrangement should facilitate the financial management process. Too often the organizational chart is assumed to have perpetual status, and the process is made to conform to the organizational structure. However, changing concepts of management often require changes in organizational structure. The structure exists so that processes can be carried out; the process does

75

not exist to maintain the structure. Of course, any organizational structure must accommodate multiple processes, yet the importance of the financial process demands first-order consideration. An example of contemporary organizational adaptation can be found in the many cities that have formed planning and budget units to accommodate the functional relationship between certain planning and executive budget activities. This relationship was, in turn, derived from the PPBS (Planning-Programming-Budget-Systems) movement of the 1960's.

The organizational structure should facilitate direct management control by the chief executive. Although the legislative body holds the ultimate responsibility for overall government and particular elements of the financial system (such as budget adoption and external audit), the financial management system's staff activities should be under the control of the chief executive. This is only consistent with the chief executive's responsibility for the administration of city programs and thus for the administration of city finances to carry out programs.

The organizational structure should allow for flexibility and the maintenance of horizontal ties between "finance" and other operating units, particularly with the planning unit. The tie with planning is based on the inherent connection between the policy and plan components of planning and finance. The ties to other units are based on the service function that "finance" has with line departments. For example, the finance department normally handles purchasing, payroll, fee collection, accounting, and other such operations for line departments.

The National Municipal League recommends a model organization that is based on its "Model City Charter."[1] All financial operations, except the external audit, are grouped into a department of finance under the direction of a director of finance and, in turn, under the city manager. The independent audit is the direct responsibility of the city council. Financial activities are distributed among five functional divisions: accounts, assessments, budget, purchasing, and treasury. The budget division can be operated as one of the divisions of the finance department or as a separate unit directly under the manager. The latter arrangement reflects the policy emphasis of the budget as opposed to the line emphasis of the other divisions. Either way, a functional tie must exist between the manager and the budget because the formulation and administration of the budget is the manager's responsibility.

Such an organization is appropriate for many medium-size cities, but small and large cities may require different organizational arrangements. Small cities may rely on a city manager, mayor, or an individual staff or council member to carry out most of the financial activities, with the help of some internal record-keeping (for example, city clerk) and occasional external consultants (such as accountants). Local banks may also provide some of the required services. Larger cities may have a more detailed organizational articulation of financial functions as shown in Figure 4-1.

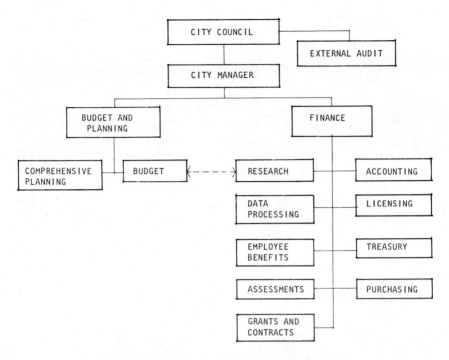

Figure 4-1. Large City Financial Organization

Roles and Responsibilities

Most local government officials and administrators have roles in the process of financial management. Although roles and responsibilities vary among cities, some common or generally accepted ones are listed below.

1. Council, commission, assembly, or other legislative body
   a. authorizes programs
   b. identifies sources of revenue
   c. appropriates funds
   d. adopts annual budgets
   e. orders and reviews an external audit
2. Manager, mayor, or other executive officer
   a. maintains overall management
   b. prepares and submits annual budgets
   c. administers adopted budgets

3. City attorney
   a. prepares ordinances
   b. reviews contracts
   c. ensures legality of financial operations
4. Finance officer
   a. directs department of finance; including numbers 5 through 8 below
5. Assessor
   a. assesses property values
   b. maintains property tax maps and records
6. Budget officer
   a. assists chief executive in preparing budget estimates and in budget administration
   b. conducts economic and fiscal analysis
7. Controller, comptroller, or accountant
   a. maintains general accounting records
   b. issues bills, taxes, and assessments
   c. issues payments and payrolls
   d. maintains inventory of city property
   e. conducts the internal audit
8. Treasurer
   a. collects revenues
   b. disburses funds
   c. maintains city treasury
   d. issues licenses
9. Auditor (external)
   a. conducts audit of financial operations
   b. prepares and submits report to the legislative body
10. City planner
    a. conducts basic economic research and policy analysis
    b. assists with planning and programming functions
    c. prepares capital budget
11. Department head
    a. assists in formulation of programs
    b. assists in budget estimates

The Fiscal Planning System

The fiscal management system is approached here as a subsystem of the overall process of management, as a series of specific financial activities that are symbiotically related to individual elements of the overall management process. Figure 4-2 shows these elements and their specific interrelationships.[2]

MANAGEMENT   FISCAL PLANNING

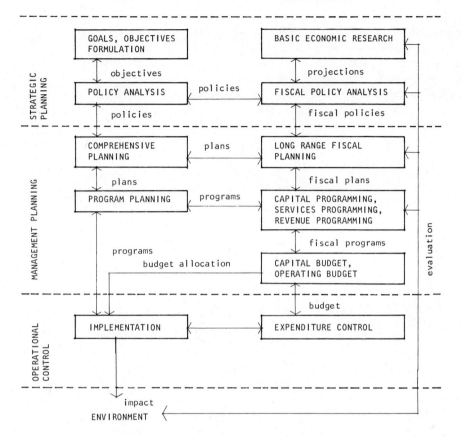

Figure 4-2. Fiscal Planning Process

The strategic planning phase includes the financial elements of basic economic research and fiscal policy analysis. Basic economic research provides the estimates or projections of future population, employment, income (estimates of demand for public goods and services), and other economic parameters as inputs to the activity of fiscal policy analysis. Fiscal policy analysis includes two essential activities: (1) the estimation of probable and potential economic and financial consequences of overall public policy alternatives being considered at the strategic planning level, and (2) the formulation and evaluation of specific alternative financial policies in terms of accomplishing public goals and objectives.

Thus the strategic planning phase of the management process produces public policies, including specific financial policies, for the management planning phase. For example, a selected overall policy might involve "the improvement of the quality of existing housing stock through the mechanisms of selective area code enforcement and rehabilitation." Presumably, this policy would have been selected from among alternative policies, because the policy analysis function showed this policy to be best in terms of satisfying goals and objectives; the estimated consequences of this alternative, including the economic and financial consequences, appeared to match the desired consequences most closely. Analyzing these economic and financial consequences is part of the fiscal policy analysis function. Likewise, a specific fiscal policy may be formulated that is consistent with and supportive of overall policies, such as "the financing of housing development programs primarily from community development block grant funds and other categorical grant program funds."

These and other policies are accepted as given in the management planning phase, where the financial activities include the formulation of long-range fiscal plans, capital, service, and revenue programs and the capital and operating budget. Long-range financial planning involves conducting a fiscal outlook study to project future levels of required expenditures and revenues, as well as formulating expenditure and revenue plans to ensure a balanced budget for future periods. This financial plan must be scaled to the comprehensive plan; in fact, they are simply two parts of the same future plan. The financial plan is then translated into shorter range and more detailed capital, service, and revenue programs. The financial programs must be integrated with the overall programs of the local government. That is, the financial programs represent the financial articulation of the capital facilities, services, and revenues required to carry out the programs of local government over some time period (often five or six years). The financial programs also serve as guidelines for the formulation of the operation and capital budgets, which in turn, allocate dollars to specific programs over a one-year period.

As programs are implemented, some control is required to ensure that expenditures are not exceeding budgeted amounts and that the revenues are not below previous estimates. Variances often exist because both are based on estimates rather than fact. Although some flexibility is built into the budgets, major variances may require readjustments in budgets, programs, plans, policies, and/or goals and objectives.

This description has moved through one cycle of a continuous financial management process. Implemented programs affect the environment in some way—it is hoped in a way that moves the environment in the direction identified by the public goals and objectives. If the environment is observed, the effect of the management process cycle is observed and can be evaluated. Adjustments are made via the feedback function (policy, plan, and program evaluation). Each cycle learns from the previous cycle; adjustments are made in successive cycles.

Using this general description of the financial management system, the following sections discuss each of the financial planning elements in more detail. Budget elements are covered separately in Chapter 5.

Basic Economic Research

Basic economic research, in the context of the local government's financial planning system, essentially involves the estimation of future levels of demand for public goods and services.[3] The local government is the producer; the citizen is the consumer. Therefore, the fiscal impact of alternative public policies will depend heavily on the future economic composition of the city. Policy formulation relative to capital investment (such as extension of public utilities, construction of roads, and land acquisition), service program development (health, education, and recreation), and revenue (taxes, user charges, and grants) will depend on estimates of future levels of population, income, land use, and other economic variables. For example, the policy relative to new school construction will depend on the projected school-age population over the span of the life of the school facility. Likewise, the financial resources required for the extension of water and sewer lines will depend on the projected area and density of new physical development, and the fiscal impact of a property tax rate reduction will depend on the future size of the tax digest.

The process of generating these estimates involves the application of certain quantitative techniques and the skills of economists, statisticians, and urban/regional planners. A complete presentation of these various techniques is beyond the scope of this text and is, indeed, a course of study of its own. However, some basic notions are presented here with references to other work in the area.[4]

First, some general comments on the use of quantitative economic analysis techniques are appropriate. Quantitative projection techniques range from the simple and inexpensive to the extremely complex. The more extensive techniques might be expected to yield more accurate or sophisticated estimates than simpler techniques in many situations. However, there is always a trade-off between the cost of analysis and the benefits promised by incrementally better analysis results. Thus, one should match the technique to the need for information; the sophistication of the technique and the level of analysis effort should vary with the importance of the decisions that will be based on the analysis results. One should select the least costly technique that will yield adequate results. Also, most of the more complex projection techniques, and to some extent all the techniques, tend to yield better results for large areas than for smaller areas. That is, a technique used to project future levels of economic activity for a state or subregion may be essentially worthless when applied to a middle-size city. In fact, most "models" (in this context, jargon for complex techniques) are developed and used at state, regional, and metropolitan levels. This size problem exists because many techniques depend on projecting future activity from past activity, which must in turn be estimated from the analysis of statistical data.

Statistical analysis depends to some extent on the analysis of large numbers of events where individual fluctuations tend to average out and where there exists some stability in population descriptors such as the average or mean. At the level of specification of many analysis techniques, most middle-size and smaller cities simply do not represent large numbers. For example, the growth rates in large metropolitan areas are generally more stable than in small rural communities, which makes it easier to project population in the former. The introduction of one unforeseen event (such as the introduction of one new industry) could drastically change the population and income levels in the small rural community, but have little overall effect on the large metropolitan area. This does not mean that smaller places must do without the benefit of basic economic projections. It does mean that smaller places where fiscal policy decisions are perhaps not overly complex and critical can rely on simpler, less extensive analysis. Larger regions and metropolitan areas where fiscal policy is more critical may rely on a more extensive program of basic economic research.

It should also be mentioned that most of the techniques covered here yield inputs to more than just fiscal policy analysis but rather to all policy analysis. For example, population projections are useful for estimating future land development and transportation demand, as well as for formulating private sector marketing projections. Likewise, an economic base study can be used to estimate future income or as an input to an industrial development program. However, in the context of financial management, the techniques are useful in projecting future levels of demand for public goods and services. Demand (see Chapter 1) is affected by the factors of population, income, distribution of income, prices of goods and services, and preferences. Thus, most of the techniques involve generating estimates of future levels of population, employment, income, and to some extent preferences and price levels. The following is a brief overview of some of the applicable techniques.

Population Projections

Statistical Methods. There are essentially three statistical approaches to projecting future levels of population: (a) the linear model, (b) the nonlinear model, and (c) the ratio method. The linear model assumes that the absolute amount of future population growth per time period will equal absolute amounts of growth in past time periods. For example, if a city has been growing by an average of 2,000 persons per year, it is assumed that it will continue to grow by that amount. The model takes the form of a simple linear regression, with the form:

$$P_{t+n} = P_t + g(n) \tag{4.1}$$

where
P = population number
t = time index
n = number of years
g = absolute growth per year

83

For example, a city of 200,000 persons, with an annual growth of 4,000 persons, would have the following model:

$$P_{t+n} = 200,000 + 4,000(n)$$

A ten-year projection would be:

$$P_{t+10} = 200,000 + 4,000(10)$$

$$P_{t+10} = 240,000$$

The actual model equation (values for P_t and g) is derived by applying a specific statistical technique (regression analysis) to historic population figures.[5] The technique (found in any statistical analysis text) essentially "fits" an equation or line to the data points, as shown in Figure 4-3. Once the line is found, it is extended to provide future estimates (dashed line).

The nonlinear model involves the same general approach except that the fitted equation or line represents some characteristic curve rather than a straight line. One such curve, the exponential, is based on the assumption of a constant rate of growth.[6] This assumption leads to a compounding effect on the total population, with the form:

$$P_{t+n} = P_t(1 + r)^n \qquad (4.2)$$

where P, t, and n are defined as in the previous equation, and where r equals the rate of growth.

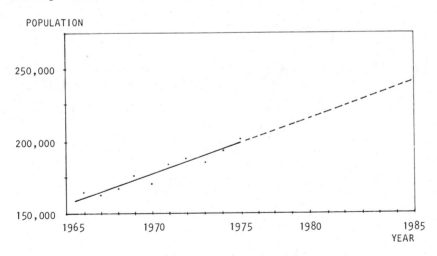

Figure 4-3. Linear Regression Population Projection

For example, a city of 100,000 persons and an average growth rate of 4 percent would have the following model:

$$P_{t+n} = 100,000(1.04)^n$$

A ten-year projection would be:

$$P_{t+10} = 100,000(1.04)^{10}$$

$$P_{t+10} = 148,024$$

This model is shown in Figure 4-4.

These two statistical models (linear and nonlinear) have the advantages of being relatively simple and inexpensive. The historical data on which the models are formulated are generally available from U.S. Census publications and from numerous other sources. Assumptions can be altered (for example, increasing rate or decreasing rate) to generate high, medium, and low population projections. In addition, the same basic techniques can be applied to the estimation of other economic variables. For these reasons the statistical methods are heavily relied upon at all levels of city size. However, they are subject to the problems inherent in the assumption that future growth is a simple function of past growth. This assumption may be acceptable in large cities exhibiting historically stable growth, but less acceptable in small areas with more variation in growth.

The third statistical technique, the ratio method, utilizes a different assumption: the future population of a particular area will be a constant percentage of

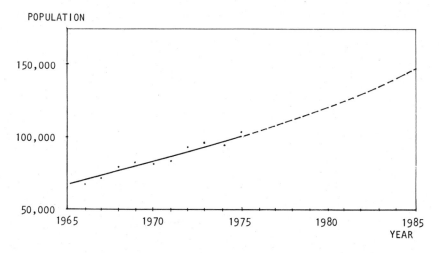

Figure 4-4. Exponential Curve Population Projection

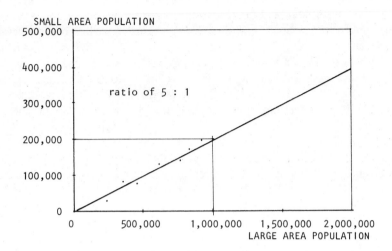

Figure 4-5. Ratio Projection

the future population of some larger area. This further assumes, of course, that future estimates exist for the larger area. That is, the larger area (whether state, region, or metropolitan area) may conduct sophisticated projection studies that yield reasonably accurate estimates. The ratio method allows the smaller unit to use those estimates. This model takes the form:

$$_1P_{t+n} = \frac{_1P}{_2P} \, _2P_{t+n} \tag{4.3}$$

where
$_1P$ = population of the study area
$_2P$ = population of the larger area

For example, a particular city may historically represent 12 percent of the state's population, or a suburban jurisdiction may historically capture an additional 1 percent of the metropolitan area's population growth in successive years. Estimates derived for the larger units can be converted to estimates for smaller units via the ratio method. Actual ratios or trends in ratios must be derived statistically from historic data (see Figure 4-5).

Composite Methods. The statistical population models yield aggregate estimates of total population based on the rather simple assumptions of stable absolute growth, rate of growth, trend in rate, and/or ratio. Estimates so derived may be satisfactory for some purposes but insufficient for others. A more sophisticated approach involves using the causal components of population change (that is, birth rates, death rates, and net migration) to project population by categories of age and sex. These composite models are usually called "cohort-survival" models, either with or without a migration element. The analysis involves dividing the total population into age categories (U.S. Census categories of five years; 0–4, 5–9, etc.) and sex categories, called "cohorts." Each cohort is projected separately to future dates (multiples of five years) by applying the effects of birth, death, and migration. For example, the 0–4 year age group is projected five years into the 5–9 year age group by multiplying the number of persons in the former group by the survival rate (1 minus the death rate). New births are projected into future 0–4 year age groups by applying birth rates to the number of women of childbearing age. Thus, each cohort is projected forward in steps of five years to yield a total population estimate that is subdivided into age and sex categories. Such projections are usually presented as an age-sex pyramid, as shown in Figure 4–6.

Because birth and death rates tend to be relatively stable, the cohort-survival model tends to yield reasonably accurate estimates in and of itself. However, the other element of change, migration, is less stable and more difficult to estimate. One estimation procedure involves comparing actual population figures for past periods with estimates of what the population would have been with only the effects of natural increase (births and deaths)—the "residual" representing the net migration. Other estimates may be derived or projected statistically from the previously discussed population methods (linear, nonlinear, and ratio) or more complex research that often occurs at the state planning levels or within universities. The cohort-survival/migration models are most useful because they yield detailed breakdowns of projected growth that can be helpful in policy analysis. For example, the long-range need for schools and facilities for the elderly clearly depend on the future populations of those age groups.

However, these techniques, like the statistical techniques, are more appropriate at the larger scale than at the smaller scale. Therefore, smaller cities usually depend on both simple statistical projections with high and low estimates and on policy formulation that is not highly dependent on accurate population projections. Middle-size cities with some growth stability can utilize both statistical and composite methods to yield reasonably good estimates for the purposes of policy analysis and planning. Larger cities and regions may use any and all methods, including complex urban growth models, to generate estimates.

Projection of Economic Variables

Statistical Methods. The basic statistical methods utilized above to estimate future population levels can also be utilized to estimate future values for a num-

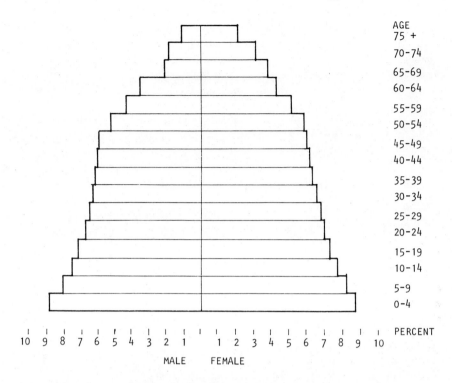

Figure 4-6. Typical Age-Sex Pyramid

ber of economic variables. That is, some economic variables exhibit sufficient stability over time to allow for statistical projection. For fiscal policy analysis, these include the elements of supply and demand: for example, income, distribution of income, price levels, cost of resources, and preferences. Linear, nonlinear, and ratio methods are all applicable. For example, future levels of aggregate income may be projected as a function of historical trends or as a ratio of estimates derived at some larger scale; the local rate of price inflation may be based on the national rates; and the preferences for public bicycle paths may be a function of the growth of sales of bicycles. Of course, the simple statistical projection of economic variables suffers from the same problems as the statistical projection of population as discussed above, but it also represents the least costly way to generate future estimates that are often sufficient for policy analysis purposes. Thus cities of all sizes tend to rely heavily on these methods.

Macroeconomic Models. There are several complex approaches to projecting future levels of economic activity, each with a number of variations. The basic approaches include the economic base model, the input-output model, and the econometric model. Several general points can be made about these more sophisticated approaches. First, they apply to large areas (such as states, regions, and standard statistical metropolitan areas) rather than to smaller, individual governmental jurisdictions, because the approaches involve the use of "economic" regions as the units of analysis—the importance being the relationships that exist between a subject economy and external factors. An individual local government seldom represents a complete economic entity, but rather a part of a larger metropolitan or regional economy. Second, the complex models tend to be many times more complex and expensive than the simpler statistical models. They require the skills of specialized economists and extensive data collection and analysis. Third, they tend to be useful for more purposes than just the projection of economic variables. That is, the more complex models involve rather extensive research efforts that can be utilized to describe the composition and performance of an economy, project future levels of economic activity, and evaluate the potential impacts of alternative policies and plans. For these reasons, the more complex approaches can be utilized on a nonroutine basis by the in-house staff of larger governmental units, by consultants, and/or by university research personnel.

The economic base model addresses the estimation of levels of income, employment, and economic output on a simple aggregate basis. The urban economy is divided into two components: the "basic" (export or nonlocal), and the "service" (local). The basic component includes those industries that sell primarily to markets outside the urban area, whereas the service component consists of those selling to local markets. The assumption is that the size of the service component is a function of the size of the basic component. The relationship is articulated as a "multiplier" that is estimated as a ratio of total activity to export activity. The demand for export goods is determined outside the urban area, and thus the total effect of a change in demand on the urban economy can be estimated as the effect on the basic component plus the effect on the service component via the multiplier. Thus, the economic base model yields gross estimates of changes in income, employment, and other factors from estimates of changes in demand for exports, with the assumption that total economic activity is solely a function of export activity. No consideration is given to growth that might occur as a result of changes in government expenditures or basic or service component composition and productivity.

The input-output model involves a more detailed examination of the economy, dividing the economy into sectors (that is, groups of similar industries) and estimating the relationships among sectors, including exports. The analysis framework includes an accounting procedure that identifies the values of inputs (such as primary resources, intermediate products, or taxes) and outputs (such as intermediate sales to other sectors, final sales to government, or exports) for each sector over a given time period. Thus, flows in dollar values are estimated among all sectors and to final use. The total value of inputs plus profits and losses equals the total value of outputs. Any change in the demand for exports can be traced back through the relationships to estimate changes in income, employment, and final output for each sector and the total economy. Thus, input-output analysis yields a more specific and conceptually complete estimate of future economic activity than the economic base analysis, but also has a correspondingly higher requirement for data collection and analysis effort.

Econometric model approaches involve the construction of complex, multi-variate statistical models that are based on historically observed relationships among economic variables and/or their proxies. Econometric analysis is technically the most complex of the economic methods (although not necessarily the most expensive) and exhibits a satisfying logical framework because it deals with a number of complex, interacting causal factors rather than with single indirect measures associated with simpler statistical projections. A complete model might consist of a number of equations, each describing the relationship between a particular economic variable (such as income) and a number of independent variables that are thought to affect the dependent variable. For example, the level of income can be predicted from levels of consumption, investment, government, exports, and imports. The values for the independent variables are derived from the statistical analysis of historical data. The simultaneous solving of the equations represents a description of the economy. Once such a model has been constructed, it can be utilized to estimate the effects of changes in any of the model's variables.

The success of econometric models at regional levels is uncertain because the development and application of such models is relatively recent, and because the understanding of the complexities or urban economies is still limited. However, the sophistication of the technique and the logical desirability of dealing with causal elements appear to offer good promise for future applications.

Summary—Basic Economic Research

In summary, basic economic research yields the future projections for population and other economic parameters that are inputs to the policy analysis function and the long-range fiscal planning function. The extensiveness of the analysis and the methods used will depend primarily on the size of the analysis unit. Smaller local governments will tend to rely on simple statistical projections and adaptation of the estimates of larger units (such as the region or state). Middle-size cities can generally support an ongoing economic research effort using in-house, consultant, or university personnel, employing a variety of techniques, including the occasional use of macroeconomic or related models. Larger cities and metropolitan areas can generally employ the full complement of techniques, including the ongoing development and conduct of sophisticated macroeconomic models and other simulations. The selection of specific techniques depends on the availability of data and staff, on the desired specificity of results, and on the critical nature of the decisions that will be based on the analysis results. The question of required accuracy in a given situation is always one of degree and is thus a matter of judgment. Policy analysis will always be conducted in the context of future uncertainty and imperfect projection techniques —yet with a substantial belief that policy formulation with better information leads to more rational policy in the long run.

Fiscal Policy Analysis

Policies are general guides to action formulated to identify the desirable or acceptable means for achieving goals and objectives and articulated at the local government level as legislation or as administrative procedure. General policy analysis addresses the formulation and evaluation of alternative policies. More specifically, fiscal policy analysis involves the formulation and evaluation of alternative fiscal policies and the estimation and evaluation of the probable economic and financial consequences of alternative general policies.

For example, a local government might want to formulate a consistent policy relative to the amount and quality of future growth. Policy analysis of this issue would involve estimating the probable effects of existing policies on past and future growth, and the formulation and evaluation of alternative growth policies (such as no growth, maximum growth, or controlled growth). The economic and financial consequences of particular growth policies would certainly be included in the analysis. That is, local government decision-makers should know the probable public and private economic and financial consequences of each policy before adopting a set of policies.

The availability of basic economic projections and some analysis techniques allow for this type of analysis. The specific techniques are not discussed here because they are structurally similar to the techniques covered in more detail in Part III, Techniques of Analysis. The major difference is that policy analysis is more general, whereas program analysis is more specific. For example, policy analysis of "growth through annexation" (for an example city) might reveal that the annexation of residential areas generally leads to a short-run net financial deficit. The program or project analysis of particular areas to be annexed might identify the exceptions to the general policy.

In addition to the general policies, fiscal policy analysis deals with the formulation and evaluation of specific fiscal policies. That is, a local government may have goals and objectives relative to economic growth, stability, equity, and efficiency, articulated as expenditure and revenue policy. For example, a city might want to reduce reliance on the property tax as a major revenue source because of the apparent inequity and inefficiency of that tax. Fiscal policy analysis would formulate and evaluate alternative revenue sources as total or partial substitutions for the property tax. On the expenditure side, analysis might be directed at estimating the economic impacts of alternative budget allocations. For example, policy analysis might explore the extent to which a city should be debt-financing, using funds for matching federal or state grants, or supporting quasi-governmental activities.

Long-Range Fiscal Planning

Long-range fiscal planning takes place in the management planning phase of the overall management system (Figure 4-2), assumes the basic economic projections and fiscal policy as given, and runs parallel to the comprehensive planning process. The fiscal plan has three functions:

1. It provides the financial dimension to the comprehensive plan.
2. It identifies the sequence of actions required to carry out fiscal policies.
3. It generates the necessary inputs to the capital, service, and revenue programs.

Long-range fiscal planning starts with the basic economic projections (that is, changes in population and other economic parameters) and the adopted fiscal policies (for example, shift of emphasis from the property tax to other existing and new revenue sources or increased reliance on user charges where possible) as outputs from the strategic planning phase of management. The development of a fiscal plan must coincide with the development of the comprehensive plan in that the overall plan of capital improvements and services must be scaled to financial feasibility. The primary element of the fiscal plan is the "fiscal outlook" study, which compares future expected levels of revenues and expenditures, identifies potential fiscal problems, and formulates actions to overcome problems. The following sections describe the sequence of fiscal planning activities.

Inventory of Activities. The first step in the "fiscal outlook" study is the construction of an "inventory of activities" composed of all existing activities and proposed activities that are included in the comprehensive plan. These items are organized on a line item or program basis with all associated costs and/or revenues (data from the accounting system).

Capital and service activities are treated separately because of the tendency to finance capital items through debt while financing service activities through operating budgets and because expenditures for many capital items are "one time only." This separation also yields a reasonable context for "balancing the budget." A balanced budget does not strictly imply that total revenues equal total expenditures within a particular time period, but rather that total revenues equal the nondebt-financed expenditures plus the "debt service." That is, a local government may finance a large capital facility via a bond issue (debt) and pay for the facility (repay the debt) over a period of years. The amount of the debt repayment, rather than the entire capital sum, is considered as an expenditure in a given year. Thus, it is possible to show a "balanced" budget each year while incurring higher levels of debt. The separate treatment of capital and service (or operating) activities provides a better overall picture of financial condition (see Chapter 8, Debt Financing).

Activities are also categorized by priority. The "required incremental" category includes the activities that are required by law and/or convention, and are considered to constitute the absolute base of local government activity. Examples would include all the basic local services, such as fire and police protection, waste collection, and utilities. The "required additions" category includes those facilities and services beyond the "required incremental" that are required to carry out previously adopted plans and programs. Examples include increases in service quality, capital elements of the comprehensive plan, and successive activities for multiyear programs. The "desirable additions" category includes essentially new facilities and programs that have not previously received financial commitment which can be postponed if necessary.

Analysis of Service Standards, Methods of Operation, and Cost Factors. After the inventory of activities is constructed (or revised from the previous year), three related activities are required. Each activity should be evaluated in terms of standards of service, methods of production and supply, and unit cost factors. The objective is to select the appropriate level of service and to relate unit cost to output for existing and alternative methods so that revisions can be made in the inventory.

Should the level of a particular service be increased or decreased? Limited resources often mean that an increase in the level of service for one activity yields a decrease in level of service for another. Intercity comparisons are sometimes useful, and standards are often suggested by national associations for particular functional areas. However, the basic process is one of setting priorities among services. The analysis of production and supply methods essentially involves scanning alternative methods for performing activity tasks, especially new technology that might yield increased efficiency. The analysis of cost factors involves identifying trends in the prices of the resources of production (such as labor and materials prices) and assessing unit costs for each existing activity and for alternative methods of performing those activities.

Estimation of Expenditures. The levels of expenditure for each fiscal year are usually estimated for future periods of five to ten years. The expenditure required for each activity, by category (from the inventory of activities), is projected by adjusting the existing expenditure with respect to expected changes in the base of the activity and the cost of the activity.[7] That is, the total expenditure equals the base multiplied by the cost per unit of base:

$$E_t = b_t(c_t) \qquad (4.4)$$

where
E = total expenditure
b = number of base units
c = cost per base unit
t = time index

For example, a solid waste collection service for 10,000 households, with a cost of $45 per houshold, would yield a total expenditure of $450,000. A five-year estimate requires a projection of changes in the number of households and changes in costs over that period. Population projections, adjusted by the number of persons per household, yields an expected number of households. Adjustments to cost figures must be based on estimated changes in factor prices (land, labor, and capital), service standards, and productivity (changes in methods of operation or technological innovation).

The general equation is:

$$E_{t+n} = b_t(c_t)\,[(1 + d)(1 + f)(1 + s)(1 + p)]^n \qquad (4.5)$$

where
E_{t+n} = total expenditures in year $t + n$
b_t = number of base units in year t
c_t = cost per unit of base in year t
d = rate of change in base (per year)
f = rate of change in factor costs
s = rate of change caused by change in service standards
p = rate of change in productivity
n = number of years

In equation (4.5), if the number of households is increasing at the rate of 6 percent per year, factor prices are increasing at 8 percent per year, service standard increases require 2 percent per year, and productivity is assumed to be constant (over the projection period), then a five-year estimate would be:

$$E_5 = 10,000\,(\$45)\,[(1 + .06)(1 + .08)(1 + .02)(1 + 0)]^5$$

$$\qquad (4.6)$$

$$= \$978,190.$$

Estimation of Revenues. Revenues are estimated in much the same way as expenditures. Total revenues include taxes, user charges, administrative fees, short-term investment returns, grants, and other transfers. Taxes, the largest revenue class, are projected to future time periods by assuming the existing rates and changes only in the tax base. Tax bases generally include the value of real estate (the property tax digest), the level of consumer expenditure (the sales tax), or income (income taxes). The rates of change of these bases, and the bases of other revenue sources can often be projected statistically, using the economic parameters covered in the previous section.

Total revenue equals the base multiplied by the rate:

$$R_t = b_t(r_t) \tag{4.7}$$

where

R = total revenue
b = number of units of the base
r = the rate applied to the base
t = time index

For example, a local income tax with a $1 million taxable income base and a 1 percent flat rate would yield a total revenue of $10,000:

$$R_t = 1,000,000 \, (.01)$$

$$= 10,000$$

Future projections are made by adjusting the base only. For example, a five-year projection assuming a 6 percent annual increase in taxable income would be:

$$R_5 = 1,000,000 \, (.01) \, (1 + .06)^5$$

$$= \$13,382$$

The general formula is:

$$R_{t+n} = b_t(r_t) \, (1 + d)^n \tag{4.8}$$

where

d = rate of change in the base

and

$R, b, r, n,$ and t are defined as above.

If the estimation of the rate of change for the base is made from the estimation of other more basic economic variables (such as income, population, or consumer expenditure), then the "revenue elasticity" of the particular tax must be considered.[8] The revenue elasticity is the percentage change in revenue relative to the percentage change in the economic variable. For example, the revenue from a local income tax may change more slowly than the level of income because of differences in taxable income and total income, or it may change faster because of a progressive tax rate. Estimates of elasticity can be derived from the analysis of historical data and may be available to local governments from state revenue agencies.

The Fiscal Outlook. Expenditures are projected for each category of activity, assuming changes in expenditure bases and costs. Revenues are likewise projected, assuming changes in the bases, without changes in rates. Thus, the projections yield an estimate of what can be expected in the absence of additional changes in policy, program, plan, or activity. These estimates can be plotted as in Figure 4-7.

   Actually, a number of such calculations and graphs are required to produce a sufficiently detailed fiscal outlook. Individual inspection should be given to each expenditure and revenue fund and/or other financial entity (such as general fund, specific capital funds, trust funds, debt repayment funds, or public utilities). The appropriate consolidation of these charts provides a summary fiscal outlook. Collectively, these estimates exhibit the expected relationships between expenditures and revenues. If revenues cover expenditures, then no exceptional action is required. However, the more typical local government situation (given recent levels of inflation and the expansion of the scope of local government services) will involve an estimated deficit in some categories, if not in the overall budget. Once the magnitude of the differences is known, alternative solutions can be formulated and evaluated. Solutions are seldom simple because of the numerous variables that can be adjusted. The level and composition of public

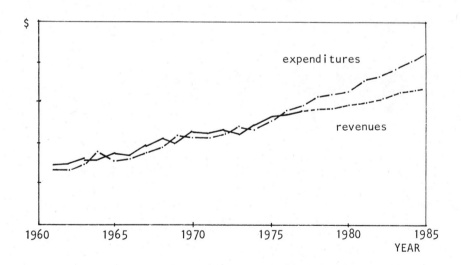

Figure 4-7. Fiscal Outlook Graph

services and the timing of capital improvements can be changed to increase or decrease the level of expenditures. Tax structure and tax rates can be adjusted to yield more or less revenue. The probable impact of any such change can be estimated by redoing the expenditure and/or revenue analysis with the changes included. Thus, alternative fiscal solutions can be evaluated in terms of fiscal impact.

The estimates, along with the required fiscal actions, constitute the long-range fiscal plan. Of course, no plan should be so rigid as to preclude subsequent change; rather the process of fiscal planning is continuous—in order to adjust the fiscal system periodically in response to changing conditions. The long-range fiscal plan is a response to future uncertainty, and is designed to provide lead time for rational fiscal decisions.

In summary, the long-range fiscal plan includes:

1. inventory of activities, by category
2. analysis of service standards
3. analysis of methods of operation
4. analysis of cost factors
5. estimation of future expenditures
6. estimation of future revenues
7. a combined fiscal outlook, the identification of problems
8. analysis of alternative solutions
9. recommended set of fiscal actions, in sequence, with the probable effects, leading to a balanced budget and a good financial condition

Capital, Service, and Revenue Programs

A program is a statement of a set of interrelated resources and activities, ordered in sequence, that is required to carry out some part of a plan. Capital, service, and revenue programs are formulated to carry out the long-range fiscal plan. In other words, fiscal programs translate the fiscal plan into shorter range (five years in one-year increments) financial components of the program activities of local governments. For example, the capital program includes a list and description of each proposed capital project with an assignment of resources (dollar amounts) over a five-year period. This display is useful in that capital projects may take more than one year to complete, and once started, represent a commitment to a certain level of expenditure. All the projects and the related expenditures make up the total capital program. Often, the first year of the five-year capital program is adopted directly as the fiscal year's capital budget.

The capital program includes:

1. list and description of each capital project including the purpose of the project

2. estimation of the costs for each project over a five-year period
3. source of funds for each project
4. corresponding service costs for each capital project
5. interrelationships among projects, including physical, financial, and timing
6. priority list
7. summary of the total capital program

The service program and the revenue program are essentially similar to the capital program, including a list and description of services and tax sources, and covering a five-year period. They have a similar function of grouping expenditures and revenues at the level of specific activities. However, they are generally not adopted directly as budgets, but rather guide the formulation of the operating budget and its related tax legislation.

The formulation of the budget is treated extensively and separately in Chapter Five.

Notes

1. The International City Managers' Association, *Municipal Finance Administration,* 6th ed. (Chicago: The International City Managers' Association, 1962), p. 23.

2. As with the management model of Chapter 3, the management side of this figure was derived from the work of Munson and Anthony; see note 10, Chapter 3.

3. Basic economic research is also applied to broader economic aspects such as "growth," see note 4, Chapter 1.

4. An excellent and general text in the area of quantitative methods is Donald A. Krueckeberg and Arthur L. Silvers, *Urban Planning Analysis: Methods and Models* (New York: Wiley, 1974).

5. Regression analysis actually involves several variations, but the most common is "simple least squares linear regression" which in most population projection cases can be performed rather simply by hand and calculator. Large data sets may require the use of a computer; most statistical package program sets will include regression analysis. Also, several statistical measures are available to assess the accuracy of the regression model; see the standard error of the estimate and the coefficient of correlation.

6. Other curves often used include the modified exponential, the Gompertz curve, and certain linear transformations; see Krueckeberg and Silvers, *Urban Planning Analysis,* Chapter 2.

7. The expenditure and revenue estimation framework can be found in Werner Z. Hirsch, *The Economics of State and Local Government* (New York: McGraw-Hill, 1970), pp. 280-290.

8. See Chapter 1, Elasticity.

5 Budgeting

Introduction

This chapter covers the process of budgeting as an integral part of the overall fiscal planning and management system described in Chapter 4. The functions of basic economic research, fiscal policy analysis, long-range fiscal planning, and capital, service, and revenue programming are assumed to have been essentially completed before the actual preparation of a budget. The reader should be aware, however, that the term "budgeting" is often used to refer to the overall process of allocating resources as well as to the preparation of specific documents.

The budget historically referred to "the leather bag in which The Chancellor of the Exchequer carried to Parliament the statement of the Government's needs and resources."[1] Eventually the meaning shifted to refer to the document itself. Today, the budget is the central element of public fiscal management as well as a major element in the overall process of local government; it is both a document and a complex, collective decision process. It can be defined as the financial articulation of the activities of a governmental unit that at the local level takes the form of an ordinance or resolution which recognizes anticipated revenues, authorizes activities, and appropriates expenditures for a one year time period.

Budget formulation is a complex process involving aspects of planning, politics, economics, and accounting. It is a planning process because it involves making decisions under conditions of uncertainty that have consequences for future time periods. Goals and objectives must be formulated, policies analyzed, and comprehensive plans and programs delineated before the budget can be formulated (see Chapter 4). It is not unusual for a local government to initiate the budget planning process a full year before the budget adoption. Budgeting becomes a political process because it is the collective mechanism whereby decisions are made about "who gets what" in the local public sector—how the resources of local government are to be allocated. Furthermore, budgeting is an economic process because allocating resources is a primary function of any economic system. Budgeting is therefore the public substitute for the automatic allocational mechanisms of the private market system. Finally, budgeting is an accounting process whereby revenue and expenditure information is structured to facilitate continuous inspection, evaluation, and management control. This complex process works at the local level of government largely because of a systematic procedure—although there is a great deal of disagreement about the best procedure. A typical step-by-step budgeting process is presented here. However, any single governmental unit may vary from this process in a variety of ways depending on its own situation and needs.

The Budget Process

Budgeting process commonly involves four major activities:

1. executive preparation
2. legislative review, modification, and enactment
3. executive implementation
4. postaudit

The chief executive (such as a strong mayor or manager) is responsible for preparing budget estimates and a preliminary budget document. Depending on the size of the city, the executive may prepare the budget alone or may rely heavily on the staff work of a budget officer, the finance department, and the planning department. This "executive budget" is presented to the legislative body (such as a council or board) and to the public before the start of the fiscal year. The legislative body reviews the proposed budget, holds public hearings, and makes changes if necessary or desirable. The final budget is adopted with a resolution or ordinance that authorizes activities, appropriates monies, and sets tax rates. The chief executive then administers the final budget. Changes may be necessary during the budget year because of differences between estimated and actual revenues and expenditures, emergencies, and shifting priorities. Typically these are affected with amendments to the budget ordinance. The last general activity is the postaudit, which is an external accounting of the actual financial activities for a budget year; this is presented to the legislative body. Each of these general activities can be broken down into a number of specific activities and set in a time sequence of a budget calendar.

The Budget Calendar

Local government budget authority, and sometimes procedure, is set in state law or local government charters or both. Detailed budget procedure is usually presented in an administrative document at the local level. This budget manual normally outlines several budget activities and a budget calendar or cycle. Budgets are effective for a one-year period, either as a fiscal year from July 1 to June 30 or as a calendar year from January 1 to December 31. Other years can also be used, but in general there is a coordinative advantage in utilizing a calendar that is the same as that used by higher levels of government. Figure 5-1 shows a

101

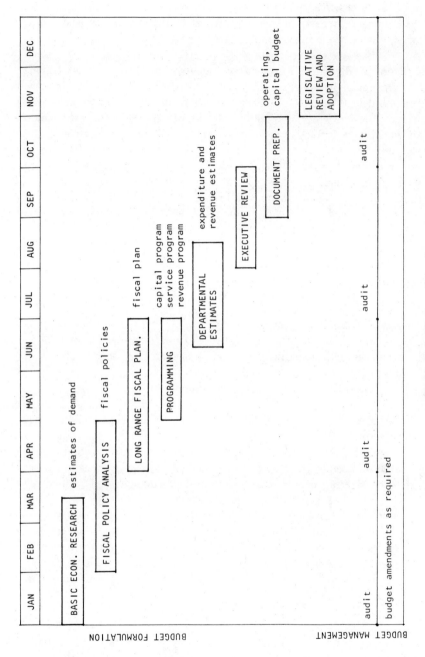

Figure 5-1. Budget Calendar

sample activity chart/calendar for a budget cycle on a calendar year basis with a one-year budget preparation sequence. Each of these activities is described below, starting with the first steps of executive preparation.

Basic Economic Research, Fiscal Policy Analysis, Long-Range Fiscal Planning, and Programming. In actuality, the analysis, planning, and programming activities discussed in Chapter 4 are the first steps in the budgeting process. Basic economic research, which is often an ongoing process, generates estimates of future population, income, employment, and so on; these factors are used as measures of future aggregate demand for public goods and services. Fiscal policy analysis provides estimates of the probable economic and financial consequences of public policies and formulates specific fiscal policies. Long-range fiscal planning uses these estimates and policies to consturct a long-range fiscal plan for revenues and expenditures, based on the fiscal outlook. This fiscal plan is then converted to more detailed five- or six-year programs for revenues and capital and service expenditures. These prebudget activities are not strictly sequential, but rather overlapping, concurrent activities whereby the important parameters of the budget are identified. In this example, a full six months (or half the overall budget cycle) is devoted to these activities.

Departmental Estimates. Given the outputs of the above activities, the chief executive issues a budget memorandum to all department heads and to others with expenditure responsibilities. This communication lays the groundwork for the detailed budget requests of each department.

The memorandum includes the following items:

1. *Anticipated fiscal policy.* A summary of the overall fiscal situation, with policies that will affect departments, such as changes in total or particular revenues and expenditures or changes in personnel policies and salaries.
2. *Capital and service programs.* A summary of anticipated activities over a five- or six-year period, including continued, discontinued, and/or new programs, with expenditure and revenue estimates
3. *Departmental activity inventory.* The activity inventory described in Chapter 4 for each department organized by budget category, including projected service volumes, service standards, methods of operation, and cost factors
4. *Request for departmental budget request.* A standardized set of forms, designed to facilitate executive review, which is consistent with budget and accounting format

The department head reviews the budget memorandum and completes and submits the budget request forms. In effect, the department head is formulating a budget for his own department and planning the assignment of the resources of personnel, equipment, and supplies to the programs and activities of the department within the constraints identified in the memorandum. This task yields an estimate of the budget amount required by the department. Of course, this activity is not carried out in isolation; the department head has been involved in much of the previous planning process, including the formulation of the activity inventory, setting service standards, selecting methods of operation, and formulating capital and service programs. These uniform departmental requests bring all of the budgets together in a common format that can be analyzed and adjusted.

Executive Review. Every local government operates in a situation of limited resources, and many operate under relatively severe fiscal constraints. That is, there is simply not enough revenue to allow a city to do everything it would like to do. Therefore, one of the major budgeting tasks for the chief executive involves balancing total required expenditures with total expected revenues. (State laws usually prohibit a city from budgeting expenditures that exceed expected revenues or some percentage of expected revenues.) Department heads, primarily concerned with their own units, will generally submit and argue for budget amounts that, when taken collectively across all units, exceed the estimated revenues. The executive must combine these requests into a single budget; thus the process at this stage is one of budget cutting. Therefore, department heads will often submit artificially high requests in anticipation of inevitable cuts. The extent to which this occurs depends on the specificity of the constraints imposed by the fiscal policies, plans, and programs (in the budget memorandum), on the extent of the overall fiscal crunch, and on the working relationship between the department heads and the chief executive or other designated budget officer. The chief executive must work closely with department heads to make adjustments that will bring the total budget into line with overall constraints. A dissatisfied department head may have another chance at the budget later, in the legislative review process. In summary, the chief executive, relying on planning estimates, plans, and programs, has the responsibility for assembling the budget from the departmental requests and nondepartmental items (such as fixed costs and debt service).

Document Preparation. Once the executive budget has been formulated, it is submitted to the legislative body and the general public. Budget documents include the following:

Budget Message and Summary. This document presents a clear summary of the important features of the budget. It covers past, present, and estimated future economic parameters (growth, income), financial condition, revenue and expenditure levels, as well as needed changes in fiscal policy, and a brief description of the operating and capital programs. Generally, the summary will also present total estimated revenues by source and total planned expenditures broken down by departments or programs. This document is typically prepared in multiple copies and made available to the public.

Detailed Operating Budget. Like all budget documents, the detailed operating budget can take a variety of forms: program or line item, unified or separate capital. The typical line item budget organizes expenditure amounts by departments, funds, and category of expenditure: for example, personnel, supplies and materials, and contractual services. The program budget is organized by program, activity, and category of expenditure.

Capital Budget. Items of expenditure that are generally nonrecurring, large, of a fixed investment nature, and long term are called "capital items." Such items include street improvements, water and sewer lines, new buildings, purchase of land, and new major equipment. These are sometimes organized into a separate budget because of their increased reliance on planning periods of more than one year. The capital budget is derived from the capital program, with each project identified and described and total costs programmed over a five-year period. The first year of the five-year estimate is the capital budget for the coming fiscal year.

Ordinances. The budget package generally includes all the legal documents needed to adopt the budget including appropriations, authorizations, and resolutions.

Legislative Review. The chief executive submits the budget documents to the legislative body accompanied with a verbal presentation of the budget message. Copies are made available to the press, libraries, organizations, and interested groups and individuals; public hearings are then scheduled and advertised. The council reviews the budget as a complete body or by subcommittee. Public hearings are conducted; citizens have the opportunity to provide additional information and criticism. Department heads may also testify to clarify parts of the budget and sometimes to request a higher level of expenditure. After the public hearings have been held and the review completed, the legislative body may make changes in any part of the budget within normal legal constraints.

Adoption. As the final budget is formulated, the legislative body adopts it by resolution or ordinance. If changes to the executive budget have been extensive, the adopted budget is reprinted; if not, only the changes are printed and attached. The adoption should occur before the start of the fiscal year, although this is not always the case. The inherent complexity, the political focus, and typical bureaucratic processes may delay the adoption beyond the start of the year. In this case, legislation is adopted that allows expenditures to be made at the previous year's rate until a budget is adopted. The adopted budget is sent to the chief executive for implementation.

Budget Management, Amendments, and Audit. The chief executive has responsibility for administering the adopted budget. Three basic mechanisms facilitate this process: the allotment system, the accounting system, and financial reports. The allotment system provides a basic spending control by releasing funds to departments on a quarterly or monthly basis. This system is tied into the accounting system, which in turn is designed to record all financial transactions and to show the total financial condition at any given time. Periodic reports, taken from the accounting information, are submitted to the chief executive. Thus, the executive can periodically assess financial condition including the comparison of budget estimates with actual expenditures and revenues. For example, actual revenues may exceed or fall short of previous estimates, indicating the opportunity to increase expenditures or the need to order spending reductions. One department may be underspending while another is overspending, indicating the need for budget or activity shifts. The budgeting/accounting system should be flexible enough to allow for routine adjustments. This is sometimes accomplished by appropriating monies to a contingency fund and/or an executive's emergency fund. However, major adjustments will generally require an amendment to the budget in the form of legislation that must be passed by the council.

Part of the management system is the audit—a formal examination and verification of the accounts. There are two types: internal and external. The internal audit is conducted quarterly or semiannually by city staff or consultants and produces reports for internal management purposes. The external audit or postaudit (normally required by state law) is conducted by external certified public accountants after the fiscal year has been completed; it is submitted to the legislative body and the regulating state agency. The legislative body then reviews the audit to ensure that revenue and expenditure activities were conducted according to the intentions of the budget.

Budget Problems and Approaches

There is a great deal of variability in budgeting mechanics among local governments.[2] Legal requirements in state law and local charters may determine and constrain the process for any particular unit. Generally, the larger a city, the more complex the process. In very small cities, the entire budget might be formulated at a single meeting of the city council, where allocations are made intuitively by knowledgeable members. But in most cities the budget is a major management function. In large cities, a full-time commitment of a considerable staff may be required.

In any case, a number of problems exist in the budgeting process. Recognition of deficiencies has led to considerable debate and disagreement over the normative aspects of the budgeting process. There are essentially two opposing views of budgeting on a continuum, with a number of intermediate positions.

The critical issue between the extremes is the extent of central control over budget formulation. Historically, budgeting has been a decentralized process.[3] At the federal level, until the Budget and Accounting Act of 1921 established the executive budget, departments submitted their budget requests directly to Congress. In 1949, the Hoover Commission forwarded the concept of "performance budgeting," which required strong central budget planning and management. In 1961 the Defense Department adopted a planning-programming-budgeting-system (PPBS), and in 1965 twenty more federal agencies followed. Budget responsibility, through the president and the Office of Management and Budget (OMB), has increasingly shifted towards central control. This issue again surfaced in 1973 and 1974 when President Nixon impounded funds that had been appropriated by Congress. Congress reacted by passing legislation in 1974 that provided for some budget staff functions and increased budget control within Congress. The federal question remains unsolved and the debate continues: central control or decentralized process?

The federal experience with strong central mechanisms such as PPBS has been far short of initial expectations—to the point where formal PPBS has all but been abandoned at that level. However, many state and local governments are following the trend of the federal government to more centralized budget control. Many have adopted, or are in the process of adopting, central systems with varying but considerable success.[4] At this level there is much disagreement over whether more central control is desirable. The opposing views can be labeled as the "rational" approach and the "leave it alone" approach. The rational approach is an attempt to reform budget processes by incorporating certain concepts of central planning and management to increase allocational efficiency. The leave it alone approach is derived from a careful examination and evaluation of actual budgetary practices with the conclusion that reform measures often do more harm than good. This is not just a difference between the normative (what ought to be) and the positive (what is), because advocates of both approaches believe that their view leads to better budgeting outcomes.

The Rational Approach

Popular terminology for the rational or contemporary approach inclues systemic planning, program budgeting, cost-benefit, cost-effectiveness, and PPBS. All these terms describe a general approach that has been synthesized from the contributions of a variety of disciplines including economics (microeconomics, marginal analysis, public finance), public administration (organization and administration), operations research (quantitative analysis, decision theory, systems analysis), and urban planning (concern with future uncertainty). Approaches vary in application, but all have the common element of attempting to improve the rationality of the decision processes in the public sector by introducing both structural and procedural changes. The major focus is on the financial or budget decision, with the objective being the achievement of the best, or at least a better, utilization of limited resources. The approach involves direct ties among public policy formulation, comprehensive planning, and financial operations often in one organization under the central control of a chief executive.[5]

Several elements are dominant in the rational approach:

1. concern with process
2. program structure
3. quantitative analysis
4. extended time horizon

The concern with process is important in several aspects. First, the approach is not substance or "end-state" oriented. That is, it deals with the procedure rather than the end product. The emphasis is on establishing a rational process of decision-making, which then produces more rational decisions. The process is relatively value-free in that it aids the decision-maker by providing organized, factual information. Of course, any decision is based on both value and fact; yet the marginal contribution of contemporary techniques deals mostly with facts. Second, the introduction of new techniques and processes to an existing institution involves both organizational and administrative changes. This implies that the existing process is understood and found wanting and that the process can be altered in the desired direction through the incremental introduction of changes to the existing structure. Again, the emphasis is on the resultant process, not the structure itself.

The second dominant element is program structure. This involves a change from the traditional line item or departmental grouping of expenditures to groupings that reflect efforts aimed at particular public objectives. The emphasis in the former is on inputs such as expenditures for capital and labor for a particular department, regardless of the multiple missions of the department. The latter emphasis is on both inputs and outputs for a particular activity or program, regardless of multiple departmental involvements. This structure allows the comparison of program outputs to inputs in terms of cost-benefit or cost-effectiveness measures. Alternate programs can then be ranked with respect to their ability to satisfy objectives, and rational expenditure decisions can be made.

The third element of the contemporary approach is quantitative analysis. This usually involves the application of scientific techniques to the public decision problem—the application of systems analysis and specific mathematical techniques to the analysis of public programs, with the objective of generating factual information that can be utilized by decisionmakers. Part III of this text, Techniques of Analysis, addresses specific techniques.

The last element is the extended time horizon, which affects the planning component in the budget process. The traditional process relies on a one-year cycle, and places very little emphasis on the kinds of approaches identified in Chapter 4 (such as basic economic research, fiscal policy analysis, and long-range fiscal planning). Rather, it relies heavily on the political and legislative aspects of budget formulation. However, most public programs extend for periods of more than one year, and thus considerable lead time is required for major decisions. Program decisions in a particular year will affect consequences in future years. Therefore, contemporary approaches rely heavily on planning techniques to extend the time horizon of the budget from one year to five or six years. Although the fiscal year budget remains as the primary tool, multiyear programs provide inputs to each year's budget decisions.

The Leave it Alone Approach

The leave-it-alone approach is best represented by the writings of Wildavsky and Lindbloom.[6] This approach argues that the budgeting process works primarily because of, not in spite of, its decentralized process. Attempts to rationalize the budget process are thought to be counterproductive. Budgeting is essentially a "political' process in an environment of uncertainty about the future consequences of current decisions and competition for resources. In this situation decisionmakers (council members) do not attempt to maximize total welfare (as with rational systems), but rather attempt to "satisfice."[7] Council members consider only a limited set of practical alternatives and accept the first one that satisfies the objectives, thereby attempting to save time and energy. Complex questions are "muddled through" by fragmenting issues and relying on the specialized knowledge of individual council members or staff experts.[8] The process works because of "partisan mutual adjustment" and "disjointed incrementalism."[9] Partisan mutual adjustment holds that people can coordinate among themselves without being coordinated by an external source. Persons with different bases of power and different views of the problem can arrive at solutions through bargaining with one another in a give-and-take format. In this "fair share" ethic, council members "win some" and "lose some" and everyone is somehow satisfied over the long run. Departments and agencies compete for budget resources and in so doing arrive collectively at a satisfactory budget allocation. Disjointed incrementalism is the process whereby decisionmakers view decisions on a continuum rather than as simply correct or incorrect. Budget allocations are not made from a zero base but rather as incremental changes from previous budget allocations. Departments are essentially requesting a little more or a little less. All these mechanisms allow budget participants to arrive at reasonable, although not optimal, budget decisions. The imposition of rational mechanisms tends to subvert this process.

Few proponents of the leave it alone approach argue that long-range planning and quantitative analysis are inappropriate tools. Rather they argue that these tools should only be used so far as they provide useful information to the decisionmakers in the traditional budgeting process. They argue that the imposition of the structural and procedural change implied by a full rational approach is unproductive and even destructive.

Considerations for Local Government

Given these polar views of the budgeting process, local governments, their managers, and planners must decide whether or not they should attempt to adopt a contemporary budgeting structure and process. The answer can not be a simple yes or no; rather it is complicated by a wide range of alternative routes between extremes. A rational decision depends on the local government's particular situation and on a careful assessment of specific financial management needs. Very small cities may utilize a traditional, decentralized process with considerable success, because budget management problems are not so complex that they cannot be solved intuitively. Larger cities may find that it is to their advantage to adopt only some of the aspects of a contemporary PPBS, while other cities may find it better to adopt a complete system.[10] In any case, the decision depends on specific management needs.

Although it is impossible to identify and review all the possible financial management situations, several critical needs appear to be quite common among local governments.[11] They include:

1. response to uncertainty of future time periods
2. response to current problems or issues
3. formulation of a balanced budget

Noticeably absent from this list is "the overall, efficient allocation of resources"—one of the major objectives of a completely contemporary system. Although this is, in fact, the overall goal of financial management and planning, it is not one of the immediate, critical problems perceived at the local level. Many local government services are required by law and must be supplied to all residents. Marginal changes in routine expenditures for particular services are usually made in response to a need to maintain an existing level of service for a changing population or area or to change the desired or required quality of service. Nonroutine expenditures are made in response to unexpected crises or opportunities and to problems related to the timing of interrelated capital investments. Contemporary systems (such as PPBS) establish the structure for optimal allocation (marginal principals), yet the state of the art is such that efforts are more successful when applied to the suboptimization of smaller scale problems, and less successful when applied to overall allocational efficiency. For example, it is easier to decide which make of police vehicle to buy than to resolve the allocation of resources among public safety, public health, and education.

Future Uncertainty. Appropriate response to future uncertainty is a critical problem at the local level. The budget is the chief fiscal tool and is traditionally formulated on yearly basis. Concern with the future is incorporated in the five-year capital program and the loose mechanism of incrementalism. That is, it is assumed that with minor adjustments each department will continue to need its current proportion of the budget. Decisionmakers concern themselves with the incremental amounts rather than the total quantities. There is, however, a real need for an extended time horizon. Projects and programs are generally continuous in that they operate over a period of years, with costs and benefits often accruing far into the future. The future impacts of current decisions are affected by trends in:

1. basic economic parameters (economic growth and stability)
2. the demand for public goods and services (such as population, geographic area, income, and prices)
3. revenue capacity and expenditure requirements
4. intergovernmental relations (federal and state grants and aids)
5. unforeseen emergencies

Systematic fiscal planning allows for the identification of potential future problems and opportunities so that appropriate fiscal responses can be formulated. Solve the problems before they reach crisis proportions and exploit the opportunities.

The question is then, How should these concerns be incorporated into local government management? Effective planning requires considerable time and effort, for which only future results are promised. Therefore, a substantial commitment is required over the long run. More importantly, fiscal planning must be considered as an integral part of the overall process of local government management rather than as a separate activity. The general management model of Chapter 3 and the fiscal management model of Chapter 4 together represent a complete guide to essential fiscal planning activities. The extent to which each activity should be performed will depend on the needs and resources of each individual governmental unit. The smallest units of local government must often rely on the expertise of members of the city council, the city manager, or outside consultants (urban planning or public management firms) to perform certain planning tasks. Larger governments with a planning department will probably assign fiscal planning activities to that unit; planners are likely to have the skills required for data analysis and future projections, in addition to concern with other nonfiscal planning matters. However, most professional urban planners have limited training in the more practical aspects of public finance, and therefore, some additional expertise (public administration, accounting, or economics) may be required. Larger cities with substantial management resources can support combined organizational units of "budget and finance" specifically to carry out fiscal planning activities.

Response to Current Problems or Issues. Not all problems are anticipated so far in advance that solutions can be planned and activated. Rather, a great number of problems arise on a short-term basis in the sense that they are unanticipated or that they have existed for some time but have remained previously unidentified and unarticulated. Local governments must respond to these situations, often in a financial context, and often without adequate information or resources. The process is known as "fire fighting," and related expenditures must come from contingency or emergency accounts or budget shifts. Money is not the only problem, however, because cities must also decide how to respond to particular problems. What is the problem? What are the alternative responses? What are the related costs and benefits? What is the cost of delay? How should it be financed? These and other questions require specialized analysis.

Contemporary approaches usually establish this analysis capability in a core unit under the chief executive. However, there are other options for local government. For instance, existing staff might be assigned to an interdepartmental analysis unit on an ad hoc basis. Persons with training in public administration, business, industrial management, engineering, and city planning are likely to have some applicable analytical skills. Another option might involve assigning analysis tasks to a particular department or office such as city manager, finance, or city planning. Cities can often establish a current problems analysis capability without major reorganization or structural change. The applicable techniques of analysis are covered in Part III of this text.

Balanced Budget. Another and perhaps the most critical need at the local level involves balancing the budget. Increasing levels of demand for public goods and services, rapidly increasing public employee wages, general price inflation, citizen tax resistance, and contrained fiscal authority combine to create a situation where revenue capacity falls short of required expenditures. This is the inevitable problem of scarce resources, and neither the traditional or the contemporary approaches to budgeting can totally solve the problem. Budget cutting remains a complex problem of hard choices among alternatives—affected by individual and collective values, precedent, and other factors. However, some activities within the contemporary approach can contribute to the rationality of the budget decision. Much of the approach is designed to create better information about the potential consequences of alternative decisions. Better information presumably promotes better decisions. Goals, objectives, and policies are developed to serve as general guides to decisions. Plans and priorities relate decisions to each other in a comprehensive context, so that one can estimate the effect of a decision in one area on decisions in other areas. Program analysis yields alternatives for decisions with estimates of relative costs and benefits. All these elements are essential to good decisions, whether in a traditional or full PPBS system. Of course, many of the above elements are characteristic of comprehensive or land use and transportation planning systems. However, the intent here is to go beyond that— with the suggestion that fiscal and other planning activities be integrated into the overall system of local government management.

Capture the Best. To summarize the previous four sections, local governments need not adopt a complete PPBS system to develop and maintain an efficient financial management and planning system. In fact, the wholesale adoption of such a complete contemporary system can create a variety of problems, including:

1. the imposition of unnecessary structural or organizational change
2. the overreliance on quantitative techniques
3. unnecessary staffing and expense

The rational or contemporary approach, including the adoption of a program format budget, attempts to establish an overall central control and a systems context for public fiscal management. The system, theoretically, looks across all activities, and assigns resources (the budget decision) to those activities that exhibit the highest marginal net benefit, thus maximizing the total benefit given the resources at hand. This is simply putting the money where it does the most good. The overall systems view, however, requires structural or organizational changes. Changes may include the creation or dissolution of departments, the reassignment of staff, authority, and responsibility, and the revision of administrative procedures. Because these changes involve all units, they must be imposed from the top of the management hierarchy and accepted down the line. However, institutional change is a difficult process, especially when it is not self-initiated, large in magnitude, and when the benefits are marginal and long range.[12] The change is complicated by the fact that the uncertainty of a new system and legal constraints may require that traditional systems and documents be maintained, thus creating a dual system. Local officials are likely to view this as a duplication of effort and needless additional work for already overworked staff.

The concept of better public decisions in this context is based on the systematic design and evaluation of alternate decision paths. If the consequences of alternate decisions can be estimated, then decisionmakers can presumably select the best alternatives. Program structures of inputs and outputs relative to particular public objectives at least allow the decisionmakers to view the problem in a rational way. There is obvious benefit to this alone. However, the "correctness" of the decision relies heavily on the estimates of the costs and benefits. This is where quantitative techniques are applied, usually in the form of cost-benefit or cost-effectiveness analysis. This is perhaps the most promising part of the general approach, but at the same time the weakest.

Decisions have both "factual" and "value" components, and at the local level the value components are often dominant. This enhances rather than reduces the importance of the factual. Analysis addresses this need. However, analysis in the public sector is in its early stages of development, and successes at the local level are marginal. Where the major costs and benefits associated with an alternative program can be formulated in dollar terms, analysis is likely to produce good results. Such is the case with the evaluation of physical systems such as water, sewer, and street programs. However, when "social" and "quality" factors dominate, analysis results in less precise estimates. The fact that contemporary approaches are often sold on the basis of analysis coupled with the fact that analysis has had only limited success, produces a credibility gap that may constrain progress in fiscal management.

The introduction of a new system also requires considerable effort in terms of staff and expense. The system must be designed, introduced, operated, evaluated, and modified to meet the needs of a changing environment. Large units of government may be able to absorb this expense and even find qualified staff persons within existing departments. The more common case with smaller units of government is that additional activities require new, specialized staff without offsetting reductions in existing staff. This means that units adopting contemporary approaches must carry significant expense over a developmental period without immediate, tangible benefits.

So, in fact, the hasty adoption of a complete system can lead to some problems. Yet utilizing a contemporary central budgeting system seems to provide many significant advantages. The financial management system, as described in Chapter 4 and in the first part of this chapter, can serve as a guide to a reasonably complete system. The details of specific application in a particular local government situation will depend on the particular needs and resources of that local government. Local governments may find the most satisfactory approaches are those which attempt to capture appropriate benefits without incurring the cost of a total reform. Aaron Wildavsky is probably the most influential advocate of this general approach. He writes, "We wish to argue that cities do not have to swallow the whole system to improve decision-making and enhance resource allocation."[13] Further, Meltsner and Wildavsky recommend that most budgeting remain on a line item basis and program budgeting be utilized only in specific situations where costs and benefits are easily identifiable; a group of policy analysts should work directly under the manager or mayor, and elaborate studies should be left to consultants. This type of approach avoids the imposition of major organization and administrative changes such as the creation of new organizational units and adoption of program structure in favor of modest procedural changes within existing structure. New procedures can be introduced, developed, evaluated, and if successful, adopted. Once adopted, they become building blocks to a larger system. Thus, the system can grow incrementally, from the bottom up, to meet the changing needs of governmental unit.

Budget Types and Formats

Budget types and formats may vary considerably among local governments to meet particular needs. Small cities may utilize a line item approach in typed copy, while larger units of government may utilize a modified program budget approach with a complex computer-oriented accounting system printout. In

GENERAL FUND EXPENDITURES

DEPARTMENT OF STREETS

Account Number	Account Title	Actual Expenditures		Appropriations
		1974	1975	1976
4501	Sign Division			
A1	Salaries	132,451.13	137,691.75	150,000.00
B1	Operating Supplies	8,388.12	9,115.10	10,000.00
C3	Auto Expense	12,053.14	13,751.76	14,000.00
.	.	.	.	.
.				
	Total	283,151.60	299,452.12	310,000.00

CAPITAL FUND EXPENDITURES

STREET IMPROVEMENT

Account Number	Account Title	Actual Expenditures		Appropriations
		1974	1975	1976
7315	Construction			
P1	Purchase Bell St. R.	–	–	121,000.00
P6	Realign Bell St.	–	–	200,000.00
P8	Smith St. Widening	76,181.50	84,051.78	76,000.00
.	.	.	.	.
.				
	Total	872,155.61	931,899.13	1,100,700.00

Figure 5-2. Combined Operating and Capital Budget

general, the format should be consistent with the unit's accounting system. However, the final format is not so important if the governmental unit has a systematic budgeting process that includes the elements covered previously in this chapter.

General budget types include (1) combined operating and capital budget, and (2) separate operating and capital budgets, as well as (1) line item budget, (2) program budget, and (3) modified program budget. That is, budgets can be either combined or separate, and can be line item, program, or modified program, for six possible combinations. Some typical formats for these are outlined below.

Figure 5-2 shows a combined operating and capital budget with a line item format. Monies are budgeted by department and by object of expenditure. Actual expenditures for the previous year and the current year (estimated) are shown, as well as the fiscal year's budget appropriations. Capital funds are shown in the same format. Figure 5-3 shows the same format for revenues. Figure 5-4 shows a program budget format with the identification of program, program category, and program activity (with reference to the program descriptions in the service, capital, and revenue programs), and with monies budgeted by activity. If an activity is split among departments, it is indicated. A modified program budget (not shown) utilizes the basic program structure, but assigns monies within categories or activities by object of expenditure (such as salaries or supplies).

Figure 5-5 shows a typical capital program and budget, where the first year of the program is the budget appropriation. Generally, such budgets will

GENERAL FUND REVENUES

TAXES

Account Number	Account Title	Actual Receipts		Expected 1976
		1974	1975	
1001	Tangible Property	4,132,790.15	4,351,701.31	4,400,000.00
1002	Intangible Property	16,551.71	17,321.89	18,000.00
1003	Real Estate Trans.	6,894.51	7,159.16	7,300.00
.	.	.	.	.
.	.	.	.	.
.	.	.	.	.
	Total	7,389.415.10	8,661,873.34	9,150,000.00

Figure 5-3. Revenue Budget

```
PROGRAM:            PUBLIC SAFETY
DESCRIPTION:        P. A17

PROGRAM CATEGORY:   POLICE SERVICES
```

PROGRAM ACTIVITY	DEPARTMENTS	EXPENDED		APPROPRIATED
		1974	1975	1976
Administration	Police	61,489.21	72,143.11	80,000.00
Investigation	Police	46,221.51	44,110.55	45,000.00
Apprehension	Police	12,581.67	14,158.10	15,000.00
Traffic Control	Police	21,451.50	26,121.51	28,000.00
.	.	.	.	.
.	.	.	.	.
.	.	.	.	.
		221,381.45	252,411.17	270,000.00

```
PROGRAM CATEGORY:   EMERGENCY MEDICAL CARE
```

PROGRAM ACTIVITY	DEPARTMENTS	EXPENDED		APPROPRIATED
		1974	1975	1976
Discovery	Police	6,890.10	8,112.51	10,000.00
	Fire	18,614.46	19,446.11	20,000.00
First Aid,	Police	--	10,152.51	15,000.00
Transportation	Fire	31,451.60	35,289.10	40,000.00
	Contract			
Trauma Care	City	96,181.50	112,101.51	120,000.00
	Hospital			
.	.	.	.	.
.	.	.	.	.

Figure 5-4. Program Budget

Priority Level	Project Number	Project Description	Source of Funds	Budget 1975	Program 1976	1977	1978	1979
1	S63	Traffic signal installation, Bell St. from First Ave. to 21 St.	A B	40,000 40,000	40,000. 40,000.	10,000. 10,000.	- -	- -
1	P19	Purchase ROW for realignment of Snyder Ave.	B	112,000.	85,000.	10,000.	-	-
1	C110	Realign Snyder Street, increase to 4 lanes	C D	21,000. -	110,000. 40,000.	220,000. 60,000.	50,000. 10,000.	- -
2	C111	Construct 100 car parking lot at Fifth St. and City Park Ave.	H	40,000.	30,000.	-	-	-
2	C171	Improvements to structures in City maintenance yards	A	20,000.	20,000.	21,000.	21,000.	22,000.
. .		. .	. .	. .	. .	. .	. .	. .

Figure 5–5. Capital Program and Budget

include a priority assignment, a project description, the source of funds, the five year program, and often the total project cost.

The complete budget package, whatever the format, generally includes the legal documents required for adoption, some summary sheets (general financial condition, total revenues and expenditures, debt level, and the like), and budget tables for each fund, department, or program. Where capital program format is utilized, it is a separate document.

Notes

1. Robert D. Lee, Jr., and Ronald W. Johnson, *Public Budgeting Systems* (Baltimore: University Park Press, 1973), p. 17, citing Jesse Burkhead, *Government Budgeting* (New York: Wiley, 1956), pp. 2-4.

2. Much of the material of this section was previously published in James C. Snyder, "Financial Management and Planning in Local Government," *Atlanta Economic Review* (November-December 1973), pp. 43-47.

3. A good historical sketch can be found in Bertram M. Gross, "The New Systems Budgeting," *Public Administration Review* (March-April 1969), and other articles in the same issue.

4. A survey (1971) by the International City Management Association and The Urban Institute estimated that 16 percent of cities with more than 50,000 population were conducting program-type analysis. Likewise, a survey by the National Association of State Budget Officers reported that 65 percent of the states were conducting related analyses. See Harry Hatry et al., *Program Analysis for State and Local Governments* (Washington: The Urban Institute, 1976), p. 5.

5. A comprehensive treatment of contemporary budgeting approaches can be found in Alan W. Steiss, *Public Budgeting and Management* (Lexington, Mass.: D.C. Heath, 1972), Chapters 7, 8, and 9. Also see Harry P. Hatry, "Criteria for Evaluation in Planning State and Local Programs," in *Decision-Making in Urban Planning,* ed. Ira M. Robinson (Beverly Hills: Sage Publications, 1972).

6. See Aaron Wildavsky, *The Politics of the Budgetary Process* (Boston: Little, Brown, 1964); Arnold J. Meltsner and Aaron Wildavsky, "Second Thoughts of the Reform," in *Financing the Metropolis,* ed. John P. Crecine (Beverly Hills: Sage Publications, 1970); and Charles E. Lindbloom, "The Science of Muddling Through," *Public Administration Review* (Spring 1959), Vol. 19.

7. The concept of "satisficing" was developed by Herbert Simon, in James G. March and Herbert A. Simon, *Organizations* (New York: Wiley, 1958).

8. Lindbloom, "The Science of Muddling Through."

9. The derivation of these terms is covered in Steiss, *Public Budgeting and Management,* pp. 302-308, as developed from Wildavsky, *The Politics of the Budgetary Process,* and Lindbloom, "The Science of Muddling Through."

10. Chapters 4 and 5 of this text present a rather complete rational system. However, the extent to which it is utilized, the relative effort applied to each management task, is the important variable.

11. These elements were observed in an informative case study covered in Meltsner and Wildavsky, "Second Thoughts."

12. Some of these problems are addressed in Donald J. Borut, "Implementing PPBS: A Practitioner's Viewpoint," in *Financing the Metropolis,* ed. John P. Crecine (Beverly Hills: Sage Publications, 1970).

13. Meltsner and Wildavsky, "Second Thoughts."

6 Revenue

This chapter addresses the revenue component of local government finance with emphasis on taxation and other revenue sources. Debt financing and intergovernmental fiscal relations are covered in separate chapters. Revenue structure, principles, and economic effects are discussed as background for a more detailed coverage of particular tax instruments.

Revenue Structure

Local governments have responsibility for providing a variety of public and quasi-public goods and services that are financially articulated as items of expenditure in governmental budgets. These authorizations and appropriations are central to the political process of determining who gets what. However, for every dollar of expenditure, there is a dollar of revenue—a dollar that must be withdrawn from private sector consumption or saving and transferred to the public sector. There are a variety of mechanisms for collecting this revenue, but the number of mechanisms is far fewer than the number of expenditure categories. Particular revenue instruments are seldom tied to specific expenditure items, with the exception of certain earmarked taxes and intergovernmental transfers. Revenue instruments also tend to be highly constrained and less subject to change than expenditure items. For these reasons, the revenue component of the local financial situation often receives less political attention than the expenditure component. Also, officials and politicians would rather talk about what they are providing for the voter than what they are taking away from them. However, revenue issues do become politicized as tax increases or cuts and bond issues in a nonroutine way. The revenue component usually appears in the local budgetary process as a simple breakdown of revenue estimates for each source with emphasis on the total revenue estimate. The task is then one of selecting and adjusting expenditure items so that total expenditures do not exceed total revenue estimates.

The citizens and institutions of a community are subject to a variety of taxes and charges from a number of governmental and quasi-governmental units, in varying forms and amounts, all of which sum to the required governmental revenue. Some of the taxes are highly visible (income, sales taxes), while others are nearly hidden (corporate and business taxes); few are directly and visibly related to a specific good or service. Within this complexity, citizens exhibit a seemingly inconsistent increasing demand for public goods and services while resisting tax increases. This further compounds the problem of determining the true demand for government economic activity.

Local governments often exist in a fiscal crunch in which expenditure requirements far exceed the available revenue. Thus revenue policy is one of the critical factors in the successful financial management of local governments. No prescription can be given for an optimal revenue policy, but certainly revenue decisions must be made as part of the financial management function with due consideration of the factors here described.

Legal Constraints

Revenue authority is established by both the federal and state constitutions. Local governments, as creations of the state, are governed by the state and by local government charters and legislation at all levels. In addition, local governments are permitted only those revenue tools specifically designated by the state governments. Constraints may include maximum rates, uniform assessments, requirements for public referendum, maximum debt limits, accounting procedures, and the like. Consequently, only marginal (but often important) tax changes can be made independently at the local level, while major changes generally require state legislation. However, local communities have considerably more latitude in matters of user charges and administrative fees.

The preparation of local revenue policy (legislation and administration) is, like the budget, generally the responsibility of the chief executive. The enactment of legislation is the responsibility of the city council or other legislative body.

Categories of Revenue

Categories of revenue include taxes, user charges, administrative fees, debt, and intergovernmental transfers. Taxes are compulsory charges against some person or other entity, which are eventually paid by people, for the purpose of financing the activities of government. It is not a price paid in exchange for any particular good or service. Earmarked taxes are simply taxes for which particular classes of expenditures have been identified (such as gasoline taxes for road expenditures). User charges are prices paid to government for some particular good or service. They are not taxes, but charges associated with an exchange. The user is identifiable and, therefore, can be excluded from consumption for nonpayment as with a market situation. Examples are numerous, including charges for public utilities, solid-waste collection, toll roads, and parking meters. Administrative fees are charges against persons or other entities for the provision of some administrative function where the user can be identified. No exchange takes place. Examples include licenses, inspection fees, application fees, permits, fines, and lotteries.

Tax Base and Rate

Taxes are usually expressed as an amount or rate to be charged against a base. The tax base is usually some measure of wealth, income, or expenditure. The tax rate is expressed as a percentage, a mill (1/10 of 1 percent), or as dollars per $1,000. If the rate is applied uniformly to each unit of the base, the tax is "proportional" (such as a typical sales tax). If the rate increases with successive units of the base, the tax is "progressive"; if the rate decreases, the tax is "regressive" (Figure 6–1).

Taxes can be made progressive or regressive by varying the marginal rate (i.e., the rate on successive units of base) from the average rate. The marginal tax rate equals the average rate for a proportional tax, exceeds the average rate for a progressive rate, and is less than the average rate for a regressive tax. Progressivity and regressivity can also be affected by making adjustments to the base, such as with exemptions, deductions, and loopholes. Tax rates can be described in three ways:

TAX RATE

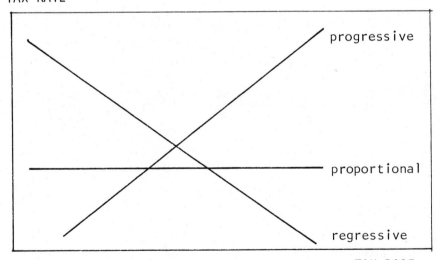

TAX BASE

Figure 6–1. Proportional, Regressive, and Progressive Tax Rates

1. average tax rate: average rate applied to the taxable base
2. marginal rate: rate applied to successive units of the taxable base
3. effective rate: total tax liability divided by total base

Thus, a progressive income tax with adjustments to the base via deductions and exemptions would have different average, marginal, and effective tax rates.

Often, progressive and regressive taxes are referred to in terms of a common base of income (as a measure of ability to pay). For example, a retail sales tax is income regressive because low-income persons spend a larger proportion of their income on sales tax than do higher income persons. Thus, one must differentiate between technical and income progressivity and regressivity.

Principles of Taxation

One of the central questions of taxation concerns the equitable distribution of the tax burden among persons and institutions. Of course, what is equitable is essentially a value judgment and therefore cannot be technically answered. However, there are several constructs or principles of equity upon which taxes can be based. Two principles are ability to pay and benefit. That is, one way to address equity is to tax persons in some way relative to their ability to bear the tax burden; another way involves taxing relative to the amount of benefit received.

The ability-to-pay principle includes two concepts of equity: horizontal and vertical. Horizontal equity requires that equals be treated equally, and vertical equity requires that unequals be treated unequally. Income is the most often used index of ability to pay, and thus persons with higher incomes should bear more of the tax burden than persons with lower income. The question is, How much more? It is known that money has a decreasing marginal utility. That is, an additional dollar of income is valued more highly at a low-income level than at a high income level (Figure 6-2). Therefore, the sacrifice or burden in terms of utility lost to a dollar paid in taxes is less to a millionaire than to the poorer person. An equal sacrifice would then require the rich members of society to pay more absolute dollars than the less fortunate. However, "more dollars" might be accomplished by an income progressive, regressive, or proportional tax, depending on the slope of the marginal utility of money curve. The problem is that each individual will have his own utility function, and the collective societal function is not known.

If, however, the required sacrifice is proportional to income, with higher income persons bearing a greater, rather than equal, sacrifice than low-income persons, then a progressive tax rate must be utilized. A more than proportional sacrifice can be effected by increasing the progressivity of the tax rate. None of this leads to the identification of an optimum or equitable tax rate. Rather, the

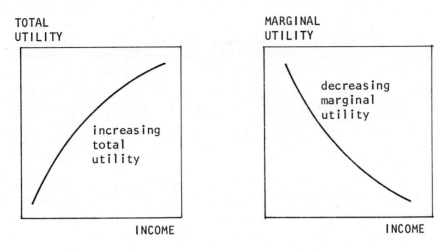

Figure 6-2. Total and Marginal Utility of Money

progressivity of tax rates must rely on the general concept of ability to pay and on society's values relative to the distribution of wealth and income.

The benefit principle of taxation requires that the tax burden be borne by persons in amounts relative to the amount of benefit they receive. A person would pay a tax as a price that reflects the average cost of providing the service or the value of the service to the taxpayer. However, this would require that the value of each good and service be assessed for each person, and that he or she be taxed accordingly. This is inoperative in the case of public or collective consumption goods and services because of the incentive for individuals to hide their preferences. If quasi-public goods exist where an exchange is required, then the benefit principle is appropriate and can be operationalized with user charges. There may be some other situations where the benefit principle may be appropriate, such as with some earmarked taxes. However, its practicality is too limited to provide a sure guideline for overall tax policy.

The ability-to-pay principle addresses more directly the concepts of equity, whereas the benefit principle addresses a goal of market efficiency. Actually, both find their way into our tax policy and instruments. It is not strictly necessary that each and every tax instrument satisfy both the equity and efficiency criteria. It is really the effect of the entire package that is of ultimate concern. The regressivity of one tax may be countered by the progressivity of another. For example, state and local taxes (sales, property) tend to be regressive, whereas federal taxes (personal and corporate income) tend to be progressive. A unified comprehensive tax policy would attempt to capture efficiency in individual tax instruments while maintaining an overall standard of equity and distribution. Needless to say, no such "comprehensive" tax policy exists within the federal system. The problem is that the tax structure with its variety of tax instruments, rates, bases, and authorities is hopelessly complex. It is difficult to assess the total impact of the system; comprehensive control is impossible. Local governments are left with the task of carefully estimating the consequences of each marginal tax change while supporting federal and state tax reform measures.

Economic Effects

A full discussion of the economic effects of taxation is beyond the scope of this text.[1] However, some of the major effects that will be of concern to local governments can be identified here. More detailed effects are discussed with specific tax instruments in later sections.

Distributional and Equity Effects

Each tax instrument and thus each tax change will have some distributional impact on the incomes of persons in the community. Although the exact tax incidence is difficult to measure, estimates can be derived through a careful study of the characteristics of the tax rates and the tax base. For example, the effects of a proposed local income tax can be assessed by applying the tax to the statistical income distribution of the jurisdiction.[2] The results of such study should be evaluated in terms of the community's goals relative to equity. Likewise, tax structure can be designed to approach the desired distributional consequences.

Some of the burden of a tax may not fall on the initial tax base object because of tax "shifting." The property tax on owner-occupied housing units can not be shifted, and the burden falls to the owner. However, the property tax on renter-occupied housing units can be partially shifted forward from the owner to the occupants in the form of higher rents. Likewise, some of the burden of corporate and business taxes are shifted forward to customers through higher prices and backward to stock owners in the form of lower profits.

Allocation and Efficiency Effects

Taxes affect the allocation of resources and economic efficiency in several ways. First, taxes may distort the economic decisions of individuals and institutions. If taxes are not tied to specific public goods and services, the individual can not accurately assess the benefits and costs of those goods and services. Thus, he or she can not easily formulate demands for public activities and may choose a suboptimal quantity. This may lead to an imbalance in the allocation of resources between and within public and private sectors. For example, if a person knew the exact cost and benefit of each of the many public goods and services, he or she might prefer that resources be reallocated to produce more of one service and less of another, and he or she might prefer to shift more of the total resources into or out of the public sector.

Likewise, taxes may distort the relative prices of goods in the private sector. For example, the local property tax may be viewed as a consumption tax on housing, increasing the effective price of housing such that the demand and supply are artificially low. Also, differential tax rates among geographic jurisdictions may induce persons, businesses, and industries to move to suboptimal locations.

A second type of effect centers around the efficiency of the administration of a tax system. That is, each tax will have an associated administrative cost that effectively reduces the revenue yield. Each tax can be evaluated in terms of this cost, as well as target efficiency, compliance, and flexibility. Target efficiency deals with the accuracy with which the tax burden falls on the intended persons. Does it fall on every intended target, and does it fall on some unintended persons or groups? Compliance deals with the rate of uncollected taxes and the associated enforcement costs. Three terms are useful here:

1. tax avoidance: legal minimizing of tax liability
2. tax evasion: fraudulent behavior
3. tax delinquency: failure to pay, unspecified reason

Flexibility is the ease with which tax structure can be changed to respond to changing revenue policy.

Growth and Stability Effects

The concerns for growth and stability relative to tax policy reside more at the national and regional levels than at the local level. Local governments are, of course, concerned with growth and stability, but they have very little taxing prerogative that can affect economic output, income, and unemployment. However, some local governments do engage in tax competition whereby industries and businesses are given various tax incentives to locate within respective jurisdictions.

Local governments are primarily concerned with the stability of the flow of revenue. That is, local government has the responsibility of providing many basic essential services that cannot fluctuate widely in quantity or quality with overall economic fluctuations. Goods and services such as waste disposal, utilities, fire, police, and general government fall into this category. Thus, local government must plan and operate its entire revenue structure (taxes, user charges, fees, debt, and intergovernmental transfers) in such a way as to yield a consistent amount of revenue.

Property Tax

The property tax is overwhelmingly the most important source of revenue for local government, accounting for 36 percent of all local revenue and 83 percent of all local tax revenue in 1972.[3] State governments have relied on the property tax in the past, but its state importance has been reduced by shifts to income and sales taxes. Only 2 percent of state tax revenue came from property tax in 1972. The property tax is a type of "wealth' tax levied against the value of property; it is based at least partially on both the ability to pay and benefits concepts. The property tax has been used since colonial times in the United States by all three levels of government. These early taxes were usually levied against specific classes of property such as land and houses. The federal government dropped the tax first, reserving its use for state and local governments. Since then, the tax has been modified to include a broader range of property, and most states have effectively dropped the tax. It remains today as the primary local government tax.

The property tax is generally thought to be the worst single tax in the revenue system. Studies of the tax read as an extensive list of defects. Not only is it an unpopular tax with citizens, it is also regressive with respect to income, inequitable in a number of ways, administratively inefficient, and responsible for a number of distortions in economic decisions. Increasing realization of this is evidenced in a growing movement for local property tax reform. Even so, there is every indication that the property tax, in some form, will remain as an important source of local revenue.

Property Tax Structure

Property is classified into two categories: real property and personal property. Real property includes land and improvements to land. Improvements include buildings and other structures that are permanently affixed or practically immovable. Personal property includes tangible and intangible property. Tangible property includes movable objects that have inherent value such as machinery, inventory stock, furniture, and automobiles. Intangible property includes objects that have no inherent, tangible value but rather represent or lay claim to value, such as bank deposits, stock certificates, and bonds. All property can be categorized by these descriptions and, in addition, can be differentiated for tax purposes by class of ownership (such as government, religious, or tax free), and by use (such as residential, commercial, industrial, and agricultural).

Most states utilize both a real estate and a personal property tax, although some use only the former. Most states also exempt intangible and certain types of tangible property because of the difficulty of discovery and enforcement. In addition, most states grant exemptions or partial exemptions to certain classes of ownership. Each state, then, has its own property tax structure. Once the base is defined, a variety of governments within the state apply tax rates to the base. The state, county, municipality, school board, and other authorities may tax a given jurisdiction.

The process of taxation includes three steps: (1) assessment, (2) determination of rate, and (3) collection.

Assessment. Assessment involves the discovery and valuation of property. Because personal property is difficult to discover and because of the exemptions that are allowed, the assessment task is mostly one of evaluating real property. The task is generally carried out by local government assessors who are elected or appointed. (Some area-wide properties such as railroads are often assessed directly by the state.) Each parcel of property is evaluated to determine its market value. The property is then assessed at some percentage of the market value. States generally require that this ratio be uniform. There is no real functional value to assessing at a lower than market value, because rates are variable to produce the required revenue. However, this traditional practice continues.

Assessment practices and quality vary widely among local governments; the general quality is thought to be poor. The task of estimating current market value for each parcel is inherently difficult and time-consuming; assessors are often inadequately trained and poorly paid. Because of the high administrative cost and time required, reevaluation of properties can only occur at lengthy intervals, leaving much of the property assessment out of date. Assessment is accomplished every year, but often by merely carrying previous figures forward. All this leads to a high level of variability in assessment values and thus to a high level of inequity.

Underassessment is also a problem at the local level. That is, local governments often find that it is to their advantage to systematically undervalue and underassess property. In this way, a city can apply a higher tax rate to generate the desired amount of local revenue, while the state and other taxing authorities' application of given rates to the artificially lower base results in a lower total burden on local residents and businesses. Also, certain intergovernmental transfers, such as state aid to schools, may be inversely related to per capita property assessment values, and many property owners intuitively appreciate a low assessment for their own property. Many states provide a review of local assessments and utilize equalization procedures to balance the state's burden among local governments.

Determination of Rate. The assessed values of all taxable properties (the tax digest) are summed to determine a total assessed value. Then each taxing authority applies a rate to that value to produce a given revenue. The rates are expressed as a percentage, as a mil (1/10 of 1 percent), or as number of dollars per $100 or $1,000 dollars of assessed value. The typical procedure for rate setting involves estimating all other revenues, comparing that figure with the total required revenue, and estimating the amount of revenue required from the property tax. Then the required rate is obtained by dividing the required revenue by the total assessed value. The decision to set the rate (higher, lower, or the same) is made by the legislative body and may be constrained by a variety of personal and political factors as well as by state rate restrictions, public referenda, and the like. Of course, both the rates and the level of budget expenditures can be varied so that expected total revenues exceed the total budget expenditure.

Collection. After the tax rate is set, it is applied to each property in the tax digest. Tax bills are computed and issued yearly, semiannually, or quarterly. Delinquent payments become liens on the property. Usually only one government, the county, collects all the taxes, and then distributes shares to all participating governmental units. The example in equation (6.1) shows how property tax is calculated.

$$
\begin{array}{ll}
\$50{,}000 & \text{market evaluation} \\
\times\ .40 & \text{40\% assessment ratio} \\[6pt]
20{,}000 & \text{gross assessed value} \\
-\ 5{,}000 & \text{exemptions (homestead, veterans, etc.)} \\[6pt]
15{,}000 & \text{net assessed value} \\
\times\ .10 & \text{tax rate, 100 mils} \\[6pt]
\$\ 1{,}500 & \text{tax liability}
\end{array}
$$

$$
\text{tax rate} = 0.10
$$

$$
\text{effective tax rate} = \frac{1{,}500}{50{,}000} = 0.03 \tag{6.1}
$$

Economic Effects

Equity and Distribution. The property tax relates poorly to both the ability-to-pay and to the benefit principles of taxation. It affects ability to pay in that ownership of property constitutes wealth that can be utilized to produce income that is, in turn, an index of ability to pay. It affects benefit in that the benefits of certain public services may accrue directly to owners of property (such as fire protection). However, the property tax, as currently utilized, is not a general property tax, but rather a limited real estate tax. It does not relate well to tax principles. First, income is not always derived from property. For example, elderly and retired families with small or fixed incomes must pay taxes on the appreciating value of homes that were purchased in past years. Undeveloped land may produce no current income, although it is taxed as if it were. It is true that some public services accrue to landowners, but these services can be financed with user charges (such as garbage collection, water, and electricity). Many benefits, however, do not relate directly to property (police, education, streets, welfare, health, general government) and the property tax does not respond to these differences. For example, one pays property tax for education, regardless of whether or not one has children in the school system.

Another distributional problem relates to the fiscal disparities among governmental jurisdictions caused by differences in the values of the tax bases. Some jurisdictions exist with a low per capita tax base, while others have high per capita tax bases—because types of land use and development tend to be spatially differentiated, income groups tend to cluster, and metropolitan areas are fragmented into a multiplicity of governmental jurisdictions. Because approximately seven-eighths of local tax revenue comes from the property tax, those units with a low tax base are seriously constrained in fiscal ability and must often provide a low level of public service. A typical example is the relatively poor central city as compared with an upper income suburb (see Chapter 7, Intergovernmental Relations). In 1971, the California Supreme Court (*Serrano* v. *Priest*) held that financing education with the property tax discriminated against the poor because of fiscal disparities, and that such financing was therefore unconstitutional. Several state supreme courts and lower federal courts have issued similar decisions. Although the U.S. Supreme Court overturned one of these cases (*Rodriquez* v. *San Antonio School District*) in 1973, it termed the system in most states as inequitable and chaotic. This decision (to overturn) affected only the question of U.S. constitutionality, and the decisions of the state courts relative to state constitutions has remained essentially unchanged as of this writing.

There also exists a problem in that local governments often engage in tax competition for new business and industry. (In general, residences require more in government services than they produce in tax revenue, whereas business and industry produce positive net tax revenue.) This competition results in an artificially low tax rate in competing jurisdictions and consequently in a lower level of service.

Fiscal disparity requires that jurisdictions with a low or declining tax base charge relatively higher tax rates to maintain an acceptable level of service, while more fortunate areas with a large or growing tax base can either tax at a lower rate or supply a higher level of service (again, for example, the central city and the suburb). This situation tends to be self-reinforcing as residences, businesses, and industries migrate to areas with low tax rates or better services or both.

Still another distributional problem is related to the potential shifting of the property tax burden. People owning and living in a residence cannot shift the property tax burden on that residence to anyone else, although they can deduct the amount of the tax from their income for federal income tax purposes. People owning renter-occupied residential units can shift some of the tax burden forward to the occupants in terms of higher rents. The renter actually pays the tax, yet he or she is not allowed the federal tax deduction. Also, if such forward shifting of burden by means of higher rents constitutes an increase in the price of housing, and there is consequently a decrease in demand, then some of the burden may be shifted backward to owners in the form of lower profits. This is likely to occur when one jurisdiction raises taxes relative to surrounding jurisdictions. Tax on land that is in fixed supply can not be shifted. Rather, it is capitalized. In other words, an increase in the tax on land reduces the expected profit or return on that land, and thus the market value of the land decreases. The burden is then carried by the landowner.

In addition to all these problems, the property tax is strongly income-regressive. A complete property tax would be progressive because high-income persons tend to own a disproportionate share of property. However, states and local governments tend to rely heavily on a more limited real estate tax. This real estate tax is income-regressive because low-income families tend to have a larger proportion of their wealth in homes than do higher income persons.

Allocation and Efficiency. The property tax produces certain allocation and efficiency distortions, some of which have already been mentioned. Inefficiency in assessment practices, as well as the effects on locational decisions of businesses and industries, have been discussed. Industries may decide to locate in suboptimal locations to take avantage of certain tax advantages.

The property tax is both a tax on land and on the improvements to land. As such, it has some adverse effects on the pattern of metropolitan development. First, it encourages speculation—undeveloped land is taxed in amounts lower than developed land. Therefore, land for new development tends to be purchased at the fringe area and beyond, in a pattern known as "urban sprawl." This low-density scattered development places an inordinate demand on such public services as streets, utilities, police, and fire. Conversely, the property tax tends to discourage the improvement of developed property, because such improvement results in a higher tax liability. Consequently, one finds a typical pattern of central city decay while new development takes place in the fringe suburbs.

Stability. The local property tax does not produce a stabilizing effect on the national economy (as the income tax does) because it is relatively income-inelastic. The tax yield does not fluctuate directly with the level of economic activity. However, at the local level this stability of yield is an advantage because it ensures local government of the revenue base necessary to provide essential public services.

Reform Issues

There are a large number of possible property tax reforms, some of which have been adopted by various states. In view of the many faults of this tax, however, one overriding reform involves a shifting of emphasis from the property tax to more reliance on alternate sources of revenue such as the local income tax, sales tax, and general and special revenue sharing. Many states have affected such property tax relief by a change in emphasis. In addition to this general trend, a number of reform measures deal with changes to the property tax. They are listed and described here:

1. *Improvement in administration.* The problems in assessment and collection have been discussed. Reform measures include professional training of assessors and tax administrators, a shift in administration from local to county or state government level, state equalization of assessment ratios and burden, and the simplification of review and appeal procedures.

2. *Review of exemptions and exclusions.* Property taxes, as now administered, covered only certain classes of property and ownership. If all wealth were included (stocks, bonds, and other intangibles), the resultant wealth tax would allow lower overall tax rates and significant tax relief for low-income groups. Of course, the discovery and collection of taxes on intangibles has proven difficult, and many states have therefore exempted them. However, the revenue potential is so great that major revision in administration and enforcement may be well worth the effort. In addition, the traditional flat tax rate might be changed to a progressive rate. Several European countries tax net worth more heavily than real estate with considerable success.

With or without these reforms, many states utilize the "homestead exemption" and the "circuit-breaker" strategies to reduce the burden on residential property owners. The homestead exemption, used in thirty-two states, excludes a portion of the value of owner-occupied residential property from the property tax, for all persons or for the elderly. The circuit-breaker, used in eight states, provides elderly persons with a tax credit or rebate via state income taxes for property tax paid. The combination of these measures (wealth tax and residential exemptions or credits) would certainly counter the existing regressive nature of the property tax, simply because wealth is so concentrated in the hands of the high-income groups.

3. *Fiscal balance measures.* Problems relative to fiscal disparities among local governments have been discussed earlier. One reform strategy involves the sharing of property tax revenue across jurisdictions to reduce tax competition and to balance fiscal capacity. In 1971, Minnesota adopted the "Minnesota

Fiscal Disparities Bill" for the Twin Cities metropolitan area of seven counties. The bill provides that 40 percent of the net growth in tax valuation from each local government be pooled for distribution over the entire metropolitan area on a formula basis. Numerous other states are considering similar tax sharing or "negative aid" mechanisms.

4. *Land tax.* Another popular reform measure calls for changing the real property tax to a land tax. Alternately, but with similar effects, land could be taxed at a higher rate than improvements to land. A land tax might be expected to have several effects:

a. It would reduce the effort required for assessment (no need to assess depreciated value, etc.).
b. It would encourage good land use and growth by removing tax liability for building construction and improvement, and increasing taxes on undeveloped land. The tax on land would decrease the cost of the land by the capitalized value of the tax and thus stimulate demand.
c. It would capture the "unearned" increment of income derived from land. That is, much of the income derived from land, and thus land value, is caused by its location and public improvements (e.g., roads) surrounding and serving it, rather than to inherent characteristics of the land. The land tax would capture some of this unearned income (value) for the public.
d. It would largely reduce or eliminate the regressiveness of the existing property tax, because the ownership of land is more concentrated in the lands of high-income persons and corporations.

5. *Federal deductions for renters.* This last reform measure involves a change in the federal income tax system to establish equity between renters and owners, both of whom pay property taxes (indirectly or directly). The change would require eliminating the property tax deduction for owners or the inclusion of an imputed deduction for renters. Some states affect the latter with their own income tax.

Conclusions—The Property Tax

At best, the property tax appears to be the least satisfactory tax in the revenue system. It fails in terms of equity and efficiency; citizens tend to rate it as the least satisfactory component of the many tax mechanisms. However, it produces a significant stable amount of revenue, and it can be at least partially controlled at the local government level. For these reasons, the property tax is likely to remain as an important revenue source for some time. However, all the reform measures have substantial merit (as well as some problems), and many are in regular or experimental use presently. The actual effects of a particular reform measure will depend on the details of the reform design and on the particular local situation. The major movement is clear: there is an increasing emphasis on the local adoption of income and sales taxes as substitutes for further increases in the property tax.

Income Tax

Income-based taxes are utilized at the federal, state and local levels and, all factors considered, are probably the most satisfactory instruments in the tax system. There are two basic types: the personal income tax and the corporate income tax. The personal income tax is a relatively good tax because its allocational effects are relatively neutral, it is adjustable to distributional effects, and it has an automatic stabilizing effect (tax revenues increase as incomes rise and decrease as incomes fall). Corporate income taxes are less neutral with respect to allocation: they may reduce aggregate investment, encourage retention of corporate earnings, affect industrial location, and create differences between corporate and noncorporate businesses. However, they do produce some stabilizing influence and are generally income-progressive because high-income persons tend to own more corporate stock than low-income persons. In addition, the corporate taxes are somewhat hidden and painless, at least relative to other taxes. Both the personal and corporate taxes produce large amounts of revenue, and both are efficient with respect to administrative costs.

The federal government relies heavily on personal and corporate income taxes: 56.8 percent of all federal revenue and 82.5 percent of all federal tax revenue was derived from those sources in the 1971–1972 fiscal year. States tend to rely more heavily on the sales tax, although income taxes account for 15.5 percent of all state revenue and 29 percent of all state tax revenue. Local governments rely least on income taxes, with only 4.5 percent of all local tax revenue derived from that source.[4] A few local governments have a corporate income tax, but it is primarily the personal income tax that is becoming a popular partial substitute for increases in the unpopular property tax. Cities that have adopted income taxes show substantial revenues from that source. For example, in 1972 income taxes yielded 35 percent of the tax revenue in Detroit, 62 percent in Philadelphia, and 78 percent in Columbus, Ohio.

The federal personal income tax was first adopted in 1861, repealed in 1872, and again adopted in 1894. This second adoption lasted only one year; the Supreme Court declared the tax unconstitutional on the grounds that it was a "direct" tax. However, the 16th Amendment to the Constitution, ratified in 1913, allowed Congress to levy taxes on incomes without apportionment among the states, and therefore allowed for the adoption of both personal and corporate income taxes in that same year. State personal and corporate taxation was first initiated by Wisconsin in 1911, although Hawaii had a corporate income tax as early as 1901. Additional states have since adopted these taxes; forty-four states now have a personal income tax, and forty-six states have a corporate income tax (1971). Local personal income taxes have been adopted in ten states.[5] Local corporate income taxes exist in only a few cities and are usually supplements to the local income taxes for incorporated businesses.

Income Tax Structure

Taxes based on income have a solid footing on the ability-to-pay concept, because income is perhaps the best overall measure of one's ability to share the financial burden of government. Income is generally defined by economists as the sum of an individual's expenditures for goods and services, the value of non-market consumption, and changes in net worth. Under this definition, additions to income includes wages, rents, and profits (factor incomes), self-produced goods and services such as garden vegetables and the labor of housewives, the use of owner-occupied homes and company cars, capital gains (whether or not they are realized), gifts, public goods and services, and unemployment and life insurance benefits. Subtractions from income would include those items that are necessary expenses in realizing income, such as wages and rents paid, living expenses, and educational expenses. Of course, the "tax" definitions currently utilized are quite different. The federal income tax structure, after which most income taxes are patterned, primarily utilizes a "factor flow" concept, which includes interest and dividends while excluding many other forms of income. The practicality of this simpler definition is obvious because of the difficulty in evaluating many of the nonmonetary types of income. However, excluding some types of income produces horizontal inequity because some forms of income are taxed while others are not. For example, consider two families: one invests savings in a house, while the other family rents a house and invests the savings in an interest-bearing bank account. The first family receives a return on investment in terms of a house to live in—a return that is not taxed. The second family receives interest in return for its bank investment, but that return is taxed as income. (In addition, the owner can deduct interest and local tax payments from his income for federal income tax purposes, while the renter cannot.) Clearly there is inequity between the owner and renter.

In addition to a limited definition of income, the federal tax structure utilizes a "net income" or "taxable income" concept whereby income is modified by exclusions, deductions, exemptions, differentiated rates (capital gains versus wages), credits, allowances, and loopholes. The point is that the income tax structure levies a tax on a limited part of income, with the end result being that the ability to pay criteria is weakened and judgments about progressivity and incidence become confused. Some local governments utilize the factor flow income definition, but others use a gross income or payroll tax for ease of withholding and collection, and to capture revenues from nonresidents who work within the jurisdiction.

State Personal Income Tax. All but six states utilize a personal income tax. They are generally patterned after the federal income tax for obvious coordinative and administrative efficiencies. However, there are many variations in details among states. Most states utilize progressive tax rates (1 to 15 percent), while several use flat rates (2.5 to 6 percent), and several use a percentage of federal tax liability (13 to 25 percent). Most use exemptions and deductions; some use credits that allow the payment of dollars to low-income persons as a "negative" income tax. A variety of special provisions exist, such as Michigan's deduction for inputed property taxes paid by renters.

State Corporate Income Tax. All but four states utilize corporate income taxes. The tax base usually consists of "total receipts less expenses." Many states use a flat rate (2 to 12 percent), eight use a progressive rate (1 to 8 percent), and one state, Alaska, levies 18 percent of the federal corporate tax liability. Like the personal taxes, detailed differences are numerous.

Local Income Tax. Personal income taxes are utilized by approximately 3,500 local governments in ten states, and there has been substantial interest on the part of most of the other states. Enabling legislation has been introduced in many states, and the trend towards adoption is clear. The base of the tax is most often the gross earnings of individuals (payroll) and unincorporated businesses, although some utilize a net income figure. Maryland allows local governments to levy a percentage of the state tax liability. Rates are usually low and flat (1 to 3 percent), although a few are proportional (0.25 to 10 percent). Some cities levy a small corporate income tax as a supplement to the personal income tax.

Economic Effects

The personal income tax yields substantial revenue to the federal and state governments and promises to do so at the local level. It can be adjusted to reflect current equity standards, has relatively neutral allocational effects, is a positive stabilizer, and is efficient to administer. Adoption of a progressive income tax at the local level could counter the regressive effects of the property and sales taxes. This is not to say that this tax is free of defects. Limited concepts of income, needless complications, unrealistic deductions and exemptions, and loopholes represent areas for potential reform. However, all things considered, the personal income tax is technically a better instrument than the other major tax instruments. The corporate income tax also yields substantial revenues, but it is not as economically neutral as the personal tax. In addition to adverse effects already mentioned, some of the corporate tax is probably shifted forward to consumers in higher prices, while some falls backward to owners in lower profits. Also, the tax may constitute double taxation for distributed corporate profits—once as corporate income and once as personal income.

Some specific notes can be made relative to local income taxes. First, the local personal income tax represents a potential new source of revenue for local governments at a time when revenues are severely constrained and expenditures are soaring. Adoption requires state legislation and usually a local referendum. Once adopted, local government can capture the advantages of the tax while retaining local control. Local resistance to the income tax is sometimes substantial, as few citizens enjoy paying any tax and many view the income tax as an additional tax. However, local tax increases are inevitable for the foreseeable future, and citizens can really only exercise choice over how they pay. In this light, the income tax appears to be preferable to the property tax.

Two main factors must be considered in state enabling legislation and local adoption: selection of the tax base and jurisdictional problems. Tax base alternatives include an adjusted net income, a gross payroll income, or a federal or state tax liability. The adjusted net income figure has the advantage that it can be borrowed from the federal or state definitions and forms with resultant administrative efficiency. Using the federal or state tax liability as a base allows this same efficiency. Any such uniformity of base allows central administration and collection with distribution of revenues to the taxing units. The use of a local payroll tax has advantages and disadvantages. It is relatively easy to administer, and allows a city to tax the incomes of persons who work in the city but live outside the city. This capture of revenue is based on the benefit principle; such nonresident workers use city services. Rates can be adjusted to reflect the magnitude of benefits. However, the payroll tax is levied only on wages; therefore, it discriminates against persons who earn more of their incomes in wages and favors those who earn their incomes in rents, profits, interest, dividends, and the like.

The other major concern involves interjurisdictional problems. The taxing of the income of nonresidents (work in city, live outside) or nonresident income (live in city, work outside) can become complex in multiple government areas. Double taxation can result unless there is careful coordination and uniform standards. For example, consider two adjacent local governments. One depends heavily on a property tax, while the other relies on a payroll tax. A person residing in the first jurisdiction and working in the second would pay taxes in both areas. Several solutions are available, including credits for taxes paid in other jurisdictions and differential rates for residents and nonresidents. (Michigan cities generally charge nonresidents half the resident rate.) Another question involves the appropriate place for the local income tax—county or city. Most states place the tax with cities, which can place "urban counties" at a disadvantage. However some counties do levy an income tax.

Finally, some adverse effects may result if the adoption of a local income tax places the local government at a large tax variance with other nearby areas. For example, some residents and businesses, both new and existing, may be encouraged to migrate to locations outside the taxing jurisdiction to escape the tax. If, however, the adoption of the income tax is merely a shift in tax instruments rather than an increase in tax, or if an increase is tied to an increase in services, then the migration effect may not occur.

Sales Taxes

Sales taxes are utilized by federal, state, and local governments, with major use occurring at the state level. These taxes are based on expenditures that, in turn, make up a large part of the economic definition of income. There are two basic types: the general sales tax and the excise tax; each has numerous variations. The general sales tax is usually based on a broad range of goods (and sometimes services) and is levied as a percentage of the retail sales value. Excise taxes are charges on specific goods and are usually levied as a percentage of the sales value or as an amount for each unit of the good (for example, cents per gallon of gasoline). These taxes are usually charged to the seller as gross receipts taxes, quoted separately to the buyer, and presumably shifted forward to buyer from seller. These sales taxes are used extensively by states, and are becoming popular at the local level as a partial substitute for the property tax. They are reasonably popular with taxpayers and produce a significant amount of revenue. However, they suffer from a major defect; they are strongly income-regressive.

The federal government has always utilized excise taxes, but it has never adopted a general sales tax. Specific items subject to the tax and the tax rates have varied over the years until 1965, when Congress repealed many of the excises as nuisance taxes and lowered the rates on others. Oregon was the first state to adopt excise taxes in 1919, with most other states following within ten years. Items typically taxed, presently as well as in the past, include fuel, alcohol, tobacco, insurance, public utilities, pari-mutuels, and amusements. Mississippi was the first state to tax general sales in 1932, with other states close behind, partially as a needed revenue measure during the depression of the 1930's. Local government adoption has been a more recent phenomenon, with emphasis on creating much-needed revenue while shifting emphasis from the property tax.

In 1971, forty-five states utilized a general sales tax, while all fifty states levied excise taxes on fuel, tobacco, and insurance. Local sales taxes are permitted in twenty-four states. State general sales tax rates range from 2 to 6 percent; local rates vary from 0.5 to 3 percent. State excise taxes on tobacco range from 3 cents to 18.5 cents per pack; taxes on fuel range from 5 to 9 cents per gallon.[6] Yields from these taxes are substantial. The federal excise taxes yield 10 percent of all federal tax revenue. State excise taxes yield 13.9 percent of all state revenue and 26.1 percent of all state tax revenue, while state general sales taxes yield 15.6 percent of all state revenue and 26.1 percent of all state tax revenue. Local government excise taxes yield 3.1 percent of all local tax revenue, while general sales taxes yield 5.4 percent of the tax revenue. Local revenues from these two sources increased by 13 and 18 percent between fiscal years 1970-1971 and 1971-1972. Where local sales taxes are utilized, they represent more substantial revenues. New Orleans receives 52.5 percent of its tax revenues from the sales tax—with Denver at 47.1 percent, Dallas at 28.3 percent, and the District of Columbia at 33.2 percent.[7]

Sales Tax Structure

General sales taxes (also called "broad based," "gross receipts," and "ad valorem" taxes) are simply percentage levies on the amount of retail sales value, charged to the seller. The seller quotes the tax separately from the price of the good and passes the tax forward to the customer along with the price. Compliance is relatively easy because sales records are usually kept by businesses, and because the retailer is usually granted a discount of from 1 to 5 percent on the amount of the tax paid for his collection efforts, or he is allowed to keep the "breakage" that results from the assignment of tax amounts to brackets of sales value (for example, 1 cent for sales of 11 cents to 50 cents, 2 cents for 50 cents to $1.00, and so on).

The general sales tax is based on consumption (which is part of the broad definition of income). However, it represents only a portion of income (other parts including in-kind services, increases in net wealth, and wages not expended), and that part is further eroded by the fact that not all expenditures are taxed. States vary on what is taxed; most tax only at the retail level, while several tax at both the retail and wholesale levels. Most states tax goods, but some tax services as well. Many tax particular services such as public utilities, hotel accommodations, and admissions. Some states exempt food and drugs, while others exempt "producer goods" such as machines, raw products, farm feed, and fertilizer. So there are many variations in the use of the general sales tax. If the tax is to be a consumption tax, then it should include all goods and services at the retail level. Taxation of producers' goods (goods used in the production of other goods) would be inconsistent, because it would tax production rather than consumption. However, the exemption of services is of some practicality because the valuation and collection of taxes on services is administratively more difficult, and the exemption of food, drugs, and other necessities is warranted to reduce the income-regressive nature of the tax.

Excise taxes (also called "narrow base," "specific," or "unit taxes") are taxes on specific goods or services, charged to the seller at either the wholesale or retail level, and presumably passed on to the buyer. These taxes are, at least historically, based on one of these three reasons: (1) regulation of quantity of use, (2) ability-to-pay principle, and (3) benefit principle. However, the revenue productivity of an excise tax, rather than its economic desirability, may be the current rationale for some of the excise taxes. (For example, Dekalb County, Georgia, levels an excise tax on liquor to help finance the school system. It appears popular with the citizens, but it is not based on the principles above.)

Regulation of the use of a good or service (a sumptuary tax) or the use of scarce resources can be accomplished by an excise tax, in that the tax has the effect of artificially raising the price of the good or service and thereby reduces the amount purchased and consumed (law of demand). Alcohol and tobacco are traditionally taxed in this way with the result that consumption is lower than it otherwise might be. Likewise, an excise tax on lumber, oil, or a product using a scarce resource would artificially raise the price and lower the use. Consider also the case of the industry that externalizes part of the costs of production in the form of polluting air and water. The cost of that industry's products are artificially low, and thus consumption is artificially high. An excise tax on that industry's products could restore effective prices and consumption to normal levels, and the tax revenue might be utilized to clean the polluted air and water. Alternately, a pollution tax might induce the polluter to internalize the external costs, eliminate the pollution, and pass higher prices along to the customer, with the same overall effect.

The ability-to-pay principle has been applied for certain excise taxes—notably in the now-defunct federal "luxury" taxes on luggage, jewelry, and the like. However, the difficulty in defining luxury and the resultant discrimination against the consumption of some items has led to the virtual abandonment of this tax.

The benefit rationale is heavily used in support of certain excise taxes. For example, excise taxes on gasoline and tires yield revenue for highway trust funds that are in turn expended for highway construction and so on. This arrangement constitutes an earmarked tax, in which the revenues are assigned a specific fund and expenditure category. The highway users, the beneficiaries of the highway system, pay these taxes in approximate proportion to their use of the highway, and thus the excise tax has a benefit basis. Likewise, excise taxes on utility services and pari-mutuel operations can be related to the benefit principle.

Economic Effects

The sales taxes are attractive as revenue instruments at both the state and local government levels. As well as yielding substantial revenue, they are administratively efficient and relatively acceptable to the taxpayer. In addition, local governments can utilize sales taxes as a partial substitute for the unpopular property tax. The general economic effects of sales taxes include income and substitution effects. That is, a general sales tax has the effect of raising prices to the consumer, or effectively lowering income. However, all goods are not taxed equally; the general sales tax applies to only certain goods and services, and the excise taxes apply only to specific items. Thus some items are taxed more than others, and those items become relatively less attractive among all goods. Families may then be induced to substitute some expenditures for others. For example, a high excise tax on liquor may induce persons to buy less liquor and more beer or soft drinks as a substitute.

These general effects are not likely to be of major concern at the local level, where low sales tax rates are applicable. However, some considerations will be of concern at the local level (as well as the state level). First, the sales tax is strongly income-regressive. Low-income persons tend to spend high percentages of their income on such basic consumption items as food and clothing. Thus, most of their income is taxed through the sales tax. High-income persons tend to spend smaller percentages of their income on these items, so only a part of their income is taxed. The net result is that low-income persons pay a greater percentage of their incomes in sales tax than those with high incomes. Also, the adoption of, or an increase in, the sales tax rate will, through the income effect, reduce the consumption of low-income persons, while affecting both consumption and savings of high-income persons.

There are two popular mechanisms for reducing the regressiveness of the sales tax, and both must be initiated at the state level. The first method is exempting food, medicines, and other necessities. Although this reduces the burden on low-income persons, it also sharply reduces the total tax revenue and leads to administrative problems in determining just what can be considered a necessity. The second method is an allowance of a tax credit on state income taxes for inputed sales taxes paid. That is, each taxpayer would receive a state income tax credit for the amount of sales tax that he has paid, which would result in a lower income tax liability or, in low-income situations, a cash return or "negative" income tax.

The other major concern at the local level involves jurisdictional problems. If a local government jurisdiction adopts a sales tax or an increase in the tax rate while surrounding areas do not, some persons will travel and shop outside the area to avoid the tax. The extent to which this happens depends on the differential in rates and on the adjacent shopping opportunities. This problem is most critical at border areas where escape is easy. At the jurisdictional boundaries, merchants may not be able to pass the tax on to customers because they must lower net prices to keep the final "taxed" price at a competitive level.

Other Taxes and Nontax Revenue

The basic tax instruments at the state and local level have been reviewed: the personal income tax, the corporate income tax, the property tax, and the sales tax (excise and general). These instruments yield 88.4 percent of all state and local tax revenue, and 64.1 percent of all state and local revenues (1971–1972 fiscal year).[8] However, there are a variety of other revenue sources. Two major sources receive separate treatment in other chapters of this text: intergovernmental revenue (24.9 percent of all state revenue—from the federal government; and 34.4 percent of all local revenue—from federal and state governments), and debt financing (state and local governments had $174,502,000 or $838 per capita outstanding debt in 1971–1972).[9] Also, a number of other revenue sources are mentioned here under three categories: other taxes (3.1 percent of state and local revenue), user charges (13.8 percent), and administrative revenues (approximately 3 percent).[10]

Other Taxes

A number of less significant taxes generally are variations on the more basic taxes. Several states and some local governments levy a gross receipts tax on businesses as a way of capturing the income of nonresident-owned and noncorporate businesses. Some states levy a capital stock tax. In general, these taxes are thought to perform less well than the corporate income taxes. In addition, some states levy severance taxes on the production of natural resources to compensate for the depletion of these resources; some states charge special taxes on insurance premiums and public utilities as substitutes for the sales tax. Local governments often levy a flat fee business tax on businesses, with the fee being differentiated by the type of business.

User Charges

Collective consumption public goods are not supplied in the private market because producers cannot exact payment from each consumer. The benefits of such goods and services fall to everyone, and no one can be excluded. Therefore, the collective demand for public goods must be satisfied through the public sector, with payment exacted through taxation. The public sector also involves itself with the production and supply of goods and services that are not primarily "public," and where the "exclusion" principle holds. (Conditions under which this might be justified were reviewed in detail in Chapter 2, The Public Sector.) Two of the more important conditions are the existence of quasi-public goods for which private consumption yields significant external benefits and economies of scale. Examples of the former include education, public health, fire protection, garbage collection, sanitation, and many other local government services. The economies of scale condition is best represented by the publicly owned or regulated utility. Streets, electrical power, storm systems, sanitary sewer systems, water, and some other services generally exhibit significant long-range economies of scale (marginal costs below average costs, decreasing average total costs), whereby a monopolistic producer is more efficient than smaller competing producers. For example, it is obviously inefficient for competing water systems to provide overlapping water lines to serve the same area. This economy of scale generally exists where production is capital-heavy (large fixed investment), a characteristic of public utilities.

Where these conditions exist, and where providing the good or service is in the public interest, government can undertake production and supply, identify direct users, and utilize a user charge. The operation is very much like a monopoly within the market system with an exchange taking place between buyer and seller. However, it differs from the market situation in that government normally does not operate under the objective of profit maximization. Rather, the objectives might include maximum consumer benefit, break-even, limited profit, redistribution of income, or the rationing of supply. For example, there is a strong and traditional belief that government should not be in business to make money, but should charge a "fair" or break-even price for services. A fair price would presumably include the economists "normal" profit—that profit or return required to induce investors to buy public capital improvement bonds. For example, a utility must charge user fees sufficient to pay the principal and interest on the bonds that have been sold to finance the capital facilities.

However, a fair price ethic may give way to a limited profit or revenue raising objective under certain conditions. Profits are not distributed to individual owners, but are returned to the "public." Thus profits from one public enterprise may be used to finance another worthy program. Government liquor sales would fall into this category. The economic effects of this use of user charges are equivalent to the use of excise taxes.

User charges can also be applied to ration the supply of a good or service. When the demand exceeds the supply, an increase in price can reduce consumption. For example, peak hour demand for roads causes congestion where roads are insufficient to handle the required volume of traffic; the high demand for and use of water in summer months may lead to shortages; and peak hour electrical loads may cause "brownouts." Prices can be adjusted upward during peak periods to induce people to consume less. Although sometimes administratively difficult, peak season and peak hour rates are being used with success in a variety of problem situations. An alternative to peak-time pricing is a marginal price scheme whereby users are charged marginally higher rates for increasing increments of quantity consumed. For example, residential water users could be charged a relatively low rate for "necessary" quantities of water and successively higher rates for step increases in additional "unnecessary" quantities. Conversely, prices can be lowered to induce greater consumption. For example, bus fares might be priced below operation costs to induce persons to use the bus system. This might be economically justified on grounds that increased patronage results in an external social benefit of less auto pollution and congestion. Education and public health are additional examples.

Such use of the pricing mechanism represents a promising and insufficiently used tool in urban fiscal management.[11] However, it assumes that the services in question are relatively price-elastic—that a significant increase in price will lead to a significant decrease in consumption. Such is not always the case. Many public services are perceived as essential, at least up to a given quantity. Families and businesses generally require certain quantities of electricity and water, and changes in price would not have a great effect on consumption. The demand for other nonessential goods and services, such as recreational facilities, may be more price-elastic and responsive to price changes.

The use of a pricing mechanism can reveal the demand function for particular goods and services, information that is difficult to obtain without such a mechanism. With or without pricing, the demand function must be estimated to make rational production and pricing decisions. Some public services have traditionally been underpriced relative to the full social costs of production, and thus consumption has been inordinately high and wasteful. Water and the provision of services to "sprawl" physical development might be examples.

User charges relate well to the benefit principle in that direct users can be charged in accordance with their levels of consumption. Transactions for nonessential services are presumably voluntary, and users buy only if they perceive a net positive benefit. Public golf courses and other recreational facilities might fall into this class. However, many services are perceived as "essentials." Therefore, one must participate and pay the charge regardless of the level of the charge. One constrained by income is excluded. Thus, user charges for essential goods and services are income-regressive, and low-income persons are excluded at the margin.

Within this general framework, the three conceptual pricing alternatives for the financing of user charge services include (1) profit pricing, (2) average cost pricing, and (3) marginal cost pricing.

First, assume that the average total costs of production are decreasing in the long run, or that production is operating in the downward sloping part of the short-run cost curve. These assumptions are consistent with the belief that economies of scale exist in production. Also, in this situation, the assumption is made that the demand function and production costs can be estimated. The resultant cost and revenue functions might be as shown in Figure 6–3.

A profit maximizer would produce at point A, where the marginal cost of production equals the marginal revenue ($MC = MR$), where profit is maximum, and at price P_1, and quantity Q_1. Average cost pricing would require production at point B, where the average revenue (price) equals the average cost of production at price P_2 and quantity Q_2. This average cost pricing would allow the service to break even, including the normal profit required to attract bond purchasers. Production at points between A and B would yield a limited profit. Marginal cost pricing would require production at point C, where the average revenue (price) equals the marginal cost of production, with price at P_3 and quantity at Q_3. This is the point of short-run "social optimum" where con-

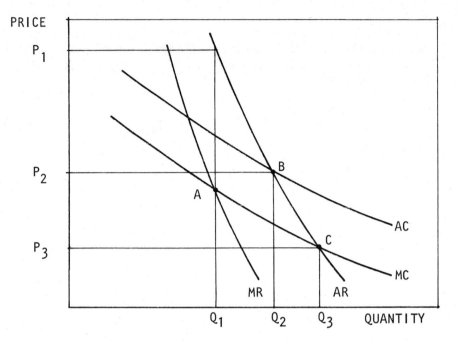

Figure 6–3. Alternative User Charge Pricing Schemes

sumers obtain the maximum quantity of the service at the lowest price. However, if government duplicates this, it will sustain a loss (price below average cost) that will have to be made up with a subsidy from other revenue sources. In this case, production at points beyond *B* will require such a subsidy.

If the previous assumptions are changed to include production with increasing average total costs (diseconomies of scale), then the situation depicted in Figure 6–4 exists. Here, profit pricing would occur as with the previous example, with maximum profit at point *A,* where *MC = MR.* However, marginal cost pricing (point *B*) would yield a profit as the price (average revenue) at that point exceeds the average costs. Average cost pricing (point *C*) yields the highest quantity/lowest price combination. Of course, under these conditions, the private market might be more efficient in the production and supply of this good. If excess profits exist, competitive firms would enter the market, increase the supply, and lower the price. Assuming a perfect competitive market, the service would be provided at the lowest possible cost.

It is sometimes the case that local government has no control over the quantity of certain services and must provide an essential level. In this case the demand curve is perceived as being vertical, as in Figure 6–5. If the average cost is declining, then the marginal cost will be less than the average cost, and marginal

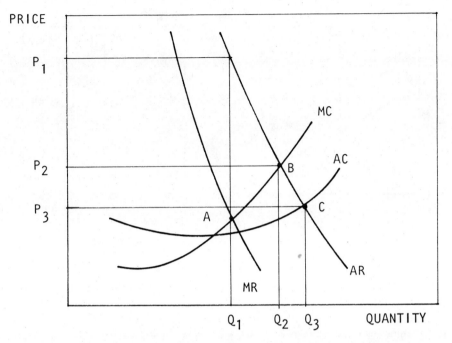

Figure 6–4. User Charge Pricing with Increasing Costs

cost pricing will require a subsidy. If the average cost is rising, then marginal cost pricing will yield a profit. Thus, with short-run variation and uncertainty in demand and cost functions, it becomes apparent why average cost pricing is so heavily relied on. Average cost figures are readily available and nothing is simpler than adjusting user charges to reflect this break-even position. However, any policy or strategy towards redistribution, rationing, increasing consumption, or raising additional revenue will require a closer look at the marginal picture.

Administrative Revenues

Administrative revenues include licenses, fees, permits, fines, forfeitures, and special assessments. Most are charges to people to cover the administrative costs of some type of regulation. They may represent a small but positive net revenue for many local governments. Examples are numerous, including hunting and fishing licenses, zoning application fees, building permits, traffic fines, and performance bond forfeitures. The underlying principle is that persons who engage in activities that require regulation should pay for the cost of such regulation.

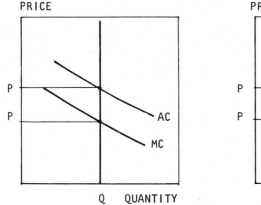
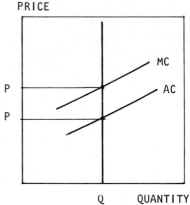

Figure 6-5. Costs and Pricing for Fixed Quantities

Special assessments are charges against property to cover the costs of certain public improvements that serve the property—such as street paving, street lights, sidewalks, or sewer lines. Assessments are levied on a front-foot or areal basis, sometimes within a special assessment district. These improvements constitute an improvement and an increase in value to served properties, and the amount of the assessment should reflect each property's share of the benefit. Some large improvements have both a general public benefit and individual property benefits, in which case the costs are divided between assessments and general revenue sources. Assessments are sometimes pledged to repay capital improvement bonds, but because of a historically high level of defaults, the bonds tend to carry high interest rates. Thus, the use of assessments appears to be declining, although they are certainly appropriate in some circumstances.

Summary

In summary, many local governments exist in a "fiscal crunch" situation where rapidly inflating costs are outrunning revenues. Future estimates reveal substantial deficits. Resolution of this problem requires difficult political and management decisions relative to both expenditure and revenue structures. Holding the line on expenditures is often the first response, simply because of taxpayer resistance and because local government exercises more control over expenditures than revenues. That is, local revenue decisions and instruments tend to be more constrained by state and local legislation. However, any long-run solution to local government finance will depend on judicious management of the revenue system.

Local governments find themselves with an overwhelming reliance on the property tax—a tax that is considered to be one of the least efficient and most undesirable of instruments. Although it yields substantial revenues, it does not relate well to "benefit" or "ability to pay" principles. There is a strong trend away from total reliance on the property tax in favor of adopting local income and sales taxes, and increasing the use of user charges. Each alternative has its advantages and disadvantages; yet when appropriately mixed and tailored to individual situations, they can substantially improve the overall revenue picture. Even with the adoption of other taxes, the basic property tax is likely to remain for the indefinite future. Thus, there are continuing efforts to improve the tax by introducing exemptions, changing assessment practices, and the like.

For example, some cities have developed property "tax breaks" for owners of redeveloped inner-city houses to reverse the usual disincentive effect of the property tax on housing improvement. In addition, some rather innovative uses of the property tax have surfaced; cities in California, Iowa, Minnesota, and Oregon have utilized "tax increment financing" for redevelopment purposes. This method allows a redevelopment authority to issue bonds that are repaid from the property tax increments (increases) generated by the new development. Another innovation is the "Minnesota Fiscal Disparities Bill" that redistributes 40 percent of the total growth in the metropolitan area's tax digest (Twin Cities) among the individual governmental units on a formula basis.

Revenue "planning" requires substantial attention at the local level, because of the lag time associated with major changes that must be legislated at the state level. In addition, potential changes in structure must be considered in light of probable economic effects, including allocation, distribution, stabilization, and growth. It is not necessary, or even possible, that each and every revenue instrument be perfect, but the entire revenue package must be acceptable in terms of satisfying general taxing criteria and generating sufficient revenues to ensure a sound financial condition.

Notes

1. Extensive coverage of the economic effects of taxation can be found in Bernard P. Herber, *Modern Public Finance: A Study of the Public Sector* (Homewood, Ill.: Richard D. Irwin, 1971), chapters 7–13; and John F. Due and Ann F. Friedlaender, *Government Finance: Economics of the Public Sector* (Homewood, Ill.: Richard D. Irwin, 1973), chapters 9–18.

2. Applicable techniques for handling the incidence of program costs and benefits are covered in Chapter 11, Program Evaluation.

3. U.S. Bureau of the Census, *Statistical Abstract of the United States: 1974,* 95th edition (Washington: Government Printing Office, 1974), Table 405, p. 248.

150

4. *Statistical Abstract,* p. 248.

5. Advisory Commission on Intergovernmental Relations, *State and Local Finances: Significant Features and Suggested Legislation,* 1972 edition (Washington, D.C.: Government Printing Office, 1974), pp. 226–228.

6. Ibid., passim.

7. Ibid., Table 99, pp. 226–228.

8. U.S. Bureau of the Census, *Government Finance in 1971-72,* Series GF72—No. 5 (Washington: Government Printing Office, 1973), Table 4, p. 20.

9. Ibid., Tables 3 and 4, pp. 19, 20.

10. Ibid.

11. Wilbur Thompson, "The City as a Distorted Price System," *Psychology Today* (August 1968), pp. 28-33.

7

Intergovernmental Relations

Fiscal Relations

No local government fiscal management and planning system would be complete without considerable attention to the fiscal relationships that exist among units of government. Although "intergovernmental relations" is as much a political as an economic subject, treatment here must, by necessity, be limited to financial matters from a local government perspective.

With two levels of constitutional government and a multiplicity of local governments (78,218 as of 1972),[1] the complexity of intergovernmental fiscal relations is inherent in the federal system of government. "Unity and diversity" is maintained via a shifting balance of responsibilities among federal, state, and local units, often with the price of overwhelming complexity. The relative imbalance of responsibilities among governments creates intergovernmental problems termed "vertical" and "horizontal." Vertical problems stem from imbalances among the federal, state, and local levels, while horizontal problems are derived from imbalances among governments at the same level (for example, local governments). Fiscal, or financial, relationships in this context refer to flows of money among governments; in the case of local governments, this includes monies from the federal and state levels and to and from other local governments. The magnitude of these flows is significant; in the 1971–1972 fiscal year, city governments received 32 percent of general revenues and 27 percent of all revenues from intergovernmental sources.[2] Table 7-1 shows the distribution of these funds by source.

Table 7-1
City Government Intergovernmental Revenues, 1971-72

Revenues	Percentage of General Revenue	Percentage of Intergovernmental Revenue
State	24.0	73.3
Federal	7.2	21.9
Local	1.6	4.8
Total	32.8	100.0

Source: U.S. Bureau of the Census, *City Government Finances in 1971-72.* GF-72-4 (Washington: Government Printing Office, 1972), Table 1, p. 5.

151

City intergovernmental expenditures accounted for only 1.2 percent of all expenditures, the net effect being a positive flow of substantial funds from federal and state levels to city governments.[3] In addition, intergovernmental flows have been increasing. General revenue for city governments increased by 14 percent (1970-1971 to 1971-1972) while intergovernmental revenues increased by 18 percent. Funds from state, federal, and other local sources increased by 13, 35, and 27 percent, respectively. Of course, the amount of federal aid to state and local governments, and the amount of state aid to local governments, varies among states. Per capita federal aid to state and local governments averaged $115 (1969-1970) and varied from $361 (Alaska) to $79 (Florida), while state aid to local governments averaged $142, and varied from $292 (New York) to $20 (Hawaii).[4] When state aid to local governments is calculated as a percentage of local government revenue from other sources, states vary from 126.2 percent (North Carolina) to 10.8 percent (New Hampshire) (1970).[5]

These statistics reflect primarily the flow of shared revenues, grants, and other aids from higher levels of government to lower levels. In addition, substantial funds flow among local governments via intergovernmental agreements and contracts. Together they form an increasing part of the local government financial situation and thus an increasing part of the fiscal management function.

Vertical problems arise when there is a mismatch between expenditure responsibilities and revenue capacity among hierarchical levels of government. Currently, the general consensus appears to be that such a mismatch does exist (even given the level of federal and state aid), with the effect that local governments' expenditure needs exceed revenue capabilities to the extent that local governments are in a situation of fiscal crisis. In addition, horizontal fiscal problems have become major political issues in many metropolitan areas. These problems stem from an extreme fragmentation of metropolitan areas into multiple, adjacent, and overlapping governmental units that are differentiated by expenditure and revenue responsibilities. The issue is one of political autonomy versus economic efficiency and equity, with such attendant problems as externalities, tax competition, inequitable distribution of tax effort, diseconomies of scale, tax overlapping, or administrative disorganization.

Both vertical and horizontal problems combine to create major fiscal management problems for local government. Problems and solutions are explored in subsequent sections of this chapter.

Local Government Fiscal Problems

An understanding of the origins of fiscal problems at the local level depends to some extent on a historical view of the growth and distribution of population within the United States. Absolute growth in population has been dramatic—from approximately 4 million persons in 1790 to 211 million in 1974. Total

1美4美5美53

Table 7-2
Urban Population

Year	Percentage Population Urban	No. Places > 1 million	No. Places > 100,000
1910	45.6	3	50
1920	51.2	3	67
1930	56.1	5	94
1940	56.5	5	93
1950	59.6	5	109
1950[a]	64.0	5	107
1960	69.9	5	132
1970	73.5	6	156

Source: U.S. Bureau of the Census, *Statistical Abstract of the United States, 1974* (Washington: Government Printing Office, 1974), Table 17, p. 18.
[a]The definition of "urban" was changed in 1950 to include some unincorporated areas (such as fringe areas).

population is growing by approximately 0.9 percent per year (1970-1973), and is expected to reach between 251 and 300 million persons by the year 2000.[6] Given the level of absolute growth, the interesting characteristic is the distribution of the growth. In 1790, 95 percent of the population resided in rural areas, while only 5 percent resided in urban areas.[7] In 1970, the pattern was 73 percent urban and 27 percent rural, with only 5 percent of the population actually living on farms. The trend from rural to urban has been continuous (Table 7-2).

In the period from 1960 to 1970, total U.S. population increased 13.3 percent, while metropolitan population increased by 16.6 percent, urban population increased by 19.2 percent, and rural population declined by 0.3 percent.[8] In 1974, metropolitan areas covered 11 percent of the land, while urban areas utilized only 1.5 percent of the land.[9] The history is one of absolute growth and an increasing concentration of population within urban areas.

The physical growth of cities has occurred mostly at the fringe of the cities, where undeveloped land has been more readily available and less expensive.[10] In the 1800's, incorporated cities simply annexed fringe areas as urban services were provided to those areas. However, in the early 1900's, state legislatures began to pass legislation that allowed fringe areas to incorporate as municipalities, and that made annexation more difficult by requiring approval by those persons to be annexed. Much of this was in response to a growing concern with municipal corruption. Thus, the pattern of "fragmentation" was set; urban areas grew via the addition of local governmental units adjacent to the central city. The pattern continues today with the "typical" metropolitan area consisting of 85 units of government including: 2 counties, 13 townships, 21 municipalities, 18 school districts, and 31 special districts and authorities.[11]

This pattern of urban growth and jurisdictional fragmentation has led to a series of local government fiscal problems under the umbrella of "intergovernmental relations." Although the mix of particular problems varies among states and local governments, most of the problems exist to some extent in metropolitan areas. Therefore, the metropolitan context is used for the following discussion of problems; readers with primary interest in small rural cities may find that some of the "typical" problems do not apply to their own situation.

If local fiscal problems had to be characterized in just one way, they might be condensed to "required expenditures exceed available revenue," or "aspirations exceed the willingness to pay." Of course, the ever-present condition of economic scarcity necessarily prohibits the public from having everything it might want. Nevertheless, the local government situation goes beyond that economic condition; local government appears to be "starving." "Fiscal crisis" has become a common term as cities struggle each year with the task of somehow balancing the budget. High levels of price inflation and, in particular, public worker wage inflation have dramatically increased the costs of government production. At the same time, the public demands increases in the scope and depth of local services while resisting tax increases. Many cities are in the position of cutting services while raising taxes and increasing levels of debt. Mayors petition state and federal sources for increased levels of intergovernmental aid and tax reform. At the time of this writing, New York City is near default and possible bankruptcy. Many other cities face major fiscal crises without known solutions on the horizon. Almost every city is taking a hard look at the fiscal future. Meanwhile, citizens bear the burden of ever-increasing local taxes while observing a relative decline in the urban "quality of life." The aging city deteriorates but is not renewed. Transportation facilities become outmoded and congestion increases. Crime rates continue to rise. Perhaps the level of air, water, and noise pollution increases. This scenario exists to some extent in most places as real problems and perceptions on the part of an increasingly aware public. The citizen expects these problems to be addressed by the closest level of general government, the city. Yet, the city is often unable to respond. Particular problems, their causes, and potential solutions are presented in the following sections.

Vertical Problems

The major vertical problem in intergovernmental relations is the mismatch between expenditure needs and revenue capabilities among the levels of government. Federal, state, and local expenditures have all risen (as presented in Chapter 2), but only at federal and state levels have revenues generally kept pace. The federal level relies heavily on a progressive income tax that yields higher revenues in a growing economy without increases in the tax rate. That is, as the GNP (gross national product) and incomes rise, persons fall into marginally higher income tax brackets, and the total revenue yield is increased. Since the 1950's, the federal government has been able to finance larger expenditure levels and increase the level of aid to state and local governments, while lowering the tax rates. States have not been nearly so well off as the federal government and have had to raise tax rates. However, states tend to rely on the general sales tax and, to an increasing extent, on the income tax, both of which yield higher revenues with a growing economy. The local governments, however, have had to rely primarily on the property tax, the revenues of which tend to lag behind economic growth. That is, an increase in the value of the property tax base affects the property tax revenue only where it is reassessed and entered in the tax digest. In addition to other inherent problems with the property tax, this characteristic lag produces a situation where local tax revenues increase more slowly than expenditures in periods of economic growth. James Heilbrun has estimated that the GNP elasticity of local government spending was 1.40, and the GNP elasticity of local tax revenue was 1.0 or less in the period 1960 to 1971.[12] That is, a 1 percent increase in the GNP yielded a 1.4 percent increase in local expenditures and a 1 percent (or less) increase in local tax revenues. The difference was made up by increasing levels of federal and state aid and raising local tax rates. In summary, federal and state levels can generally meet expenditures in a growing economy without major tax rate increases, while local governments must rely on intergovernmental transfers and increased tax rates.

One might well ask, Why not simply raise local tax rates? Tax revenue equals the tax base times the tax rate. An expanded economy requires expanded government expenditures and thus increased revenues. Persons are required to pay more absolute taxes at all levels. At the federal and state levels the base expands to yield higher revenues, while the rates remain stable. At the local level, the base is relatively stable (or at least lags), and so the rate must be raised to yield higher revenues. There are essentially two reasons why it is difficult to raise tax rates at the local level. The first is primarily political, and is related to the fact that local governments must depend heavily on the relatively unsatisfactory property tax. Persons generally find it easier to pay additional taxes from incremental increases in income than from a stable fixed investment such as a home. That is, as a person's income rises, he or she pays more income tax; as a person's consumption increases, he or she pays more sales tax. In both cases, marginal tax increases come from marginal increases in income. More persons pay more tax as aggregate income rises in a growing economy, but a specific individual with a declining income pays less tax. However, the property tax is not directly related to income. Persons with a fixed or decreasing income (such as the unemployed) find increases in the property tax rates to be a significant burden. For this and other reasons (see Chapter 6, Property Tax), the property tax is quite unpopular with citizens. Therefore, it is politically difficult for local officials to enact increases in local property tax rates. When such increases are inevitable, local politicians can often be observed to participate in elaborate rituals of opposition, until the last possible moment when the rate is increased, with much regret.

The second reason has to do with the conflict that exists between two of the primary functions of local government: allocation and distribution. Local government must allocate resources to the production of general public goods and services. The provision of an adequate supply might require increases in the local tax rate. However, local government is also concerned with the distribution of wealth—the incidence of taxes and public benefits. The property tax is thought to be highly income-regressive. Therefore, an increase in the property tax rate falls more heavily on lower income groups. What is acceptable on allocational grounds is unacceptable on distributional grounds and vice versa, and so local government officials are reluctant to increase tax rates.

Horizontal Problems

Horizontal intergovernmental problems stem primarily from the extreme level of jurisdictional fragmentation already discussed. These problems can be categorized under the following headings:

1. externalities
2. income segregation and tax effort
3. tax competition
4. diseconomies of scale
5. area-wide decision-making

Externalities. Society is becoming more complex as it grows. The number of interacting economic units grows arithmetically; the number of linkages among units grows geometrically. Economic interdependencies become numerous and complex. Such is the economic situation among local governments. It is not unusual for a person to live in one political jurisdiction and travel through several more to places of employment, shopping, and recreation. That person may pay direct and indirect taxes and user fees in several dozen overlapping and adjacent governmental units. It is difficult, if not impossible, to relate individual taxes to particular services in exact jurisdictions. On the government side, many public benefits appear to accrue to persons who live outside the taxing authority. (Numerous examples of externalities and effects were presented in Chapter 2.) The overall effect can be summarized as one of variances between actual and perceived costs and benefits of public programs among citizens and governmental units, with the result of a nonoptimal allocation of resources—and a potential general undersupply of public goods and services.

Income Segregation and Tax Effort. The fragmentation of metropolitan areas has occurred largely on the basis of income and race. Because these characteristics tend to be statistically associated, they are often considered together. (In metropolitan areas, 11.8 percent of white families had incomes below $4,000 in 1972, whereas black families in that income category accounted for 33.1 percent.).[13] However, income segregation is the important factor in the context of intergovernmental problems. Historically, the poor have migrated to the aging central cities where low-cost housing, unskilled jobs, and social services were available. Middle- and upper-income families migrated to the new housing and better environment of the suburbs. Income groups were geographically differentiated. Political incorporations solidified distinctions, and many municipalities can now be characterized as low income, working class, high income, white, and so on.

One point of view identifies the advantages of having a quantity of small jurisdictions, each with a different mix of services. Thus, a person can select the jurisdiction that best fits his or her needs and desires.[14] That is, a large number of jurisdictions might affect a "marketlike" efficiency whereby families could select the best package of services from among a large number of alternatives. Of course, this efficiency would require the typical market conditions such as full mobility, complete knowledge, and absence of externalities, all of which are violated to varying degrees.

The problem with income segregation is that the low-income jurisdiction is left with a low per capita tax base and relatively high expenses for social maintenance programs, while the high-income jurisdiction enjoys a high per capita tax base and relatively low social overhead costs. Thus, the low-income jurisdiction must either provide a lower level of service, levy a higher tax rate, or both, relative to the high-income jurisdiction. It is clear that higher income suburbs bear less of a tax burden (taxes as a percentage of income) than lower income central cities.[15] Therefore, jurisdictional segregation by income contributes to an inequity of tax burden among governmental units and critical fiscal problems in the lower income jurisdictions.

Tax Competition. Tax competition exists among local units of government for several reasons. First, local governments often use low property tax rates to encourage businesses and industries to locate within their boundaries. These elements are desirable from a local fiscal point of view because they represent a net increase in tax revenues. That is, businesses and industries generally involve high property values, but require little in the way of public service. Therefore, they generate property tax revenues in excess of expenditures required on their behalf. Single-family residential units generally require more in services than they generate in revenue, and therefore represent a net fiscal loss.

However, if all the local governments in an area engage in tax rate competition, the tax rates will be artificially low, with the result that levels of public service will be artificially low. In addition, lower rates across all units will minimize the competitive advantage of any particular unit over another.

Another, but related, type of tax problem arises among adjacent units of government. For example, consider a central city that enacts a 2 percent sales tax to finance a rapid transit system. The effect is to increase prices by 2 percent in the central city. Metropolitan consumers may then be inclined to purchase major items in the suburbs. To the extent that this occurs, central city businesses may reduce investments in the city in favor of the suburbs, resulting in a decrease in the city tax base. The point is simply that taxes in one jurisdiction will affect every other jurisdiction; a change in one location will produce effects in other areas until some economic balance is restored.

Diseconomies of Scale and Area-Wide Decision-Making. The costs of production vary among the many public goods and services. Given the general goal of economic efficiency, goods and services should be produced at a scale that yields the lowest average cost. However, the scale of production in local government is fixed by the jurisdictional boundary. Where economies of scale are insignificant or do not exist, a local government of a given size can produce a service as efficiently as a government of any other size. Such is often the case with labor intensive and horizontally organized services, such as fire, police, and solid waste collection. For example, a single fire station represents a certain efficiency; an expansion of scale to two or more stations involves only the replication of the first fire station and its level of efficiency. However, services that are capital-intensive and vertically organized often exhibit significant economies of scale. Services such as water, sewer, and transportation fall into this category. Efficiency goals require that these services be produced at a scale that is large enough to capture lower average costs. Production at a smaller scale will yield artificially higher prices (taxes, user charges) and thus a misallocation of resources. Therefore, excessive fragmentation of metropolitan areas leads to diseconomies of scale for the production of some public goods and services.

A related point involves the efficiency with which public management decisions can be made. A large number of independent local governments, each making rational economic decisions, may not lead to a rational area-wide decision. Major problems of metropolitan education, employment, environment, or physical development require area-wide planning and management, and thus a large-scale decision mechanism.

The Central City–Suburb Exploitation Issue. Intergovernmental problems are often most apparent in metropolitan areas, where the relationships between the core city and the suburbs have become an important political-fiscal issue. The issue, termed "exploitation," arises from the twin observations that the central cities are relatively worse off than the suburbs, and that suburban commuters use the facilities and services of the central city. The suburban commuters are held to "exploit" the city—to use its facilities and services without rendering adequate compensation, with the result of a net flow of economic benefits from the city to its suburbs.

There can be no question as to the first observation—central cities are in a more severe fiscal crunch than the suburbs.[16] Central cities consist of older, often outmoded, and deteriorating physical stock (housing, streets, utilities) that requires high levels of maintenance and renewal. Central cities house the poor segments of the metropolitan population, who require high levels of public service. Middle- and upper-income groups and businesses have fled to the better conditions of the suburbs, leaving a diminished central city tax base. Areal expansion of the central city is blocked by surrounding suburban boundaries. The diminishing tax base forces a reduction in the supply of public services. The quality of city life falls; more residents flee to the suburbs. The problems build on themselves. However, none of these problems, as severe as they are, constitute "exploitation" in the strict sense. The exploitation issue involves a net flow of benefits from the central city to the suburbs. The suburban commuter (who lives in the suburbs, works in the city) uses city facilities and services (streets, police and fire protection, cultural facilities). The city must therefore provide additional facilities and services to accommodate the commuter or at least share its existing facilities and services with the commuter. The commuter pays some direct and indirect taxes and charges to the city (such as sales taxes or admission fees), but avoids the city's property tax. Of course, city residents using the suburbs produce a similar but opposite effect. In addition, the suburban commuter may support the central city via state taxes that are returned to the city in grants and aids, and the metropolitan use of the central city may create higher land values (higher tax revenues) and higher incomes in the central city. Whether or not exploitation actually exists depends on the measurement of these various flows.

A number of studies have examined the exploitation issue, with emphases on the measurement and incidence of costs and benefits to city and suburban residents. The results vary.[17] Several studies have reinforced the conclusions of suburban exploitation of the central city (Book, Neenan), while several have concluded central city exploitation of the suburbs (Smith, Vincent).[18] The variance among results has depended on what benefits and costs were included in the analysis and how these were measured. Most studies have estimated costs as "revenues paid" (such as taxes and user charges) and benefits as "cost of providing the service," as they accrue directly to city and suburban residents. However, Neenan's excellent study of the Detroit metropolitan area (1972) significantly expands on that concept of benefit.[19] The cost of service benefit was estimated and then modified by an effective demand factor. That is, citizens have a demand for both the direct and indirect benefits of public programs, and that demand varies from person to person. For example, in addition to direct benefits accruing to himself, a high-income person may place a value on redistributive benefits that accrue directly to lower income persons. The value of benefits (as effective demand) can be estimated in terms of the citizen's willingness to pay, which in turn can be estimated from voting behavior among income categories. Neenan used this inclusive "willingness to pay" benefit measure to estimate direct, indirect, and poverty benefits, and to conclude, "In every instance the revenue flows to Detroit fail to compensate fully for the public sector benefit flows from Detroit to the municipalities. . . . Consequently, each municipality enjoys a welfare gain from Detroit through the public sector. . . ."

A more recent study of the Washington, D.C., metropolitan area by Greene, Neenan, and Scott concluded that the District of Columbia received net benefit from the Maryland and Virginia suburbs when benefits were estimated on a "cost-of-service" basis, but that the reverse was true when benefits were estimated on an effective demand basis.[20]

Therefore, the exploitation issue remains unsettled. Several studies of particular metropolitan areas suggest that suburban communities may compensate central cities for the cost of direct benefits received, but that significant suburban exploitation of central cities does exist in terms of a more inclusive economic definition of benefits. Exploitation has other dimensions in addition to the flow of costs and benefits. Certainly, exploitation of the central city does exist to the extent that suburban residents have found a way to avoid direct responsibility for solving severe urban problems. Political incorporation, large lot zoning, and racial discrimination have been used to effectively confine the poor or minority groups to the central city. The suburbanite often enjoys the economic benefits of participating in the metropolitan area's economy, yet successfully avoids direct involvement in its economic problems.

Fiscal Solutions

It is difficult to divide potential solutions for local intergovernmental problems into vertical and horizontal categories, because most of the strategies involve origination, or at least participation, by governmental units both vertically and horizontally removed from the particular local government. In addition, the solutions presented here are not new; rather thay are being used to some extent throughout the fiscal system and/or in some particular state or local situation. One might ask why these strategies are not adopted with greater frequency. There are several answers. First, every state, metropolitan, and local situation is different, and thus solutions appropriate to one area might not be satisfactory in another area. Second, local governments can affect very little change in the pattern of intergovernmental relationships on their own, but rather must rely on action at the federal and state levels. Because local situations vary within states, legislatures encounter considerable difficulty in finding politically acceptable state-wide solutions. However, this does not mean that local governments cannot influence intergovernmental relations; the appropriate use of existing mechanisms (such as federal and state grants, planning, and interlocal contracts) and the formulation of reform strategies for consideration at the state level are important components of the local fiscal management function. Lastly, intergovernmental fiscal relationships that have been built over the years represent, in the aggregate, a complexity that discourages anything more than a marginal reform action. It becomes overwhelming to assess the existing situation, and therefore it is difficult to estimate the consequences of major changes with sufficient certainty. For example, the property tax is known to be an almost totally unsatisfactory tax, and yet there is a great deal of reluctance to eliminate it in favor of a better taxing mechanism. The unknown economic consequences represent too great a risk. Therefore, all the potential reform strategies tend to be incremental.

Categorical Grants

Categorical grants are transfers of money that do not require repayment from higher levels of government (federal and state) to lower levels (state and local) for expenditures within particular categories of activities. Federal and, to some extent, state categorical grants to local governments form an important part of the local budget; they serve to:

1. encourage local expenditures towards national, state, and/or regional goals
2. redistribute income among state and local governmental jurisdictions
3. correct the expenditure revenue imbalances that exist among federal, state, and local government levels

Federal grants to local governments have been primarily in the categories of income security (welfare), education and manpower training, health, and community development. State grants to local governments fall mainly to the areas of education, welfare, and highways. A significant part of the state aid involves federal funds that are passed through to local governments.

Categorical grants have both income and substitution effects at the local level. The receipt of grant moneys raises the effective income of the local unit and therefore encourages a reduction of tax effort. Also, grants that can be expended only on particular programs may affect a change in the overall allocation of resources among local activities. For example, a major grant for law enforcement activities may induce the recipient government to lower its tax rate (spend federal money instead of local money), and/or to shift monies that normally would have been spent on law enforcement activities to other areas, substituting the federal money—with the result that there is no increase in the total amount of resources spent on law enforcement. To control these effects, the granting federal agency attaches "strings" or conditions on the receipt or use of the grant. That is, grants are usually subject to a variety of administrative regulations, and often include a provision for "matching." A matching grant requires the local government to contribute some of its own resources to a program to comprise a percentage of the total program cost. For example, a 70–30 federal matching grant requires that the recipient government expend 30 percent of the total program costs from its own resources, while the grant provides the other 70 percent. This induces the recipient unit to maintain its tax effort and to expend larger total amounts on the grant category activity. However, from the local point of view, this may constitute a distortion of the optimal allocation of resources across all activities.

One of the major problems with the system of categorical grants is the complexity and uncertainty of the system. In 1970, there were approximately 800 separate grant programs at the federal level. The application and administration requirements are complex and time-consuming. Some grant programs are authorized but unfunded; the level of funding varies from year to year. Once an application is submitted, the success, timing, and amount of the grant are uncertain. Applications may require review at the regional and state levels. Often political connections must be exercised to increase the chances of a successful application. The process is so confusing that local governments must expend considerable management effort towards discovering what grant programs exist, which are funded, how and when to apply, and how to manage the grants once received.

Revenue Sharing

Revenue sharing involves the transfer of monies from higher levels of government to lower levels on a routine and/or formula basis. State-to-local sharing often takes the form of "shared" or "earmarked" taxes. For example, a state may designate that a particular percentage of a specific tax (property, general sales, or excise) be allocated to local governments (counties, cities, or school districts) on a formula basis. Formulas are often based on such measures as population, location of collection, or type of government.[21]

However, revenue sharing at the federal level is more often identified with particular programs: General Revenue Sharing and Special Revenue Sharing. General revenue sharing exists in the form of the State and Local Fiscal Assistance Act of 1972, whereby approximately $30 billion is to be transferred to state and local governments over a five-year period. One-third of the aid goes to state governments, with the remaining two-thirds allocated to local governments. The aid is divided first among states on the basis of one of two formulas (population, tax effort, relative income, or these factors combined with urbanized population and income tax collections) and, second, among local governments within a state on the basis of the three-factor formula. Applications for these funds are not required; rather they are sent automatically to eligible governments (states, counties, townships, municipalities, Indian and Alaskan villages). Expenditures must be accounted for, but constraints are minimal; funds can be utilized for capital and operating expenses in the areas of public safety, environmental protection, public transportation, health, recreation, libraries, social services (poor and aged), and financial administration. For all general purposes, this aid can be considered as "no strings attached" monies, constituting about 5 to 10 percent of city budgets. Of course, local governments are more than happy to have this money. However, the real measure of effectiveness depends on the extent to which general revenue sharing meets its stated objective of relieving fiscal pressure at the local level. The impact of general revenue sharing was certainly reduced by the cut and, in some cases, impoundment of federal categorical grant funds in 1973 and 1974. A recent analysis by Rondinelli found that revenue sharing funds have not been used to substitute for reduced categorical aid, but were used to fund existing activities and/or to reduce or postpone tax increases; the net effect was not an expanded revenue capacity.[22] Rondinelli found, on the other hand, that general revenue sharing was relatively less complex and more efficient than categorical aid.[23] Some of the problems with the early revenue sharing experience have not been problems with the act itself, but rather have been the net effects of cuts in federal categorical aid and the extreme fiscal constraints under which many local governments must operate. There is continuing federal and local support for the shift from categorical to general forms of intergovernmental aid, and it appears likely that the State and Local Fiscal Assistance Act will be extended in some form beyond 1976.

Special Revenue Sharing is a movement to combine approximately one-third of the federal domestic categorical grant programs into several broad categories such as education, manpower training, law enforcement, transportation, and community development. Although special revenue sharing has yet to be fully implemented, several programs have been enacted including the Housing and Community Development Act of 1974 and the Omnibus Crime Control and Safe Streets Act of 1968.

The Housing and Community Development Act altered a large number of existing categorical programs under eight titles: Community Development, Assisted Housing, Mortgage Credit Assistance, Comprehensive Planning, Rural Housing, Mobile Home Construction and Safety Standards, Consumer Home Mortgage Assistance, and Miscellaneous.

Community Development, Title 1 of the Act, combines six categorical grant programs into a single block grant: Open Space-Urban Beautification-Historic Preservation, Public Facility Loans, Water and Sewer and Neighborhood Facilities, Urban Renewal, Model Cities, and Rehabilitation Loans. The objective is "development of viable urban communities by providing decent housing and a suitable living environment and expanded economic opportunities, principally for persons of low- and moderate-income."[24] Eligible program activities include the acquisition of real property, the acquisition or construction of public works, code enforcement, clearance of buildings, provision of public services related to community development, payment of matching funds for other federal grant programs, and relocation payments. States, counties, and general local governments are eligible for CD (Community Development) funds. However, annual applications are required and must include a three-year plan of activities. Title 1 funding is set at $8.4 billion over three years (1975, 76, 77) plus $50 million each for 1975 and 1976, and $100 million in 1977, for transition grants to communities with urgent development needs beyond normal program funding. The allocation of funds is complicated by an 80–20 split between metropolitan and nonmetropolitan areas, and with metropolitan cities (central city or other city with population of over 50,000 within SMSA) and urban counties entitled to a formula amount based on relative population, housing crowding, and poverty. In addition, there is a "hold harmless" provision that guarantees higher levels of funding for communities with high levels of funding under the previous categorical programs. Also, 2 percent of the appropriation is allocated to a discretionary fund.

The Omnibus Crime Control and Safe Streets Act of 1968 (amended in 1973 and 1974) established another special revenue sharing program to encourage law enforcement and criminal justice research and planning and for authorizing grants to state and local units of government for improving and strengthening their justice systems. It established the Law Enforcement Assistance Administration (LEAA) within the U.S. Department of Justice, and has provided monies for a broad range of law enforcement and related activities including planning, public protection, recruitment of personnel, education and training, construction of facilities, program operation, and the like. State and local expenditures under this program must be part of an overall "plan," but constraints are minimal when compared with the categorical grant system.

Tax Reform

Tax reform measures affecting intergovernmental fiscal relations involve a number of strategies for increasing fiscal capacity at the local level. (Specific reform measures are addressed in Chapter 6.) Local tax reform involves improving the structure (for example, exemptions) and administration of the property tax and, more important, shifting emphasis away from the property tax in favor of local income and sales taxes. In addition, there is a strong sentiment in favor of redirecting educational financing to the state level and social maintenance financing to the federal level.

Planning, Special Districts, Federation, and Consolidation

The complex intergovernmental relationships that exist among local governments are largely the products of the fragmentation of areal jurisdiction within metropolitan areas. One set of solution strategies involves "internalizing the externalities" by enlarging jurisdictions for some or all purposes. The strategies include regional or metropolitan planning, special service districts, federation, and consolidation.

The question is one of political autonomy versus economic efficiency. The trade-off between the two requires a value judgment, and therefore the question cannot be adequately answered here. However, it seems clear that certain local government services (such as transportation, air quality, water, and sewer) exhibit significant economies of scale, and therefore area-wide planning and management are warranted. Additionally, the problems of externalities, income segregation, and tax competition can be affected via the adoption of area-wide jurisdiction. However, citizens place high values on local political autonomy. They rationally may view the economic inefficiency of fragmentation as a reasonable price to pay for local determination.

The areal consolidation of responsibility can take a variety of forms that vary along the dimensions of comprehensiveness of substantive concern and level of authority. That is, a metropolitan or regional mechanism can deal with only one activity or a broad range of activities, and it can exercise the authority to levy taxes and provide services, or it can remain only advisory in nature.

The strategy of regional planning most often takes the form of a voluntary area-wide council of elected officials with a professional planning staff to enhance local cooperation, provide technical aid to local units, and formulate comprehensive regional plans. Many of these councils or commissions were created in the 1950's and 1960's as relatively diluted forms of regionalization. That is, the planning output is usually advisory, and dissatisfied officials can withdraw from participation. Although the level of activity of these organizations has varied, they exist in some form in 212 metropolitan areas and 238 nonmetropolitan areas (1974).[25] Numerous federal grant programs require the involvement of a regional mechanism to perform various supervisory functions such as reviewing applications from local units and requiring that local projects be part of an area-wide plan. Many of these initially weak and comprehensive regional planning agencies have evolved to exercise more authority, including the exercise of tax power and the provision of multiple services on an area-wide basis. In addition, there has been a proliferation of special districts or authorities with the responsibility for providing a specific area-wide service such as water or sewer. It is probably fair to characterize the United States as having a significant regional governmental system, although there is a great deal of variance among the states and metropolitan areas.

Single-purpose area-wide authorities often provide satisfactory solutions in situations where a particular service need transcends local governmental boundaries. State "enabling" or special legislation is required to establish a special district; once established, service and taxation (or user charge) apply only to the functionally created area, regardless of local governmental boundaries. The problem with special districts is that they constitute additional units of government, and to some extent, may contribute to the general problem of fragmentation and overlapping of tax authorities. As previously mentioned, multipurpose authorities have grown out of the weaker forms of regional planning. They often take the form of a "metropolitan federation." Here, a federation of local governments supplies area-wide services and levies area-wide taxes, while local governments are retained to provide local services. Federation has the political advantage of retaining at least some local autonomy, while capturing area-wide economies. Another strategy, "consolidation," is the complete or partial combination of local governments into a single area-wide government. Existing local governments are either abandoned or retained to supplement the services of the consolidated government. One rather common form of consolidation involves the combination of all units within a county—termed an "urban county." The urban county is granted "home rule" powers (powers generally associated with municipalities), future local municipal incorporations are prohibited or limited, and existing municipalities continue to exist to supplement county-wide services. Of course, consolidation has the political disadvantage of severely limiting local government autonomy.

Interlocal Contracts and Agreements

Interlocal contracts and agreements provide another mechanism for intergovernmental cooperation. An agreement provides for the joint exercise of power by two or more governments (vertically or horizontally). For example, two local governments or a municipality and a county may agree to operate a joint planning commission. A contract is a business transaction between or among governmental units. For example, a contract may provide that one municipality purchase water from another municipality. Contracts and agreements usually include provisions for the nature of the agreement, the responsibilities of each unit, limitations on the agreement, service charges and other financial provisions, staffing, property arrangements, duration, termination requirements, and amendment procedures. Agreements and contracts are covered by state enabling legislation, the provisions of which vary considerably among states.[26] The use of contracts among local governments is extensive, and the arrangements are often complex. For example, a state forestry commission may lease fire fighting equipment to a county, which in turn, loans the equipment to a rural town in exchange for fire fighting service in the county's nearby rural areas. Likewise, a city may enter into contract with a county and other cities to construct and operate an area-wide water and sewer system.

The complexity of a multitude of intergovernmental agreements and contracts requires considerable attention on the part of the financial management system. A simplifying variation can be found in the Los Angeles "Lakewood Plan," whereby the county offers local governments packages of services under a single contract. Local governments are free to select the package that best meets their needs and to provide some of their own services.

In summary, intergovernmental agreements and contracts constitute heavily used mechanisms for cooperation, but require considerable management attention. They can affect "economy of scale" situations where area-wide authority, federation, and consolidation strategies are politically infeasible. They tend to promote fragmentation but offer a considerable potential for economic efficiency in local government.

Notes

1. See Chapter 2, "Size and Scope of the Public Sector" for a review of governmental composition and responsibility.

2. U.S. Bureau of the Census, *City Government Finances in 1971-72,* GF-72-4 (Washington: Government Printing Office, 1973), Table 1, p. 5.

3. The objects of the flows of funds in this context are governmental units, as opposed to persons. Since federal, state, and local governments are co-incident, a person pays taxes to all three and receives goods and services from all three. The difference in the incidence of revenues and expenditures at each level is facilitated by intergovernmental transfers.

4. Advisory Commission on Intergovernmental Relations, *State-Local Finances: Significant Features and Suggested Legislation,* 1972 edition (Washington: Government Printing Office, 1974), tables 43, 45, and 46, pp. 68–72.

5. Ibid.

6. U.S. Bureau of the Census, *Statistical Abstract of the United States: 1974* (Washington: Government Printing Office, 1974), Section 1, Population, pp. 5–13.

7. Urban areas are here defined as cities with a population of 2,500 or more.

8. *Statistical Abstract, 1974,* Table 13, 18, pp. 14, 19.

9. Ibid., Table 19, p. 20.

10. Much of this brief history can be found in Advisory Commission on Intergovernmental Relations, *American Federalism: Into the Third Century* (Washington: Government Printing Office, 1974), p. 7.

11. Ibid. p. 9.

12. James Heilbrun, *Urban Economics and Public Policy* (New York: St. Martin's Press, 1974), p. 330.

13. *Statistical Abstract,* Table 623, p. 385.

14. See Charles M. Tiebout, "A Pure Theory of Local Expenditures" in William E. Mitchell and Ingo Walter, *State and Local Finance* (New York: Ronald Press, 1970), p. 21.

15. See Robert B. Pettengill and Jogindar S. Uppal, *Can Cities Survive?* (New York: St. Martin's Press, 1974), Chapter 4.

16. Ibid. Chapter 4.

17. A review of research in this area can be found in Kenneth V. Greene, William B. Neenan, and Claudia D. Scott, *Fiscal Interactions in a Metropolitan Area* (Lexington, Mass.: Lexington Books, 1974), p. 17.

18. These major works are reviewed in Greene, Neenan, and Scott, *Fiscal Interactions;* Samuel H. Book, "Costs of Commuters to the Central City as a basis for Commuter Taxation," Ph.D. Dissertation, Columbia University, 1970; William Neenan, *Political Economy of Urban Areas* (Chicago: Markham, 1972); R.F. Smith, "Are Nonresidents Contributing Their Share to the Core City Revenues," *Land Economics,* August 1972; and Phillip E. Vincent, "The Fiscal Impact of Commuters" in Werner Z. Husch et al., *Fiscal Pressures on the Central City* (New York: Praeger, 1971).

19. Neenan, *Political Economy.*

20. Greene et al., *Fiscal Interactions.*

21. Provisions for state revenue sharing can be found in Advisory Commission of Intergovernmental Relations, *State-Local Finances: Significant Features and Suggested Legislation,* 1972 edition (Washington: Government Printing Office, 1974), pp. 73–112.

22. Dennis A. Rondinelli. "Revenue Sharing and American Cities: Analysis of the Federal Experiment in Local Assistance," *Journal of the American Institute of Planners,* vol. 41, no. 5 (September 1975), pp. 319–333.

23. Ibid. p. 331.

24. U.S. Department of Housing and Urban Development, *Summary of the Housing and Community Development Act of 1974,* p. 1.

25. ACIR, *American Federalism,* p. 13.

26. Model provisions can be found in Advisory Commission on Intergovernmental Relations, *A Handbook for Intergovernmental Agreements and Contracts* (Washington: Government Printing Office, March 1967).

8

Debt Financing

Introduction

Debt financing occurs routinely at all levels of government, and yet there is much misunderstanding about the nature, function, and extent of the debt. Part of the confusion is caused by the general lack of information that exists about public financial operations, and a portion results from misguided attempts to equate private debt with public debt. At the local government level, this problem surfaces around voter resistance to bond referendums and the often observed lack of coordination between local government "plans" and the financial means for implementing the plans. Nevertheless, debt financing is one of the central elements of local government finance and is therefore entitled to receive full planning and management consideration. This chapter provides a general overview of local government debt financing with an emphasis on debt planning and management, and includes a review of the various functions of the debt, the extent of the debt, and a description of various debt instruments.

Local Government Debt

Local governments incur both long-term and short-term debt. Long-term debt occurs in the form of the sale of fixed income securities or bonds. There are two major types of bonds: (1) the "general obligation" or "full faith and credit" bond, for which repayment is guaranteed by the total resources of the issuing unit, and (2) the "revenue" or "nonguaranteed" bond, which is backed only by particular revenues that are associated with the project to be financed. The major, unique characteristic of these long term instruments is that they are tax-exempt. That is, interest earnings from municipals are exempt from federal income tax and from state income taxes in the state of issue. The result is that the effective yield of these bonds to the bond holder is significantly enhanced. For example, consider an individual investor in an income category that requires a federal marginal tax rate of 45 percent (a single person with a taxable income of $26,000 in 1973) and a state income tax rate of 5 percent. Table 8-1 shows the results of alternate investments in municipal or corporate bonds. In this case, the municipal bond at 5 percent and the corporate bond at 10 percent are competitive in terms of the effective yield to the bond holder. This means that municipal bonds can be issued at lower interest rates and with lower interest

Table 8-1
Effective Yield of Tax-Exempt Bonds

	Municipal Bond	Corporate Bond
Principal invested	$1,000	$1,000
Interest rate	0.05	0.10
Before tax yield	50	100
Tax (50%)	0	50
Effective yield	50	50

costs to local government. This also means that tax-exempt bonds are particularly effective investments for individuals with high marginal tax rates as well as other institutions needing tax liability reduction.

Local governments also incur short-term debt, usually in the form of bank notes, to solve occasional cash flow problems created by emergencies, unforeseen expenditures, and in anticipation of tax receipts.

Most local government expenditures are made on a "pay as you go" basis. Current operating expenses for personnel, materials, supplies, and recurring minor capital items are financed from the current revenue of taxes, user charges, fees, and intergovernmental transfers and grants. However, financing through borrowing is utilized in several general situations. First, there may arise periodically the necessity for singular large items of expenditure that would result in an inordinate tax burden for a given fiscal year. For example, a city may find that it needs a city hall expansion one year, nothing significant the next year, a new water plant the third year, and so on. Debt financing in this case can be used to spread the payment burden over a period of years with some stability for the year-to-year tax burden. The second debt situation, and in fact the most common situation, involves debt financing for the construction and/or purchase of capital or productive facilities that yield benefits over an extended time period in a pay as you use context. For example, a city may construct a city hall that serves the public for thirty years before requiring major renovation. Debt financing allows the payment burden to be spread over the productive life of the facility with some equity of burden among generations and persons moving into or out of the governmental unit's jurisdiction. This is particularly appropriate for a self-financing public enterprise such as a water system that operates on user fees. Most major debt issues involve both these above rationale. However, small capital items that occur with regularity should be financed from current revenues to reduce administrative and interest costs.

Borrowing is also utilized in certain short-term situations in order to solve cash flow problems. For example, a natural disaster or an unscheduled plant failure may require an immediate cash expenditure beyond the capability of the local government. Normally, cities carry an "emergency" or "contingency" fund for this purpose. However, not every problem can be anticipated and cities must sometimes borrow cash from banks or other financial institutions, usually in the form of short-term notes. Another short-term situation involves borrowing in anticipation of tax receipts. That is, a city may find itself temporarily short of operating cash just before the receipts of tax payments or intergovernmental transfers. Again, short-term borrowing is justified. The only problem with short-term debt is that interest costs are quite high, and therefore heavy reliance on short-term borrowing should be avoided.

The Extent of Local Government Debt

At the end of 1972, the total outstanding public debt was $601 billion, or $2,889 per capita. The federal government was responsible for the largest share of $427 billion or $2,051 per capita. Local governments were next with $120 billion, and state governments followed with $54 billion, for a combined $838 per capita. The per capita interest paid on that debt in that year was $82 for the federal share, and $33 for the state and local share.[1]

The distribution of the debt among local governments by type of debt is shown in Table 8-2.[2] It also shows the extent to which local governments rely on each major type of bond. A given governmental unit with a good credit rating can normally sell general obligation bonds at lower interest rates than revenue bonds, because the "full faith and credit" guarantee represents a lower risk to the bondholder. Therefore, municipalities, counties, and townships tend to rely heavily on general obligation bonds, and utilize revenue bonds for self-financing projects. Notice that school districts, having no direct fee capabilities, rely on general obligation bonds exclusively, while special districts, usually

Table 8-2
Distribution of Outstanding Long-Term Local Debt, 1971-72

	Outstanding Debt (in billions)	Percentage Full Faith and Credit	Percentage Nonguaranteed
Counties	13.87	81	19
Municipalities	52.51	59	41
Townships	3.14	91	9
School Districts	24.48	100	0
Special Districts	26.03	31	69
Total	120.04		

Source: U.S. Bureau of the Census, *Government Finances in 1971-72*, series G-72-No. 5 (Washington: U.S. Government Printing Office, 1973), Table 16, p. 30.

172

Table 8-3
Distribution of Per Capita Debt by City Size, 1971-1972 (in Dollars)

Population: Size of City	1 million +	500,000- 999,999	300,000- 499,999	200,000- 299,999	100,000- 199,999	50,000- 99,999	Less than 50,000
Gross debt	895	496	473	485	354	295	237
Long-term issued	109	163	70	57	41	41	24
Long-term retired	46	24	22	23	18	15	13

Source: U.S. Bureau of the Census, *City Government Finances in 1971-72,* series GF72-No. 4 (Washington: U.S. Government Printing Office, 1973), Table 4, p. 8.

providing services on a fee basis, depend heavily on revenue bonds. Also, short-term debt (not included in Table 8-2) is a significant part of the debt picture, with 12.7 percent of all city debt in that category (1971-1972).

A closer look at city governments (Table 8-3) shows that the reliance on debt increases with city size.[3] The largest cities tend to have nearly four times the per capita debt of the smallest cities, and the level of debt is increasing for cities of all sizes. In fact, cities are issuing debt more than twice as fast as they are retiring debt.[4]

The level of outstanding debt at the city level has increased over the past five years (1967-1971) at an average annual rate of approximately 8.25 percent, while general revenues have climbed at the rate of 12.25 percent, behind expenditures at 12.5 percent.[5] Two of the reasons for this increased reliance on debt financing is that cities have been, and are presently, experiencing an increasing demand for capital facilities, coupled with the fact that capital facilities depend heavily on debt financing (Table 8-4).[6] This increasing demand for capital funds is caused by the general growth of urban populations, the rising demand for local governmental services, and inordinate price increases in capital construction.

The Economic Structure of Debt

Debt occurs because people have a time preference for current resource use over future resource use. That is, given the choice, individuals would rather have a new automobile, a new house, or a thousand dollars sooner rather than later. This preference affects lending and borrowing. A person wanting to increase his current resources for consumption or investment can borrow resources (land, labor, capital) from someone who is willing to forego using current resources. The inducement for lending is the "interest" or price paid by the borrower to the lender. This lender's interest rate is based on the time preference for re-

Table 8-4
Source of Funds for Capital Financing, 1969-1970

	Cities	Counties
Current receipts	20	22
Federal grants, loans	17	15
Debt	63	63
Total	100	100

Source: Advisory Commission on Intergovernmental Relations, *Federal Approaches to Aid State and Local Capital Financing* (Washington: U.S. Government Printing Office, 1970), p. 18.

sources, the amount of risk involved to the lender, the rate of inflation, and administrative costs; it is, theoretically, set in a pure market system by the laws of supply and demand for money. Like any market exchange, borrowing and lending is voluntary and leads to a net increase in value for both borrower and lender. That is, the lender is foregoing a certain amount of current resource use by transferring resources to the borrower, but he is receiving interest in return that can be used to claim additional resources in the future. He is reducing consumption now in favor of increasing consumption later. In turn, the borrower is increasing current resource use and paying interest that will decrease his future resource use.

However, one need not borrow money solely to increase current consumption, but might rather borrow money to construct or buy a productive asset. Such use of resources is called "investment." For example, a person might borrow money from a bank to buy a television set as an item of consumption. In this case his increased current consumption is at the expense of future consumption. However, a person might borrow money to buy land that is, in turn, leased to a productive enterprise. In this case, the resource has been utilized as an investment with the expectation that returns on the investment will exceed the interest cost of borrowing the money. In this case, assuming a successful investment, the borrowing of money may enhance, rather than diminish, future consumption.

Public Debt

The governmental unit can borrow money in the same context. State and local governments can borrow through the sale of bonds with the promise to pay the bondholder the principal amount plus accrued interest at some future date. If these borrowed funds are used to support higher levels of current consumption, then they are being utilized at the expense of future consumption. If however, the funds are used to finance capital investment projects, the future real output of the projects may yield a net increase in the future level of welfare.

However, there are some differences between private and public debt. Private debt is voluntary, whereas public debt may not be entirely voluntary. A public, collective, majority decision in favor of incurring debt may leave a minority of individuals dissatisfied. Also, the interest paid on the public debt must be withdrawn from future private consumption and savings in the form of taxes, with the possibility of undesirable distributional effects via the incidence of taxation. In both cases local government and the political process must appropriately articulate the public interest. Another difference involves the ability to repay debt. Local government has the power to levy taxes to repay debt, whereas the private individual does not. This means that the public sector unit sustains debt with a relatively lower risk of default than the individual.

Ownership of Debt

Local government debt issues are generally purchased by bond underwriters, or brokers, who resell the bonds to a variety of investors. Table 8–5 shows the pattern of state and local ownership.[7] The two primary holders of state and local bonds are individuals and commercial banks, collectively holding more than 75 percent of the outstanding debt. Individual holders include primarily persons in high marginal income tax brackets, where the tax-exempt status of the bonds yields a large increase in the effective after-tax return on investment. Commercial banks, taxed at full corporate tax rates, find municipals attractive for the same purpose, but tend to leave the bond market in periods of tight money when other demands on their funds are high. Insurance companies buy substantial public bonds for tax purposes and maintenance of liquidity. Government

Table 8–5
Ownership of State and Local Bonds, 1969

	Percentage
Individuals	31.5
Commercial banks	44.1
Insurance companies	13.0
State and local funds	3.4
Corporations	4.6
Other	3.4
Total	100.0

Source: Advisory Commission on Intergovernmental Relations, *Federal Approaches to Aid State and Local Capital Financing* (Washington: U.S. Government Printing Office, 1970), Table 5, p. 25.

units buy bonds for trust funds, sinking funds, and the like, because of the fixed income stability they provide.

Debt Instruments

There are a variety of debt instruments, the most common of which are the long-term "general obligation" (G.O.) bond and the "revenue" bond. These particular instruments, and variations thereof, are discussed in the following sections.

General Obligation Bonds

State enabling legislation allows local governments to issue general obligation bonds. These bonds are guaranteed by the "full faith and credit" of the issuing unit (by the full taxing power of the government unit). For this reason, they carry a relatively low risk of default, and therefore a relatively low interest rate. This low interest cost, plus some flexibility in the management of repayment sources, makes this type of bond most advantageous to local governments. They are heavily relied on for financing a variety of capital improvements, especially those projects that are not self-financing through user charges. One problem with this type of bond is that local governments are generally limited to a G.O. debt ceiling of some percentage of their assessed valuation (usually 5 to 10 percent). Many units operate at, or near, this level and would like to go beyond. Usually a local unit is allowed to incur part of this debt without referendum, while the remaining part is subject to public referendum.

Special Tax Bonds

Bonds that are payable from a specific tax source are called "special tax" bonds. If, in addition, they are guaranteed by full faith and credit, they are considered as general obligation bonds. For example, road improvement bonds may use an earmarked gasoline tax for repayment, but also carry an additional guarantee by full faith and credit. "Special assessment" bonds are repaid from assessments levied against properties that receive the benefits of a capital improvement. "Tax increment" bonds are retired with the incremental tax revenues generated by new development. These nonguaranteed special tax bonds generally carry higher interest rates than guaranteed bonds.

Revenue Bonds

Revenue or nonguaranteed bonds are not backed by the full faith and credit of the issuing unit, but rather by specific revenues that are generated by the capital project, as well as a mortgage on the property. Financially self-sufficient projects, such as water systems, solid waste systems, municipal airports, transit systems, and other public enterprises with user-charge financing, fall into this category. The advantages of revenue bonds include the indirect assessment of interest costs to the direct users of the facility, and the exemption of this type of bond from the state-imposed legal debt ceiling. The disadvantages include the higher interest rates required because of the nonguaranteed status and the additional management control required to attract investors and ensure adequate financial performance.

Given these advantages and disadvantages, local governments tend to rely first on general obligation bonds for capital investment and then on revenue bonds beyond the debt ceiling and with self-financing enterprises. However, this may not always be the case. Small cities with unstable financial conditions and poor credit ratings, but with sound individual revenue-producing projects, may find lower interest rates with a highly rated revenue issue than with a poorly rated general obligation issue.

Industrial Aid Bonds

Industrial aid bonds, issued primarily in the southern states to induce industrial development, are attempts to utilize the financial advantage of the tax-exempt status of municipal bonds to the mutual advantage of industry and city. For example, a city or a nonprofit corporation can issue a series of bonds to finance the development of an industrial facility. The industry leases the facility without incurring the heavy front-end development costs. The rents collected by the bond issuer are used to repay the bond. Although these arrangements have been used successfully by some communities, the competitive advantage in terms of attracting new industry tends to be reduced when many of the other communities in a region offer the same incentive.

Lease Bonds

Lease bonds are similar to the industrial bonds just discussed in that it is possible to charter an "authority" or other nonprofit corporation specifically for the purpose of issuing bonds, constructing public facilities, and leasing those facilities to the governmental unit. This method, which is often used to finance schools, hospitals, and the like, allows the governmental unit to effectively exceed G.O. debt limitations. These bonds remain tax-exempt.

Bond Structure

There are two general types of local government bonds: the "sinking fund" bond and the more common "serial" bond. The sinking fund bond is a promise to pay a lump sum amount at some specific future time. A sinking fund is established by the issuer; annual payments are made to the fund, and the fund is invested so as to yield the appropriate repayment amount at the date of maturity. The problem with this type of bond at the local government level is that it requires periodic actuarial computations and adjustment to ensure adequate repayment funds, and it offers little flexibility to the investor in terms of maturity dates.

The serial bond is issued with serial, or yearly, maturity dates; that is, a certain number of the bonds in an issue mature each year. The interest on the bonds is paid periodically, usually every six months. This provides the major advantage of repaying the principal and interest each year from current allocations in predetermined amounts, while allowing investors some flexibility with respect to maturity dates. Serial bond issues can be formulated as "annuity" or "straight" issues. The annuity type is designed to produce a uniform yearly repayment of principal and interest. This is accomplished by maturing successively larger amounts of principal each year while maintaining a declining interest payment. The straight type is designed to repay an equal amount of principal each year with interest payments varying.

Bonds are issued in $1,000 or $5,000 denominations with the face or "par" value as that amount paid to the holder at maturity. The interest rate is also printed on the bond. The method of repayment depends on whether the bond is a "coupon" bond or a "registered" bond. A coupon bond has a number of interest coupons attached. These are detached by the bondholder and periodically sent to the issuer or his agent for repayment. Registered bonds (registered as to principal only or as to principal and interest) have the owner's name printed on the bond and recorded so that interest payments can be made directly to the owner. Coupon bonds are more easily transferable, but registered bonds provide more security. Most municipal issues are optionally registerable.

Bonds may be "callable" by the issuer—called in and repaid before the stated maturity date—to take advantage of a change in prevailing interest rates. Exercise of this option usually requires payment of a premium or a discount in the original selling price of the bond to reflect this issuer option.

Bond Duration

Bond duration is sometimes set by state law for certain classes of facilities, but in any case, should follow the general rule that the debt period should match the "useful life" of the project, with the rate of repayment equal to the rate of depreciation. For example, major facilities, such as city halls, may serve the public for 25 or 30 years before major renovation; sewer lines, 15 to 20 years; streets, 10 years. Emergency deficit spending for current consumption should use a relatively short debt duration, such as 5 to 10 years. Duration for non-depreciating investments, such as land, are relatively arbitrary, but an excessive debt period needlessly increases interest and administrative costs. In some cases, the duration of a particular issue will depend on how that issue fits into the overall debt program and repayment schedule.

Interest Rates

Bond issues are sold to the highest bidder in a competitive bidding situation. After the basic issue is designed, it is described in an official notice of sale. A bid form is included with the notice; it typically states the principal amounts and the maturity dates. The bidders are usually allowed to set the interest rate(s) and the amount of the bid, with the resultant total interest cost to the issuer. Bids are submitted to the issuer, opened at a stated time, and awarded to the highest bidder (lowest interest cost to issuer). Bidders are usually syndicates of investment bankers, called "underwriters," who resell the bonds to a variety of customers. The face or par value (principal) and the interest rate(s) are printed on the bonds and/or coupons. However, the actual interest cost to the issuer and the effective yield to the bond holder may vary from the stated interest rate. This can happen because the underwriter may purchase and/or resell the bonds at par value, above par value (premium), or below par value (discount). For example, an underwriter may buy an issue from a local government at below par value and resell it at par value, in which case the effective interest cost paid by the issuer involves both the stated interest and the discount. The underwriter's profit is the amount of the discount, and the final bond customer receives the stated interest. However, the underwriter may purchase the issue at a premium value and resell it at a larger premium, in which case the issuer incurs a lower interest cost, and the final bond customer receives a yield below the stated interest rate. For example, a bond with a par value of $1,000 and an interest rate of 5 percent yields an effective return of 5.26 percent when purchased for $950. A typical retail bond advertisement will generally show the principal amount, the date of maturity, the interest rate, and the yield if held to maturity (Table 8-6).

In this case, the bonds are selling at a premium with an effective yield lower than the stated interest rate. Again, all of this means that the actual cost of borrowing to the issuer and the actual return to the bond holder may vary from the stated interest rate.

Municipal bond interest rates are generally two to three percentage points below equivalent corporate bond rates because of the tax-exempt provision,

Table 8-6
Typical Bond Figures, Rate and Yield

Principal	Maturity	Rate	Yield
100,000	1975	6.5	6.0
100,000	1976	6.5	6.1
100,000	1977	6.5	6.2

although there is a great deal of variability among bond issues. The actual interest cost to a issuing local government will depend on the state of the bond market at the time of the issue and the quality of the particular issue, the latter being expressed as a bond "rating."

Bond Ratings

Bonds are rated for quality by two financial services, Moody's Investor's Service, Inc., and Standard and Poor's Corporation. Issue ratings are based on an evaluation of the financial condition of the issuer, the capacity for repayment, the technical and legal provisions of the issue, and so on. In addition, Dun and Bradstreet, Inc., issues credit ratings for major issuers of municipal bonds. Bond rating symbols and approximate interpretations are shown in Table 8-7. In addition, Moody's may use an A-1 or Baa-1 to indicate superior quality within those classes, and Standard and Poor's may use an a + or − to indicate position within a class. However, in the cases of very small issuers, not all issues are rated because of a lack of financial information or inadequate financial performance records for new projects or both. The lack of a rating does not imply a low bond

Table 8-7
Bond Issue Ratings

Moody's	Standard and Poor's	Approximate Interpretation
Aaa	AAA	highest quality, lowest risk
Aa	AA	high quality, minimal risk
A	A	good quality, adequate security
Baa	BBB	lowest investment grade
Ba	BB	speculative
B	B	nonexistent investment
Caa	CCC	poor standing
Ca	CC	highly speculative
C	C	poorest standing

quality. The rating on an issue is, however, extremely important to the issuer, because the difference in an Aaa and a Baa rating can mean a difference in interest of between one-half and two-thirds percentage points.

Debt Planning and Management

The objectives of a debt management program include:

1. adequate resources for investment in capital facilities and/or revenue-producing enterprises
2. adequate reserve borrowing capacity to cover emergencies and/or unforeseen investment opportunities
3. a stable year-to-year repayment burden
4. a sound overall financial condition (to maintain a high credit rating and low interest costs)

Debt management should be considered as an integral part of the overall fiscal planning and management system as presented in Chapter 4 (Figure 4-3). Recall that the basic economic research and policy analysis functions produce a set of fiscal policies as inputs to the long-range fiscal plan, which is in turn integrated with the comprehensive plan. That is, these strategic studies project future economic conditions (such as demand levels, inflation, and interest costs), and allow for the evaluation of alternative methods of financing and debt levels. The comprehensive plan and the companion long-range fiscal plan (see activity inventory, Figure 4-8) both include the capital elements required to satisfy future demand and development goals. With fiscal policies as guides, the fiscal plan identifies those future actions required to ensure adequate capital funds and a reasonable repayment burden. The capital program identifies particular capital projects and the associated methods of financing. Total and individual capital requirements are scheduled over a period of five or six years. The capital budget (the first year of the capital program) identifies specific debt transactions for the fiscal year. This process is graphically summarized in Figure 8-1.

A number of additional activities are required for a successful debt management program. First, a local government must develop public involvement and support for the debt program. Important issues often require public referendum and always require political support. Many issues fail because of inadequate understanding on the part of the public. Second, a local government must strive to maintain a sound overall management system and financial condition to ensure a good credit rating and the resultant low interest rates and high debt capacity. In addition, a city must maintain a public relations program to "advertise" its financial condition to attract investors. This often involves the production and distribution of periodic financial reports to newspapers, financial magazines, potential investment bankers, and bond raters.

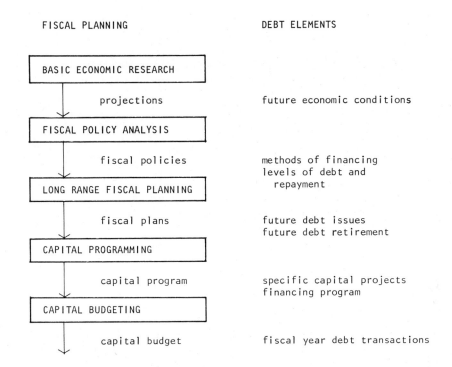

Figure 8-1. Debt Planning and Management Process

Another task involves the sound management of revenue-producing enterprises to ensure adequate revenues and avoid defaults. Most revenue issues will provide a "coverage" factor whereby the pledged revenues exceed the amount required for bond repayment. This coverage factor is one of the considerations used in bond ratings and, therefore, adequate coverage must be maintained. Also, each debt issue must be carefully designed with the aid of engineering, legal, and financial experts. Benefits from the appropriate use of consultants in financial matters can more than exceed their costs. Project costs and revenues should be realistically estimated, legal provisions must be acceptable to the issuer, underwriter, and buyer, and the financial provisions must be carefully formulated and timed. Last, a local government with a sound debt program and a good credit rating can often use its financial position to create additional advantages. A strong governmental unit may finance the projects of a weaker unit by issuing debt at favorable interest rates, constructing facilities, and leasing those facilities to weaker units. The debt is paid from the rents, and the stronger unit may retain the coverage. For example, a financially strong unit of local government might incur debt (at a favorable interest cost) to finance a water, sewer, or other system for a larger, metropolitan area. Other governmental units lease the facilities from the first unit, and in turn, levy taxes and/or user fees on the individual users of the system. Lease rates are such that the financing governmental unit realizes a positive net revenue, and the other units receive the benefit of a system that they could not finance or could finance only at a higher interest cost.

Notes

1. Summary statistics for public debt can be found in U.S. Bureau of the Census, *Government Finances in 1971-72,* series G, 72-No. 5 (Washington: Government Printing Office, 1973), Tables 3, 5, 7, and 14.

2. Ibid., Table 16, p. 30.

3. U.S. Bureau of the Census, *City Government Finances in 1971-72,* series GF 72-No. 4 (Washington: Government Printing Office, 1973), Table 4, p. 8.

4. Ibid., Table 4, p. 8.

5. Ibid., Table 1, p. 8.

6. Advisory Commission on Intergovernmental Relations, *Federal Approaches to Aid State and Local Capital Financing* (Washington: Government Printing Office, 1970), p. 18.

7. Ibid., Table 5, p. 25.

9   Accounting Systems

Accounting is essentially a method for recording and reporting the financial transactions of an organization. An accounting system contains information pertaining to the organization's past and current financial situation, and provides a mechanism for the control of financial resources to, from, and within the organization. Thus, the accounting system is of importance to managers, planners, elected officials, and others with an interest in financial affairs. This is not to say that these persons should be accountants, but rather that a basic understanding of the function and structure of accounting systems is prerequisite to effective fiscal planning and management.

Accounting is a subject and a profession unto itself; local governments must rely on professional accountants and other experts to design and maintain accounting systems. Small towns may be able to satisfy accounting needs with a staff clerk and a retained firm of consulting accountants. Larger units of government generally require a structured in-house accounting mechanism with a professional staff. Fortunately, the recent introduction of small, relatively inexpensive electronic computers to the local government scene has placed sophisticated accounting systems within the reach of many medium-sized and smaller units of government. These computer systems utilize "package" accounting programs that can be adapted to particular local government needs. In addition, such automated systems provide efficient analysis and report capabilities. The larger cities will generally utilize significant resources to maintain a complex automated accounting system and a sizable professional staff.

Accounting systems serve three basic needs: legal, stewardship, and managerial. The legal requirements for local government finance are controlled by the state governments; they include constraints on the types of financial transactions, procedures, and reports. In addition, the legislative body and certain external groups (such as federal auditors, state auditors, or municipal bond raters) periodically must assess the financial condition of the local government using reports based on data contained in the accounting system. Last, the local government manager and planner depend on the accounting system for the timely financial information needed to conduct policy and program analysis required to make sound management decisions. The accounting system also provides the mechanism for controlling the flow of resources within the organization so that activities can be carried out within the given level of resources (budget).

Some danger exists in treating a subject as extensive as accounting so briefly; errors of omission are impossible to avoid. However, the survey nature of this text precludes in-depth treatment; many standard texts are available for that purpose.[1] The purpose here is simply to familiarize the reader with an overview of accounting structure and process from which further inquiry can be directed. The remaining sections of this chapter address the structure of funds and accounts and the process of recording and reporting information in the system.

Accounting System Structure—Funds

Two important elements characterize accounting in local government: "funds" and "budgets." A fund is "an independent fiscal and accounting entity with a self-balancing set of accounts recording cash and/or other resources together with all related liabilities, obligations, reserves, and equities which are segregated for the purpose of carrying on specific activities or attaining certain objectives in accordance with special regulations, restrictions, or limitations."[2] That is, the functional activities of local government are divided into relatively independent fiscal entities called "funds." The reliance of local governments on fund structure is characteristic, although the numbers and types of funds utilized vary among governments. Local government accounting is often referred to as "fund accounting." The types of funds utilized include:

1. The General Fund. The "general," or "operating" fund is the primary general purpose fund in local government; it exists to finance the functions of general administration and the provision of general public services. Any activity not specifically included in another fund is part of the general fund. As such, it receives revenue from a number of sources, makes expenditures for a variety of activities, and, as a rule, is the largest and most active fund.

2. Special or Special Revenue Funds. "Special" funds are utilized to account for the revenues and expenditures associated with a special source of revenue or an earmarked tax. That is, certain taxes, portions of taxes, and intergovernmental grants are restricted to particular uses and must therefore be accounted for in a distinct fund.

3. Intergovernmental Service or Working Capital Funds. These funds are utilized for the departments or units within the local government that supply services to other units within the government. For example, a city garage may provide maintenance for the vehicles of all departments, and a printing shop may handle reproduction and binding services for all departments. Charges for services are made against the client departments.

4. Bond or Capital Project Funds. Capital project funds are created to account for the revenues associated with a bond issue and the expenditures of a capital project, unless those transactions are handled by special assessment or enterprise funds.

5. Debt Service Funds. These funds are utilized to account for monies committed to the repayment of the interest and principal for long-term general

obligation debt, unless otherwise included in special assessment or enterprise funds.

6. Special Assessment Funds. Special assessment funds are utilized to account for projects that are financed from special assessments levied against property owners.

7. Trust Funds. Local governments often act as owners or trustees for assets that are set aside for a particular purpose, such as employees' pension programs, utility customer deposits, and endowments. Trust funds are established to provide a separate accounting entity for each type of trust.

8. Enterprise or Utility Funds. Local governments provide certain services such as water, electricity, and solid waste collection on a self-financing user charge basis in a manner like a private enterprise. Separate funds are utilized for each such enterprise or utility.

Thus, there is usually one general fund and a number of each of the other types of funds. Each fund contains multiple accounts which correspond to the proprietary accounts of private enterprise: revenues, expenses, assets, liabilities, and net worth. However, local government is characterized by the integration of budgetary accounts with these proprietary accounts. Budget accounts record the estimated revenues, authorizations, and appropriated expenditures for the general fund and special revenue funds. However, other types of funds may be treated differently, depending on the purpose of the fund and the applicable legal constraints. Generally, enterprise, utility, intergovernmental service, and trust funds do not require formal budgetary accounts, but may utilize budgets in some other form for management and planning purposes. Likewise, capital project and special assessment funds do not require budgetary accounts, because an appropriation to a specific project is equivalent to a budget. However, budgetary accounts may be utilized to monitor the progress of capital projects. Debt service funds can also omit budgetary accounts because they must pay all interest and principal due in a particular fiscal period. Where budgetary accounts exist, actual and estimated revenues and expenditures can be compared to produce a summary of the budget situation. The actual use of formal budgetary accounts with operating accounts will depend on the purpose of the fund, as well as the management system and legal requirements.

Therefore, the accounting system is composed of a series of funds, each of which includes a number of proprietary and budgetary accounts. Before looking at these accounts in detail, consider the flow of information to and from the system. When a financial transaction occurs (for example, wages or bills paid or taxes received), it is confirmed via a "voucher." A voucher is a document that provides evidence of a transaction, such as a receipt, invoice, purchase order, tax bill, or check stub. These confirmed transactions are then entered into a "journal.' That is, the vouchers are analyzed to determine which of the accounts are affected. The journal records each transaction by date with a description of the transaction and an identification of the particular accounts to be adjusted.

This is the first place where information is converted to the "double entry" system of accounting (debits and credits to particular accounts, discussed later in this chapter). Entries in the journal are then "posted" to the "accounts." The accounts are grouped into one of three types of "ledgers": general, special, and subsidiary. General ledgers include the accounts for a particular fund. Two special ledgers are utilized: the general fixed asset accounts and the general bond debt accounts. These groups of self-balancing accounts are not, strictly speaking, funds; they are similar to funds. The general fixed asset group records the value of real and personal property owned by the governmental unit; the general bond debt group records the general obligation debt liability. These items do not fit into particular funds, because property is not the asset of any one fund (property such as a city hall may be shared by a number of governmental activities), and general debt is not the liability of any single fund (general debt is the liability of the entire governmental unit). Subsidiary ledgers are supplements to general ledgers. That is, a fund may have one or more subsidiary ledgers in addition to the general ledger. A subsidiary ledger may organize estimated and actual expenditures together by function, department, activity, object, or character to facilitate budget control. Subsidiary revenue ledgers perform the same function for "estimated" and "actual" revenues by source of revenue. Other subsidiary groups of accounts may be used for particular purposes such as customer accounts or bond registers.

In summary, financial transactions yield vouchers, which are analyzed to determine which funds and accounts are affected. The transactions are then entered into a journal as debits and credits to particular accounts. Journal entries are posted to the ledgers, which are groups of accounts within or subsidiary to a fund. The accounts are then periodically summarized in the form of financial reports to yield the appropriate managerial and planning information.

Accounts

Each fund contains a number of accounts that record specific financial information, including:

1. what the local government owns (assets)
2. what the local government owes (liabilities)
3. the difference between (1) and (2) (surplus or deficit)
4. the money it receives (revenues)
5. the money it expends (expenditures)

The first three items are called "balance" accounts; the last two are "operating" accounts (Figure 9-1). Collectively, they describe the financial condition of the governmental unit at any given time.

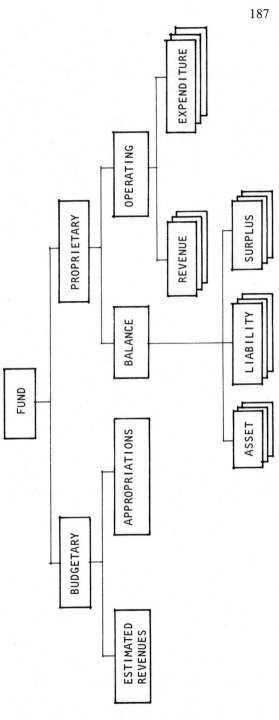

Figure 9-1. Account Structure

The balance accounts record assets, liabilities, and surplus, while the operating accounts record revenues and expenditures. Generally, there is a number of each type of account, depending on the purpose of the particular fund. Note that the budgetary accounts are combined with the proprietary accounts within a fund. Subsidiary accounts (not shown) may combine estimated and actual revenues and expenditures for budget control. Subsidiary revenue accounts combine the estimated revenues (a budgetary account) with the actual revenues according to source of revenue. Likewise, the subsidiary expenditure accounts combine appropriations with actual expenditures by function, department, character, and object. It might appear that this would require a very large number of accounts. However, the system is greatly simplified through the use of account codes. That is, each source of revenue, function, department, object, and character is assigned an alphabetic or numeric code. Therefore, a single entry can easily be identified with respect to these categories. For example, the current expenses (character) for materials and supplies (object) in the fire department (department) can be inspected by summing the entries with the appropriate code across all the expenditure accounts.

Double-Entry Bookkeeping

The process of posting transactions to the accounts involves double-entry bookkeeping. Each account is designed to show increases and decreases to that financial entity; each account is arranged in two columns: debits and credits (Figure 9-2). Double-entry bookkeeping involves maintaining a balance among the accounts; each time a transaction is posted, a value is added to one account and an equal value is subtracted from another account. A debit to one account is accompanied by a credit to one or more other accounts; the debit equals the credits. Likewise, a credit to an account effects a debit to one or more other

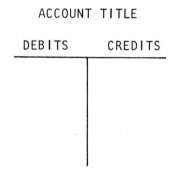

Figure 9-2. Debits and Credits Format

Table 9-1
Rules for Debiting and Crediting

Account Type	Increases to Account	Decreases to Account
Asset	Debit	Credit
Liability	Credit	Debit
Revenue	Credit	Debit
Expenditure	Debit	Credit

accounts. Recall that the particular accounts to be affected by a transaction are determined at the time of the "journal entry." The system also maintains a balance between assets and liabilities (including surplus or deficit) so that a change in one side of the balance equation must be matched by an equal change to the other side. Thus, the accounts are always in balance.

The rules for crediting and debiting accounts are summarized in Table 9-1.

The balancing feature can be shown in a simple example. Assume that a city issues two tax bills on July 1 for $5,000 each. Entries must be posted to an asset account (taxes receivable) as well as to an operating account (revenues). Following the rules of Table 9-1, the asset account is debited and the revenue account is credited (Table 9-2).

The issue of tax bills has increased assets (taxes receivable) by $10,000; revenues have also been increased by an equal amount. Assume that one of the tax bills is paid on July 10. Entries must then be posted in two asset accounts: taxes receivable and cash (Table 9-3).

The receipt of the $5,000 by the city increased the cash account by $5,000, while at the same time decreasing the taxes receivable account by an equal amount. Next, assume that the city purchases materials and supplies on July 12 for $4,000. Entries are required in the expenditure and cash asset accounts (Table 9-4).

The accounts now reflect an increase in expenditures of $4,000, and a decrease of cash assets of an equal amount. Thus, each transaction is double-entered to maintain a balance. Debits should equal credits when the account entries are summed (Table 9-5). This calculation is called a "trial balance," and is used to confirm that the accounts have been properly credited and debited. In this example, all the credits and debits were summed to create the balance. A simpler procedure for complete accounting systems involves determining the debit or credit balance within each account, and summing those figures for all the accounts to create the balance.

Table 9-2
Example 1

	Taxes Receivable			Revenues	
	Debit	Credit		Debit	Credit
7-1	5,000				7-1 10,000
7-1	5,000				

Table 9-3
Example 2

	Taxes Receivable			Cash	
	Debit	Credit		Debit	Credit
7-1	5,000		7-10	5,000	
7-1	5,000				
		7-10 5,000			

Table 9-4
Example 3

	Expenditure			Cash	
	Debit	Credit		Debit	Credit
7-12	4,000		7-10	5,000	
					7-12 4,000

Table 9-5
Trial Balance

	Debits	Credits
Taxes Receivable	5,000	
	5,000	
		5,000
Revenues		10,000
Cash	5,000	
		4,000
Expenditure	4,000	
Sum	19,000	19,000

Cash and Accrual Accounting

There are two ways of posting revenue and expenditure information to the operating accounts: cash and accrual. Cash basis accounting records revenues when they are received, regardless of when the services were supplied; expenditures are recorded when they are paid, regardless of when the services or goods were received. Accrual basis accounting records revenues when they are billed, regardless of when they are received, and expenditures are recorded when monies are committed, regardless of when they are actually paid. For example, an expenditure for the purchase of equipment would be recorded in the expenditure account when the bill is received (for accrual basis) or when the bill is paid (cash basis). Likewise, tax revenue would be recorded in the revenue account when the tax bill is issued (for accrual basis) or when the tax payment is actually received (cash basis). In general, the accrual basis is favored because it facilitates a more realistic overview of financial condition—the balance of "actual and committed expenditures" with "actual and expected revenues." It also allows the comparison of these actual figures with budgeted figures. The disadvantage of the accrual system relates to revenues; revenues billed but not yet received are reported as revenues when, in fact, they are not in hand. Thus, the actual cash position at any given time is likely to vary from the revenue position. In other words, a city could be in a good revenue position, but a bad cash position.

Cash basis accounting has the advantages of being relatively easy to administer and reflective of the local government's cash position at any given time. Its disadvantage is that the values of committed but unpaid expenditures are not recorded as expenditures, opening the possibility that total expenditures for a particular time may exceed the cash available. Because the total use of either cash or accrual basic accounting presents significant problems, many local governments utilize a modified system of both cash and accrual accounting. This often takes the form of posting revenues on a cash basis and expenditures on an accrual basis. One can then compare actual revenues with actual and committed expenditures at any given point in time, thus facilitating control of the cash position.

Reports and Audits

Sound fiscal planning and management requires timely information relative to the financial situation. Are revenues falling short of estimated revenues? Are expenditures exceeding appropriations? What is the revenue-expenditure balance? The accounting system contains the best information about the situation; periodic reporting is a routine function of the system. Monthly or quarterly reports are prepared for each fund in local government, although the content and frequency of reports may vary among funds and units of local government. These reports are called "financial statements," and include "interim statements" (periodic) and "terminal statements" (completion of the fiscal period). The three types of statements include (1) statement of revenues, (2) statement of expenditures and encumbrances, and (3) balance sheet.

Revenue and expenditure statements apply primarily to the general fund. The revenue statement compares actual revenues with estimated revenues for the "interim report" period (such as the previous month) and for the fiscal period to date. The expenditure and encumbrances statement compares actual expenditures and encumbrances with appropriations for identical periods. Together, they compare actual revenues and expenditures. Data are specific enough to allow individual inspection of revenue sources, departments, and programs. The balance statement compares assets with liabilities, reserves, and fund balance for each fund. Other items of information may be added to these reports as desired to promote a clear financial assessment and/or as required by law. Together, these reports confirm the sources and disposition of resources, and exhibit the general budgetary and financial situation.

In addition to such reports, local governments are required to conduct an external, independent post-audit of the fiscal period's transactions. An audit is essentially an examination of the accounting records, reports, and procedures to ascertain that the statements fairly represent the actual financial situation, that sound procedures have been followed, and that the financial transactions have been legal. Usually, the local government will retain a firm of independent accountants to conduct the audit. The audit report is reviewed by the local legislative body as well as the appropriate state agency. Alternately, the reviewing state agency may directly conduct the audit. Other audits may periodically be required. The term "internal audit" is often applied to interim financial statements, whether conducted in-house or by consultants. Also, the federal government (U.S. Government Accounting Office, GAO) and state government agencies may perform audits for federal- or state-financed programs at the local level (categorical grants or special revenue sharing) to ensure the legality of program activities and expenditures and to measure performance and/or effectiveness.

Notes

1. Any number of general accounting texts are available to the reader. An excellent and complete text specifically addressing public sector accounting is R.M. Mikesell and Leon E. Hay, *Governmental Accounting* (Homewood, Ill.: Richard D. Irwin, 1969). Another text useful to smaller units of government is Arthur A. Mendonsa, *Simplified Financial Management in Local Government* (Athens: Institute of Government, University of Georgia, 1969).

2. Mikesell, *Governmental Accounting,* p. 3-4 citing National Committee of Governmental Accounting, *Governmental Accounting, Auditing, and Financial Reporting* (Chicago: Municipal Finance Officers Association, 1968), p. 6-7.

193

References

Municipal Finance Officers Association and Peat, Marwick, Mitchell & Company. *Study Guide to Governmental Accounting, Auditing and Financial Reporting*. Chicago: Municipal Finance Officers Association, 1974.

Freeman, Robert J., and Lynn, Edward S. *Fund Accounting*. Englewood Cliffs, N.J.: Prentice-Hall, 1974.

Part III:
Techniques of Analysis

10 Structuring the Analysis

One of the more difficult tasks of management and planning is the translation of a problem situation into an analytic format. How can perceived problems be stated in a way that promotes understanding, analysis, rational decisions, and good solutions? A variety of personal and mechanical decision-making styles exist; some are general in application, while others are quite specific. This chapter and the three that follow present a general approach that is applicable to a wide range of fiscal planning and management situations. The purpose is to provide the reader with a guide to:

1. recognizing situations where "analysis" can be useful
2. conducting basic analysis and problem solving relative to fiscal situations
3. interpreting analyses conducted by staff experts and/or consultants

Although some measure of comprehensiveness is attempted in this chapter, the reader should be aware that large and complex problem situations may warrant more sophisticated efforts and techniques of analysis. Nevertheless, this approach should provide a sufficient foundation for a large part of the fiscal analysis that might be conducted at the local government level.

Analysis Techniques

Management is a decision process whereby choices must be made among alternative courses of action. The purpose of analysis is to facilitate good management by promoting good decisions. A decision is an intellectual judgment requiring three steps:

1. identification of alternative courses of action
2. estimation of the probable consequences of each of the alternatives
3. selection and application of decision criteria

The objective of a decision is the selection of the alternative course of action that, when followed, will leave the decision making unit "best off."[1] However, good decisions do not always guarantee good consequences, and perversely, a bad decision can yield desirable consequences. Management decisions are made under conditions of uncertainty, where future consequences are estimated rather than known. For example, consider the decision to schedule a major civic event indoors or outdoors, when outdoors is preferable and when the weather indicates a clear day. The decision to schedule the event outdoors would be, all other things being equal, a good decision. However, the weather report is only an estimate, because it might, in fact, rain. If it does rain, the consequences will be undesirable, even though the decision was sound. Analysis is therefore directed toward affecting the best decision, given the condition of uncertainty. The assumption is that better decisions increase the chances of better consequences over the long run of many decisions, if not for each and every decision. The focus of analysis is on improving the rationality of a decision by organizing and presenting information in a way that allows a reasoned and logical decision. Again, this means identifying alternative courses of action, estimating the probable consequences of each, and selecting and applying appropriate decision criteria.

It is important to note that analysis does not produce decisions; only people can make decisions. This statement is simple enough, yet apparent misunderstanding has led to a great deal of confusion as to the proper role for analysis. For example, some persons refuse to grant any credibility to quantitative analysis in the management process, while others claim that analysis is the panacea of the management process. Both these extremes are absurd. There is always a variety of determinants for any decision, and the local government decision is no exception. Local legislators, mayors, managers, and administrators may allow decisions to be influenced by personal, political, social, technological, legal, economic, and other factors. The economic-financial factors covered by the analysis methods presented in this text must be viewed as input to the decision process and a resource to the decisionmaker. The extensiveness of the analysis depends on the critical nature of the decision. The cost of a too extensive analysis may not offset the marginal benefits of a better decision. However, too little or no analysis may lead to unacceptable consequences.

Returning to the three-step decision process (identifying alternatives, estimating consequences, applying criteria), consider the example of a person planning an evening's entertainment. Assume that there is a general goal of entertainment and a budget constraint of $10. The first step in arriving at a decision is identifying feasible alternatives. The person does this by "scanning" his memory and other sources of information such as the newspaper (that is, a relatively intuitive process). The goals and constraints are "gatekeepers" for accepting alternatives as feasible. The decisionmaker will accept for consideration only those alternatives that offer entertainment costing $10 or less. The more specific the goal or objective and the more numerous and severe the constraints, the fewer alternatives will be acceptable. For example, if the person specified an objective of maximizing pleasure, and included constraints of passive activity, duration of four hours, less than five miles of travel, and less than $2 cost, then the number of feasible alternatives would be few. The point is that objectives and constraints are utilized to specify the problem to be solved and the decision to be made. Vague goals and constraints open the decision to a large number of alternatives and an extensive analysis effort. Specific objectives and constraints articulate the problem and limit the extensiveness of the analysis.

Assume that the person identifies three alternative evenings: a concert, a movie, and staying at home with the television. The second task requires that the probable consequences of each of these alternatives be estimated, usually in terms of the respective costs and benefits. Costs might include the price of tickets and the time and money for transportation. Benefits might include the expected intensity and duration of the enjoyment derived from the entertainment. Here, costs are probably easier to assess than benefits. However, this is not an uncommon situation in analysis. Costs are often inputs that are under the control of the decisionmaker, whereas benefits are often uncertain outputs that are not subject to direct control. Also, costs can often be measured in dollars, whereas benefits tend to take a wide variety of forms and therefore are more difficult to measure.

However, assume that the decisionmaker estimates the costs in dollars and the benefits as subjective ratings on a scale (Table 10-1) where the highest benefit equals 100.

Once this is accomplished a decision criterion must be selected and applied. In this case, several criteria might be utilized:

1. maximum benefit
2. minimum cost
3. maximum benefit-cost ratio (effectiveness)[2]

If "maximum benefit" is selected, then the concert is the best alternative with a benefit of 100 units. However, the maximum benefit criterion is usually accompanied by a budget constraint; maximum benefit for a given cost. In this case, the budget constraint of $10 would eliminate the concert, and the movie would be selected with 85 units of benefit. If the minimum cost criterion was utilized, then the television alternative would be selected. However, the minimum cost criterion is usually accompanied by a benefit constraint—the least cost for a given level of benefit. In this case there was no constraint placed on the mini-

Table 10-1
Example—Costs and Benefits

Alternative	Cost	Benefit
Concert	$12	100
Movie	$ 9	85
Television	$ 0	30

mum level of benefit, so the television would stand as the least cost alternative. In general, one must maximize benefit within a budget constraint or minimize cost for a given level of benefit. Trying to maximize benefit while minimizing cost is inconsistent (maximum benefit is infinite, minimum cost is zero), and hopelessly confuses the analysis.[3]

Cost effectiveness is an efficiency criterion utilizing the ratio of outputs to inputs. In the above example, the concert exhibits 100 units of benefit for $12, or a ratio of 8.334. That is, 8.334 units of benefit are obtained from each dollar of cost. Likewise, the movie exhibits a cost effectiveness of 9.444 and the television exhibits an infinitely high ratio. It appears that the television alternative ranks highest on the efficiency scale; the ratio indicates something for nothing. If there is no constraint relative to the minimum acceptable level of benefit, then the television would be the best cost effective alternative.

The decision or judgment as to the best alternative in this example depends on the criteria selected as well as the objectives and constraints. Note also that the benefits were measured as subjective ratings of the "expected" consequences of the alternatives. Although the tendency in analysis situations is towards objective measurement of both costs and benefits, there is nothing wrong with using more intuitive measures. In fact, subjective measures in a well-structured analysis may yield better results than poorly derived objective measures. Although the example analysis appears simple and intuitive, many real-world management decision problems exhibit very similar elements. However, the level of complexity and the irregularity of occurrence often constrains intuitive understanding; consequently a more systematic approach is required. Such systematic approaches to financial management and planning are variously called systems analysis, operations research, expenditure analysis, investment analysis, productivity study, benefit-cost analysis, cost effectiveness, program evaluation, and the like.[4] Whatever the name, the purpose is simply to identify and evaluate, in some systematic way, the alternative means for achieving specified objectives as an aid to decisionmakers.

Economic and Financial Analysis

Both economic and financial analysis are useful in the local government context. Although the basic structure of analysis is the same for both, there are some differences that should be noted. Economic analysis generally addresses management decisions that are made on behalf of "society at large," where the evaluation of alternatives involves the estimation of all costs and benefits, regardless of beneficiary or form (monetary and nonmonetary). It is an all-inclusive type of analysis. Financial analysis, on the other hand, refers to the monetary consequences of management decisions, and generally excludes nonmonetary effects. The variations are numerous, depending on the purpose of the analysis. It is

Table 10–2
Types of Analyses

Type	Client	Cost and Benefit Inclusion
Economic	society at large	total social
Limited economic	persons associated with the decision unit	total social
Financial	the decision unit	monetary

useful here to identify three types of analyses: economic, limited economic, and financial. Their general characteristics are shown in Table 10–2. For example, an alternative is economically desirable if the total social benefits exceed the total social costs, with the result that society (as a whole) is better off. This all-inclusive analysis is appropriate at national and regional scales, but is less useful at the local government scale. Local governments are not concerned directly with society at large as the client for analysis, but rather with those persons and institutions within their own jurisdictional boundaries. Here, a more limited form of economic analysis is appropriate. A local government project is "economically desirable" (in the limited sense) if the total social benefits exceed the total social costs as they accrue to the residents and institutions within that local government's jurisdiction. Significant external effects are considered on the side. Although the costs and benefits are all-inclusive, the client group is limited. Local governments are also interested in the financial consequences of alternatives as they affect the decision-making unit (usually the governmental unit itself). An alternative is financially feasible if monetary resources are sufficient to allow for the required cash flow. The key terms are "economically desirable" and "financially feasible."

For example, consider a proposed project alternative involving the construction and operation of a large recreational facility within the boundary of a particular local government. An all-inclusive economic analysis might reveal that the project is economically desirable because the estimated social benefits exceed social costs as they accrue to persons throughout the region. However, the particular local government needs to ask a somewhat different question. Is the new facility economically desirable and financially feasible for that local governmental unit? In other words, who pays the costs and who receives the benefits (incidence of costs and benefits)? If major portions of the benefits fall to non-residents, the net effect to local residents and institutions might be undesirable. Both limited economic and financial analysis is appropriate in this situation. Costs and benefits accruing within the government's jurisdiction must be assessed. If the proposed facility is "desirable" at the local level, the financial "feasibility" can be determined. Are financial resources sufficient to support the facility? If the project is not economically desirable at the local level, financial feasibility is superfluous.

There is no general rule covering every analysis situation; consequences to be included in the analysis will depend on the purpose of the analysis and the judgment of the analyst. In most situations, local governments will want to undertake projects that are economically desirable in the limited, internal sense as well as financially feasible. If a project is economically sound but financially unsound, then a redesign of the financial structure is warranted. If a project is economically desirable on a regional or state scale but undesirable at the local level, the larger scale government needs to accept financial responsibility via direct financing or grants and aids to the local government. The emphasis on internal effects does not mean that external effects should be neglected; contributions to regional goals and mutual externalities (such as air and water quality, law enforcement, or emergency medical care) are often as important as internal goals. It does mean that external effects (costs and benefits) should be identified and treated as such.

Program Structure

Program structure (see Chapter 5, Budgeting) is a way of organizing governmental activities and thus finances into functional categories that are related to specific governmental objectives. A program structure organizes inputs of land, labor, capital, and management (expressed as budget allocations) into productive activities. These activities yield certain outputs that relate to the goals and objectives of the program activity. Because inputs are related to outputs, and assuming that both can be measured, program activities can be evaluated in terms of efficiency and effectiveness. A typical program organization is shown in Table 10-3.

Table 10-3
Example—Program Organization

Program	Program Category	Program Activity
Public Safety	Fire Services	
Transportation	Police Services	Prevention
Environment	Emergency Care	Detection
Education		Apprehension
Recreation		Incarceration
Development		Support
General Administration		

Programs are formulated in response to broad public goals such as safe streets, high quality education, decent housing, and clean environment. Analysis at this level is seldom useful because of the lack of specificity of the goals. It is difficult to measure accurately the level of safe streets and quality of education, and identify cause and effect relationships for many complex program processes. The relationships between specific program inputs and broad, immeasurable outputs remains vague. Therefore, programs are "factored," or subdivided into component parts with more specific, measurable objectives, activities, and outputs. In this example, the public safety program is broken down into the program categories of fire service, police service, emergency medical care, and so on. Furthermore, police services can be broken down into "program activities" of prevention, detection, apprehension, incarceration, and support. At the activity level, objectives, activities, and outputs can be quite specific and measurable. For example, the activity of fire prevention might utilize the inputs of labor, supplies, and facilities, measured in dollars, to conduct educational and inspection programs. The objective might be to minimize the number of accidental fires; the output for the activity is the number of fires or the reduction in the rate of fire occurrence.

Of course, program structure does not ensure successful analysis or good management decisions. Many public program inputs, activities, and outputs have not yet been sufficiently identified and/or measured. However, program structure does provide a method of factoring complex activities into simpler activities and thus increases the opportunities for useful analysis. The drawback to this process of suboptimization is that it neglects the problem of overall optimization and coordination among activities. That is, solving each detailed problem does not ensure the best overall solution. There is always a trade-off between the specificity derived from attacking parts of problems and the need for a good overall solution. There is no ready solution to this dilemma; the degree of suboptimization will require a judgment on the part of the analyst—based on the purpose of the analysis.

Where a more traditional line item organization of activities and budgets exists (see Chapter 5, Budgeting), program information must be artificially constructed for purposes of analysis.

Systems Analysis

A system is an assemblage of objects and/or activities combined in an organized whole by some form of interaction. "Systems analysis," a broad term describing an approach to problem solving, decision-making, and design, is based on the construction and manipulation of models of systems. The origins of this type of analysis lie in general systems theory and in World War Two operations research. To define its present state, it is considered as a general approach to a wide range of problems including a sizable variety of quantitative and nonquantitative techniques. As such, a systems approach is often useful in structuring economic and financial analysis in local government. Of course, a comprehensive review of systems analysis is beyond the scope of this text. Rather, an overview and some of the central concepts as they relate to structuring analysis situations is presented here.

A central concept of systems is that all living things have certain common characteristics. They exist with some objective or purpose, have a structural configuration of component parts, perform a given function, utilize input, yield output, and so on. Any animal, plant, or organization can be described as a system. Any system can be described in terms of those characteristics that are common to all systems. Therefore any real world system can be described, and thus its description becomes a "model" of the real system. Such a description or model might take the form of physical objects, graphic representations, or written, verbal, or mathematical statements. Systems analysis involves the construction, manipulation, and observation of the "model" without disruption to the real world system.

The practice of systems analysis has developed to include three basic characteristics:

1. the scientific method
2. interdisciplinary analysis teams
3. application to decision-making for real world problems

The inclusion of scientific method implies a heavy, but not exclusive, reliance on experimentation and observation and on objective, quantitative techniques. That is, the analyst must collect and analyze data and information relative to the real world system to construct an adequate system description or model. Relationships among the model's components must be quantified. Once the model is constructed, the analyst can manipulate the model to understand the model (and thus the real world system) better and to derive problem solutions.

The reliance on interdisciplinary teams is based on the desirability of looking at problems from a number of viewpoints. Urban management problems are inherently complex and a single viewpoint is often insufficient. Sherlock Holmes theorized, "One's ideas must be as broad as Nature if they are to interpret Nature."[5] However, society has traditionally subdivided the whole of knowledge into functionally distinct disciplines with a high degree of specialization. Therefore, a "general" problem approach requires a variety of specialized experts. For example, the analysis of an emergency medical care system might require the combined thinking of a city manager, city planner, hospital administrator, doctor, fireman, policeman, ambulance driver, equipment manufacturer, engineer, and so on.

Last, systems analysis is oriented toward applied rather than pure research. The focus is on the design and evaluation of real world problem solutions, the need for which requires no explanation.

A General System Model

Models of systems can take a variety of forms. The simple conceptual model presented here is useful for structuring the economic and financial analysis of program activities (Figure 10-1). Components of the model are described in following sections.

Objectives

A system exists for some purpose, and therefore has one or more objectives. Objectives are measurable goals, which are derived from some desired end-state or condition or in response to a recognized problem. For example, if crime is perceived as a problem, then programs can be formulated with the general goal of reducing the incidence of crime. However, a system model of a crime control

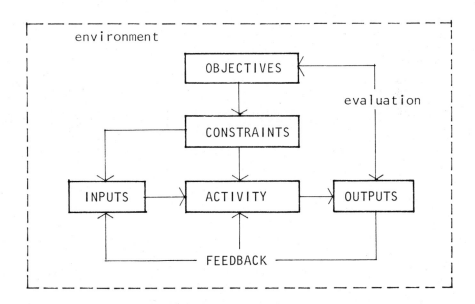

Figure 10-1. A General System Model

program would break the general goal into more specific, measurable objectives such as the reduction of the incidence of violent crime in the central business district by five percent per year. In terms of the design and evaluation of alternative programs, the objectives will be stated in a form that relates to the criteria: maximum benefit, minimum cost, or maximum efficiency. For example, the objective of a surplus cash investment program might be to maximize the net return. Obviously, such an objective for a local government investment program would be subject to certain legal constraints as well as to a low level of acceptable risk. Objectives can be stated in another way, but they must be related to one of the basic evaluation criteria. For example, an objective for an emergency medical care program might be a maximum response time of 10 minutes or less. This objective relates to the criterion of minimum cost with the constraint of a given level of benefit. That is, the best system would be the least expensive one that produced a response time of 10 minutes or less. It is important that objectives be explicit, specific, and measurable, because analysis cannot generate specific solutions to vague problems. Also, one is generally closer to a satisfactory solution when he has the wrong answer to the right question, than when he has the right answer to the wrong problem.

Environment

An inevitable problem is encountered with the use of descriptive and analytical system models. Which factors should be included in the model? How extensive should the model be? How many alternatives should be considered? There is no applicable rule of thumb; the extensiveness of the model will depend on the purpose of the analysis and the judgment of the analyst. Every system exists in an environment and is actually a subsystem of a larger system. In other words, everything is related in some way to everything else in this world, and therefore, it is impossible to describe any system as completely closed. For example, a water treatment system exists as part of a larger city water system; this in turn, exists as a part of the city utility system, and so on. For purposes of analysis, the model must include only the major relevant components and relationships. Boundaries must be established to define the extent of the model. Factors that are not directly related to the model and factors that are related but insignificant in effect are considered as external to the model. The model environment includes only those factors that are part of the model. For example, a system description of a fire suppression program might internalize the location of fire stations as an important design factor, but exclude disruption to traffic caused by the dispatch of fire fighting equipment as insignificant in terms of evaluating program performance.

Inputs

In the context of economic and financial analysis, inputs are the resources of land, labor, and capital that are transformed into outputs by a particular program activity. Inputs are variable with respect to quantity, mix (land, labor, and capital components), and incidence (who provides the resources). Local government resources are articulated in common terms of dollars of budget allocation, and are broken down by object and character (see Chapter 5, Budgeting, and Chapter 9, Accounting Systems). However, public programs also require that certain costs be borne by citizens and institutions both directly (as taxes and user charges) and indirectly (as associated costs). For example, the governmental selection of a fire safety program of a given quality requires that citizens bear direct costs in terms of taxes and indirect costs in terms of marginal fire insurance premiums.

Nonmonetary costs may also exist, in which case, the measurement of inputs may be difficult (see Intangibles, Chapter 2). However, inputs are not generally difficult to handle, because they often are measured in terms of common dollar units and tend to be under the control of the unit for which the analysis is being conducted. Some public programs are so labor-intensive that inputs are measured only as the number of personnel with an overhead factor.

Activity

Program activities vary widely in complexity. For example, the investment program activity of purchasing a certificate of deposit at an interest rate of 8 percent for 90 days exhibits little complexity. The relationship between the inputs (dollars invested) and the output (dollars returned) is known within the limits of risk. Likewise, the evaluation of alternative investments is not complex if each alternative is known. The activity of purchasing capital equipment (such as a garbage truck) or constructing a capital facility (such as a fire station) requires little analysis of the activity, because engineering specifications for the relationships between costs and outputs may be readily available and sufficient for purposes of managerial decision-making.

However, many public activities are extremely complex and, therefore, are not well understood. Often, the process of transforming inputs to outputs (and thus the relationship between the two) is not known with certainty. For example, the relationship between the level of police patrol and the rate of street crime is not well known. Likewise, the relationship between fire safety inspections and the incidence of accidental fires is not known. Often the allocation of resources to these types of activities is made on the basis of the belief that some positive relationship exists between program inputs and outputs, even if the relationship cannot be measured. However, if the relationship cannot be described and measured, it is difficult, if not impossible, to estimate the changes in outputs that would result from corresponding changes to inputs or activities. Program design and evaluation become difficult; there is little basis for altering the quantity, mix, or incidence of resource inputs in an attempt to improve program output. An all too common practice where a problem persists and the effect of a program activity is uncertain is to simply increase the quantity of resources in what may be throwing good money after bad. Of course, this does not mean that a city should cease expenditures for activities that are not completely understood. A number of public activities yield obvious benefits, but are difficult to quantify (such as certain cultural and recreational activities). It does mean that program design and evaluation depends on understanding the process of converting inputs to outputs, and that the relationship between inputs and outputs must be estimated if not known.

Outputs

Program activity outputs are generally more difficult to assess than inputs. Inputs are often known, measured in dollars, and under the direct control of the analysis unit, whereas outputs can take on a variety of forms which are difficult to measure. Outputs are expressed as physical units per unit of time (with quantity, quality, or value dimensions) or as changes in the state of nature.[6] More specifically, measures include:

1. quantity of output with a given level of quality
2. quality level with a given quantity of output
3. a combined quantity-quality value
4. changes in the state of nature

The simplest of these measures is the quantity of output, where the quality dimension is fixed or not significant. Measurements of this type are generally direct and easy to collect, and therefore are heavily relied on in analysis efforts. Table 10-4 shows some program activities and possible quantity output measures.

All these measures assume a given level of quality, at least in evaluating alternative program activities. Often, however, the quality dimension is of primary importance and the quantity is fixed. This is typically the case with public services where the quantity of persons or households is fixed at any given time. The service (whether fire, police, water, or waste collection) must be provided to everyone. The question of analysis involves selecting the quality of output. For example, society tends to think in terms of improving the quality of education rather than the quantity. Of course, quantities change over time, but in terms of evaluating programs, all alternatives assume the same quantity.

Table 10–4
Example–Quantity Measures

Program Activity	Output Measure
Local road construction	Miles of road constructed
Water distribution system	Gallons of water delivered
Solid waste collection	Tons of refuse collected
Land purchase	Acres purchased
Short term investment	Dollars of investment revenue
Printing shop	Number of copies printed
Police traffic patrol	Number of citations issued

The problem is that quality is difficult to assess because it involves varying value judgments, multiple dimensions, and indirect measures. Sometimes, accepted technical standards exist that can be applied to output. For example, there are a number of measurements for air and water quality; developed areas are given a fire service classification; educational quality is often measured by standard test scores. Where such measures exist, they can be used individually or in combined indices. Where binary standards exist, quality can be measured as a percentage of the total. For example, where housing units are standard or substandard, the measure of housing quality in a particular area might be the percentage of total units that are standard. Where these output quality measures do not exist or where they exist but are difficult to measure, the analyst can look to certain input characteristics. Here, the analyst is not directly measuring output, but is assuming that there is a quality relationship between inputs and outputs; the assumption is based on an intuitive understanding of the program activity. There is a danger in this approach if the relationship between inputs and outputs is not well known. As mentioned above, there are a number of cases where programs have been allocated increasing amounts of dollars with little or no observable results on the assumption that the quality of the output would be increased. Nevertheless, where the analyst is confident of input-output relationships, but output quality cannot be measured directly, input measures often provide the best available estimates. Input characteristics include (1) input quantities, (2) relative input quantities, and (3) input performance indicators.[7] For example, the quality of an educational program might be measured by the number of teachers (input quantity), the number of teachers for each 100 pupils (relative input quantity), or the percentage of teachers with advanced degrees (input performance characteristic). Table 10-5 shows example quantity and quality measures for the output of an emergency medical care activity. Seldom will any singular quality measure be totally satisfactory; therefore, several measures can be combined in an average or weighted index.

Sometimes, because neither quality nor quantity is fixed, there is a trade-off between the two. For example, consider the selection of a building design for a

Table 10-5

Example—Quantity and Quality Measures, Emergency Medical Care

Type	Measure
Quantity	Number of responses, number of cases treated
Quality (output)	Average response time
Quality (input quantity)	Number of ambulances, number of trained personnel
Quality (relative input)	Number of ambulances per 1,000 residents
Quality (input performance)	Percentage of personnel with paramedical training

new city hall. Both quality and quantity dimensions exist. The city can select from a number of designs, with a small high-quality structure and a large low-quality structure at the extremes. The decision requires a trade-off between quantity and quality dimensions. Several approaches can be utilized. One can tighten the constraints to reduce the number of alternatives. In this example, the minimum acceptable size and the minimum acceptable level of quality can be increased to eliminate consideration of the more extreme alternatives. This method is legitimate only where there is some rational basis for determining realistic constraints. Another approach attempts to convert quality measures into quantity measures. For example, a lower quality structure might be related to increased (life cycle) maintenance costs and a shorter useful life, which in turn, can be expressed as quantities. A third approach attempts to measure quantity and quality dimensions in terms of value. The appropriate value is measured as benefit on the demand side and as cost on the supply side. That is, the value to the consumer can be measured as the price he is willing to pay for a given quantity-quality combination; the value to the producer can be measured as the costs incurred in the production of the quantity-quality combination. For example, consider again the case of selecting a building design from among four alternatives, all of which fall within minimum size and maximum cost constraints (Table 10-6).

Table 10-6

Example—Quantity, Quality, Value; Alternative Building Designs

Alternative	Quantity (Sq. Ft.)	Quality ($ per Sq. Ft.)	Total Cost ($)
A	20,000	25	500,000
B	18,000	25	450,000
C	19,000	29	551,000
D	18,000	30	540,000

Here, quantity is measured as square feet of building space, and quality is measured as construction cost per square foot (a relative input measure). The combined value measure is simply the quantity times the quality, or the total cost of each building alternative. Notice that the alternative selected as best depends on the criteria, as well as the quantity, quality, and value measures. Alternative criteria and respective selections are:

1. maximize quantity—A
2. maximize quality—D
3. maximize value—C
4. minimize cost—B

That is, alternative C represents the highest total value—considering both quantity and quality. In this example, the maximum benefit and minimum cost criteria also lead to solutions, but a problem arises with the efficiency criterion. Quality was measured as an input characteristic; thus, the relationship between inputs and outputs becomes you get what you pay for. The total value of the output equals the cost (input) for each alternative. Therefore, all alternatives display identical efficiency. An efficiency criterion requires different measures for inputs and outputs—as cost on the supply side and as benefit on the demand side. The costs on the supply side are the values shown in Table 10-6; the values on the demand side might be measured as the relative market value, approximated by current lease rates on equivalent types of space (Table 10-7). Here, assuming no differences in maintenance cost and useful life of the building factors among alternatives, the ratio measures estimate benefits relative to costs. In this example, alternative D appears to yield the highest benefit per unit of cost, and thus, the highest efficiency.

Thus far, quantity, quality, and value measures have been described. The one other output measure is a change in the state of nature. That is, program output can be measured in terms of changes that occur to some current situation as measured by one or more indices. For example, the output of an air pollution program might be measured as a change in the technical indices of air quality.

Table 10-7
Example—Input and Output Values

Alternative	Cost ($ per Sq. Ft.)	Lease Rate ($ per Sq. Ft. per yr.)	Ratio of Rates to Cost
A	25	6.50	0.260
B	25	6.50	0.260
C	29	7.00	0.241
D	30	8.00	0.266

The output of a police patrol program might be measured as a change in the appropriate crime rates. When such measures are indirect, the casual relationships between program inputs and output indices must be known or assumed.

Constraints

Systems exist with constraints on both inputs and activities. Constraints serve to limit the values and ranges of the factors or variables that are included in the system. They are derived from one or more of the following sources:

1. policy statements
2. administrative regulations
3. legal parameters
4. political and social parameters
5. existing technology
6. resource limitations

For example, input constraints often include a maximum budget allocation, while activity constraints generally include existing technology. Such constraints limit the number of combinations of inputs and activities and thus the number of feasible alternatives to be considered.

Evaluation and Feedback

Evaluation is the assessment of the system in terms of the relationship between the system's outputs and objectives. If outputs and objectives coincide, then the system is operating perfectly; the solution is known. However, if outputs fall short of objectives, changes in inputs and activities can be changed in such a way as to yield outputs that are closer to objectives. The process of changing inputs and activities is termed "feedback" or "control." The evaluation and feedback functions can be viewed as an iterative process, whereby successive observations and changes to the system yield outputs that converge on the system's objectives.

In terms of program evaluation, the system format is utilized to describe the parameters of the analysis problem (objectives, constraints, inputs, activities, and outputs). There is a limited number of alternative sets of program inputs and activities, each leading to a unique consequence or output. Each alternative is evaluated in terms of its ability to satisfy the program objectives. The set of program inputs and activities that most closely satisfies the objectives is selected as the solution or best alternative. In a program design situation, alternative sets of inputs and activities are tested in an iterative fashion to design the best program. The use of a system model allows experimentation to take place with the model rather than with the real world system. The actual process of evaluation involves the application of evaluation criteria to the program outputs. Program evaluation is addressed in detail in Chapter 11.

The Analysis Process

The general process of analysis, within the framework of this presentation, can be summarized as follows:

1. define the analysis problem
2. identify general goals and measurable objectives
3. identify constraints
4. identify alternative inputs and activities
5. identify boundaries and external effects
6. estimate relationships between inputs and outputs, and thus, the outputs for each alternative
7. evaluate outputs (outputs vs. objectives)
8. generate analysis solution

Steps 1 through 5 are essentially the tasks of identifying the basic components of the analysis problem. Steps 6, 7, and 8 involve estimating costs and benefits for alternatives, applying decision criteria, and selecting the analysis solution. The systems approach presented above is simply a way of structuring the evaluation of alternative means for achieving specified objectives. It translates a perceived problem into an analyzable format, where the format is general and applicable to a wide range of problem situations.

Structuring Alternatives

How can the alternatives to be evaluated be generated? Theoretically, because an infinite number of alternatives might be considered, there is an infinite number of feasible solutions. However, real world constraints limit the consideration to a finite number of practical alternatives. The cost of the analysis increases with the number of alternatives considered. The problem involves generating a reasonable number of feasible alternatives without excluding new and innovative approaches. In many analysis situations, the alternatives are inherent in the purpose of the analysis. For example, a city manager may have to select one type of police vehicle from among three types available on the market or decide to purchase or lease a given amount of office space. Where such alternatives are few and easily identifiable, the problem of finding feasible alternatives presents little problem. However, in such situations it is often useful to consider the possibility that additional, unidentified alternatives may exist. In program design and other complex evaluation situations, the identification of feasible alternatives requires considerable effort. The analyst can depend on the use of multidisciplinary teams of experts to generate suggestions from various viewpoints. A review of the literature for previous research and the approaches taken by other local governments can also be helpful. However, to a great extent, the generation of alternatives will depend on the personal experiences and subjective judgments of the decision-makers and analysts.

Another method for identifying alternatives involves the consideration of all the system's variables or factors that fall under the control of the decision-making unit. Combinations of these variables constitute possible alternatives. For example, consider the evaluation of alternative solid waste collection activities. Activity variables might include:

(1) organization   (a) city-operated
                       (b) contracted to private firm
(2) frequency   (a) once per week
                       (b) twice per week
(3) pickup   (a) curbside
                       (b) backyard
(4) technology   (a) automated truck
                       (b) simple truck

Each combination of these four variables represents a unique waste collection program activity; each has an associated cost and benefit (input and output). The combinations can be shown graphically as in Figure 10-2. Each path of the "tree" represents a distinct alternative. However, the number of combinations increases rapidly with the number of variables and values, and thus, complex situations can exhibit an unmanageable number of alternatives. Nevertheless, this approach is often useful in exploratory stages of the analysis.

The Do-Nothing Alternative

Analysis situations seldom start from nowhere. Some current system or activity usually exists, and the analysis deals with evaluating that activity and alternative activities. This relates to the "do-nothing" alternative. That is, one alternative is to do nothing and to continue with the existing situation. However, to do nothing does not mean that nothing will happen. Doing nothing means accepting the output of the status quo. Therefore, alternatives must always be compared to each other as well as to the existing situation.

215

(1)   (2)   (3)   (4)

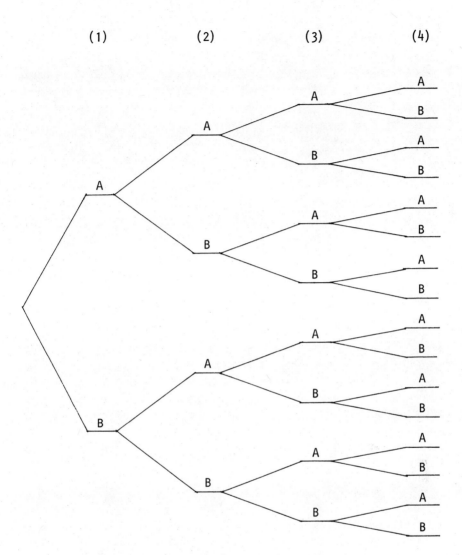

Figure 10-2. Alternatives from Combinations of Variables

Interrelationships Among Alternatives

Alternatives are sometimes related to each other in ways that must be taken into consideration. Two common types are the "mutually exclusive" and "complimentary" alternatives. The selection of an alternative from a set of mutually exclusive activities precludes the subsequent selection of others in the set. For

Table 10-8
Example—Complimentary Alternatives

Alternative Program Activities	Estimated Reduction in Crime Measure
A. Foot patrol	0.02
B. Vehicle patrol	0.01
C. Street lighting	0.02
D. Foot and vehicle (A & B)	0.02
E. Vehicle and lighting (B & C)	0.03
F. Foot and lighting (A & C)	0.06
G. All three (A, B & C)	0.08

example, consider the alternate uses of a particular parcel of land: an industrial park, a recreational park, and retained surplus. The first and second uses are mutually exclusive. Once an industrial park is selected, the recreational park option is no longer available.

Complimentary alternatives result in more or less than additive costs or benefits. For example, consider some of the alternative means for reducing street crime in a central business district: improved lighting, increased foot patrols, and increased vehicle patrol. Each might result in an estimated reduction in the frequency of street crimes, but when used in combination the resultant reduction might exceed or fall short of the sum of the individual effects. A simple example is shown in Table 10-8. Here, each program (*A, B,* and *C*) results in an estimated decrease in the frequency of crime. The combination *D* results in a less than additive effect, *E,* in an additive effect, and *F* and *G* in a more than additive effect. These types of interdependence can be handled in analysis by the judicious identification and separate treatment of each combination as an alternative.

Notes

1. Decision analysis has become formalized as a field of study and application; two applicable works are Morrie Hamburg, *Statistical Analysis for Decision Making* (New York: Harcourt, Brace and World, 1970), and Rex V. Brown, Andrew S. Kahr, and Cameron Peterson, *Decision Analysis for the Manager* (New York: Holt, Rinehart and Winston, 1974).

2. The selection of appropriate criteria is covered in detail in Chapter 11, Program Analysis.

3. It is certainly possible that a particular alternative will offer both the maximum benefit and the minimum cost, but trying to select an alternative from among many alternatives using that criteria is unproductive. The established criteria will identify a maximum benefit-minimum cost alternative if it exists.

4. These terms refer to specialized areas of study and application which relate to the material of this text, but which when taken individually and collectively, cover a far broader context. A selection of applicable references is included at the end of this chapter.

5. Arthur Conan Doyle, *A Study in Scarlet,* in *The Complete Sherlock Holmes* (Garden City, N.Y.: Doubleday, 1930), p. 37.

6. For a more complete treatment of government production-output see Werner Z. Hirsch, *The Economics of State and Local Government* (New York: McGraw-Hill, 1970), p. 147.

7. Ibid.

References

Catanese, Anthony J. *Scientific Methods of Urban Analysis.* Urbana: University of Illinois Press, 1972.

Catanese, Anthony J., and Steiss, Alan Walter. *Systemic Planning: Theory and Application.* Lexington, Mass.: D.C. Heath, 1970.

Drake, Alvin W., Keeney, Ralph L., and Morse, Philip M. (eds.). *Analysis of Public Systems.* Cambridge: The MIT Press, 1972.

Hatry, Harry P., Winnie, Richard E., and Fisk, Donald M. *Practical Program Evaluation for State and Local Government Officials.* Washington: The Urban Institute, 1973.

Hatry, Harry P., Blair, Louis, Fisk, Donald, and Kimmel, Wayne. *Program Analysis for State and Local Governments.* Washington: The Urban Institute, 1976.

Hinrichs, Harley H., and Taylor, Graeme M. *Systemic Analysis: A Primer on Benefit-Cost Analysis and Program Evaluation.* Pacific Palisades: Goodyear Publishing Company, 1972.

International City Management Association. Report for the Department of Housing and Urban Development. *Applying Systems Analysis in Urban Government: Three Case Studies.* Washington: The Association, 1972.

Krueckeberg, Donald A., and Silvers, Arthur L. *Urban Planning Analysis: Methods and Models.* New York: Wiley, 1974.

Kraemer, Kenneth L. *Policy Analysis in Local Government: A Systems Approach to Decision Making.* Washington: International City Management Association, 1973.

de Neufville, Richard, and Stafford, Joseph H. *Systems Analysis for Engineers and Managers.* New York: McGraw-Hill, 1971.

11

Program Evaluation

Evaluation of Alternative Consequences

Chapter 10 presented an approach to structuring analysis situations as "decision problems." Recall that the decision process includes three interrelated steps: (1) identification of alternate courses of action, (2) estimation of the probable consequences of each alternative, and (3) selection and application of decision criteria. A program format and systems model were used to translate perceived problems into a formal decision framework. The first step, the identification of alternatives, was also presented in Chapter 10. This chapter addresses the second and third steps. The estimation of probable consequences is essentially a process of identifying and measuring the costs and benefits associated with each alternative. The selection and application of decision criteria is a task of selecting the appropriate criterion for each decision problem.

Measurement

The estimation of probable consequences of alternatives implies "measurement"—one of the more difficult and critical tasks of analysis. Alternatives must be compared to one another in terms of a common measure. One cannot compare easily the qualities of apples to oranges or the level of health care to the durability of road pavement. Often, this means that costs and benefits must be converted to the common measure of the dollar. However, this approach is not always possible or necessary. Other approaches presented later in this chapter can be utilized.

The appropriate concept for estimating costs is "opportunity cost," which for many situations can be measured as the market values or prices of the resources to be utilized.[1] However, there are situations where differences occur between opportunity cost and market price. Where such differences occur, the more inclusive economic analysis utilizes opportunity cost, whereas financial analysis utilizes monetary cost. For example, a project that employs unemployed labor has a cash cost equal to wages, but an opportunity cost of zero. The opportunity cost is that benefit which is foregone by not using the resource in its alternate use; in this case the alternate use of the labor is unemployment or zero productivity. The employment of unemployed labor results in a net benefit to society in terms of increased productivity, even though there

219

is an associated financial cost. Another common situation involves the use of land for a proposed project when the land is already owned by the decision-making unit. The cash cost for the land may be zero, but the opportunity cost may be substantial. Once the land is utilized for the particular project, it is unavailable for other uses. The opportunity cost of the land is the benefit (or value) of the land in its next best use. The resource of land is utilized for the proposed project, although there is no associated cash cost. Economic analysis would include an imputed cost to the land, whereas financial analysis can treat the cost of the land as zero.

Costs that have been incurred in the past are called "sunk costs." Although they mistakenly find their way into decisions, they should not be included in program analysis. Decisions should be based on future consequences, rather than on consequences that have already occurred. For example, consider a city that spends $50,000 for an option to purchase a tract of land for a planned new airport for $450,000 (total cost, $500,000). Within the option period, another equally attractive tract becomes available for a total price of $400,000. The "sunk cost" of $50,000 should not influence the decision; the tract with the lower future cost should be selected. In this case, the $400,000 tract should be selected even though $50,000 has already been expended for the original site.

It is generally more difficult to measure benefits than costs. Some benefits are easily measured, as in the case of physical units (such as gallons of water, tons of solid waste, and acres of land) or dollar values (such as for market substitutes or cost savings). However, problems arise with "public" goods and services, as well as with certain other services, that are heavily affected by human and social values. Collectively consumed public goods and services have no close substitutes in the private market on which to base estimates of dollar values; human and social values are difficult to quantify because they vary greatly among persons and groups, and are often unrevealed (the value of human life, health, security, or quality of the environment). To the extent that benefits cannot be measured, the relationships between program inputs (costs) and outputs (benefits) can not be quantified. Evaluation is, then, impossible. Therefore, the assumption for program analysis is that both costs and benefits can be measured in some way. If inputs and outputs can be measured in common terms (such as dollars), then the net consequences can be determined. That is, if both costs and benefits can be measured in dollars, then the net result can be measured in dollars. If both inputs and outputs can be measured, but only in different terms, then the net effect is uncertain. However, this does not mean that alternative programs can not be evaluated relative to one another. Several strategies can be utilized:

1. force the major costs and benefits into dollar measures, consistent among alternatives, while treating immeasurables as "intangibles" to be considered "on the side"

2. measure the major costs and benefits in "common" but not dollar terms (such as the number of persons served, lives saved, and percentage decrease in incidence for all alternatives
3. where measurement of costs are impossible, assume equal costs among alternatives, and select the alternative with the greatest benefit; where benefits cannot be measured, assume equal benefits among alternatives, and select the least cost alternative.

These particular evaluation strategies are explored more fully later in this chapter.

Uncertainty

The problems of uncertainty are closely related to the problems of measurement. That is, estimates of benefits and costs are always limited in accuracy, and are therefore uncertain. Simple analyses require only that one utilize the values of the best estimates, but more complex problems may warrant the calculation of "expected values" and/or "sensitivity analysis." The expected value approach utilizes historical, technical, or subjective probabilities (relative frequencies over the long run) of particular outcomes to calculate a weighted estimate of the outcome. For example, consider the problem of selecting police vehicles from among several types. In comparing car A to car B, the benefit might be calculated as months of service before salvage. However, there exists some uncertainty as to the useful life of any particular vehicle. Historical probabilities (from past experience with a particular type of vehicle) can be used as shown in Table 11-1.

Previous experience (historical records or manufacturer's specifications) indicate that 20 percent of the vehicles stay in service for 18 months, 40 percent for 24 months, and so on. The relative frequencies sum to 100 percent; the probabilities sum to 1.0. The numbers of months are multiplied by the proba-

Table 11-1
Example—Calculation of Expected Value

Months before Salvage	Relative Frequency, Probability	Product
18	.2	3.6
24	.4	9.6
30	.3	9.0
36	.1	3.6
	1.0	25.8 months expected value

bilities; the results are summed to determine the expected duration of service. In this example, the expected duration of service is 25.8 months.

The "sensitivity analysis" approach is utilized when there is uncertainty about any of the variables in the analysis (such as costs, benefits, interest rates, or rate of consumer use). The question becomes: how sensitive is the solution (choice between alternatives) to various values assumed for the uncertain variable? For example, one alternative may be "best" if consumer use of the program output is high, but another solution may be preferable if consumer use is moderate. In such cases, the analysis calculations may be conducted several times, using various values for the uncertain variable. The sensitivity of the solution to the different values can be observed. If one alternative always looks best regardless of various values, then the solution is "insensitive," and the importance of that variable can be discarded. If solutions vary, then one must examine the value of the subject variable where one solution switches to another solution. For example, assume that a sensitivity analysis reveals that program A appears best if the rate of inflation is 8 percent or more, but program B appears best if inflation is less than 8 percent. The sensitivity analysis has simplified the overall analysis, because the analyst is not required to estimate a specific inflation rate, but rather to select more or less than 8 percent. Inasmuch as such a judgment can be made, the uncertainty of inflation rates has been reduced in the analysis.

Benefits and Costs

Types of Benefits

Benefits from public programs and projects are usually many and varied. The analysis of small and relatively uncomplicated problems may require only the identification and measurement of the major direct benefits. However, more complex problems may have indirect, secondary, and intangible benefits that are significant and critical to the management decision. The analyst must decide which benefits to include in, and omit from, the analysis, depending on the importance of the decision and the extensiveness of the analysis. The following sections identify and provide examples for each type of benefit.[2]

Direct benefits accrue to users of the project or program in terms of increased income or reduced costs. They are measured in physical units or market value in dollars, or in the absence of market values, as the cost of providing the service in the next best way. They are viewed in terms of satisfying program or project objectives. Examples include:

1. a surplus cash investment program—dollars in revenue or rate of return
2. a summer recreational program—market prices for equivalent recreational activities, such as the rental rate for a private tennis court

3. construction of an urban highway—dollars saved due to reduced travel time and distance
4. water supply system—gallons of water supplied
5. an emergency medical care program—the cost of supplying an identical service via contracts with private sector companies
6. a job training program—increased income of program participants

Indirect benefits accrue to persons outside the direct aspects of the program or project from "physical" or "technological" spillovers (externalities), and can be measured as with direct benefits. Examples include:

1. construction of an urban highway—dollars saved in reduced travel cost resulting from reduced congestion on adjacent streets
2. construction of a power company dam—dollar value of recreational use on the lake resulting from the dam, and cost savings in downstream flood control
3. a new recreational park program—increased park use at other park programs because of better geographic distribution of recreational opportunities

Property value benefits accrue to owners of land which is enhanced in value because of its proximity to a public project, and can be measured in dollars of increase in land value, or as a capitalization of an increase in income derived from the land. For example, the construction of a new park may have the effect of increasing the values of residential or commercial sites adjacent to the park. Likewise, the provision of urban services (such as water, sewer, fire, or police) may increase the value of property. If such an increase at one location occurs at the expense of another location (public improvement causes development at one location rather than another), then there is no net benefit to society as a whole. Only real increases in productivity of land constitute a net benefit to society at large (for example, a flood control project increases agricultural yields). However, local governments are concerned with land value increases within their own jurisdictions, in which case even transfers of land value may represent substantial benefits to a local government. In fact, a large part of local government land use planning and capital improvement programming is directed towards inducing private development and increasing land values.

Secondary benefits accrue to persons outside the direct aspects of the program or project from economic, rather than physical, externalities, measured as with direct benefits. Such economic benefits stem from or are induced by the program. For example, the construction of a central business district mall may increase commercial activity at that location, and secondarily benefit suppliers of goods sold there as well as consumers who pay lower prices caused by competition. Such benefits may be significant at the local scale, but represent mostly shifting at the larger scale.[3]

Intangible and other benefits are those benefits that are perceived but impossible to measure. Examples include the satisfaction of public goals, redistribution of income, aesthetic effects, or local political autonomy. Other benefits include such items as employment, where a particular project or program creates job opportunities. Like other benefits discussed, employment benefits may represent only shifting (moving jobs from one location to another) or actual benefits because of increases in productivity (employing the unemployed).

In general, financial analysis will include only direct monetary benefits as they accrue to the decision-making unit. Economic analysis, on the other hand, can include the full range of types of benefits if the project is sufficiently large to warrant an extensive analysis. However, many indirect and secondary benefits are difficult to quantify and, therefore, most local government analysis will concentrate on direct benefits and major indirect and property value benefits. Other perceived but unmeasured benefits are treated as intangibles.

One must be careful not to "double count" particular benefits by considering them in more than one category. For example, consider a local government surplus cash investment program, the returns from which are counted as a direct benefit to the governmental unit. These returns to government represent revenue and have the effect of lowering the tax burden on local citizens. However, this reduced tax burden should not be counted again as an indirect benefit. There is only one benefit; it accrues to citizens through their governmental unit. The analyst can avoid such mistakes by parsimoniously identifying benefits by type and incidence.

Types of Costs

Program costs for financial analysis are easier to estimate than program benefits, because they are generally under the control of the decision-making unit (such as a budget allocation, a contract fee, or a purchase price). The two major categories are "capital" and "operating." Capital costs include those program inputs associated with the construction of a public improvement, the purchasing of a nonrecurring item or real asset, or setting up the initial provision of the service. Operating costs include expenditures for the recurring operation of the program (such as supplies, labor, and maintenance). However, the more inclusive economic analysis may include costs in any of the categories identified in the previous "benefits" section of Chapter 10. Programs may create adverse direct, indirect, secondary, intangible and property value effects that are measured as economic costs.

Intangibles

Consequences of alternatives that cannot be converted reasonably into common measures of value should be excluded from the central analysis and held aside for separate consideration. Such consequences might include the impact on income distribution, aesthetic effects, local political autonomy, or any category of cost or benefit that cannot be measured because of the limited nature of a particular analysis. These effects should be neither neglected nor forced into common values, but rather identified and presented to the decision-makers along with the quantitative economic and financial analysis. The decision-makers can then include these factors with all the other factors required for a decision. In fact, the intuitive evaluation of intangible factors clearly presented is often preferable to poorly constructed quantitative factors.

The Distribution of Benefits and Costs

The purpose of the analysis (complete economic, limited economic, or financial) will determine to some extent what benefits and costs are to be included in the analysis. Another major consideration involves "who" receives the benefits and "who" pays the costs. Seldom does any program activity distribute benefits and costs uniformly among affected persons. Therefore, the distributional question should be treated explicitly in analysis. Generally, the incidence of benefits and costs for an alternative program activity can be estimated by subdividing affected persons into geographic, racial, income, age, and other groups. Once the incidence pattern has been estimated, it can be included in the analysis in several ways:

1. by setting the distributional impact as an explicit objective for the system analysis, perhaps combined with other objectives into a weighted multiple objective
2. by setting the distributional impact as a system constraint, such as a "maximum acceptable level of regressiveness"
3. by setting the distributional impact aside as an "intangible"

The mechanics for (1) and (2) are covered later in this chapter.

Criteria and Evaluation

The fundamental evaluation criterion is "maximum net gain." That is, the best alternative program or action is the one that contributes the maximum net gain to the decision-making unit or the constituency for whom the analysis is being conducted. However, net gain can be calculated only when costs and benefits are measured in common terms. For example, consider two investment alternatives, each costing $100 and returning $110 and $120, respectively (Table 11-2).

The net consequences can be measured in terms that are common to both costs and benefits. Here, alternative B appears best because it exhibits the maximum net gain to the investor. However, common cost and benefit measures cannot be obtained in every situation. Often, costs appear as dollar measures, while benefits appear as nondollar measures. In such situations, benefits must be measured in terms that are common among all the alternatives to be evaluated (such as the quantity, quality, or value measures discussed in Chapter 10).

Three basic criteria can be utilized where net consequences are uncertain:

1. minimize cost within a given level of benefit
2. maximize benefit within a given level of cost
3. maximize cost effectiveness (benefit-cost ratio)

Once the consequences of alternative programs, with whatever common measures, have been estimated, the alternatives can be ranked relative to one another using the above criteria. The minimum cost criterion is useful in local government, because the level of benefit for many public service programs is fixed by a given service population and standard of quality. The analysis task involves finding the least cost for providing a particular service. The maximum benefit criterion is likewise useful, because the local government budgeting process often allocates a specific amount of money in advance of program initiation, and the analysis task involves maximizing benefits within that budget constraint. The cost-effective criterion is useful in promoting the efficient use of local government resources. It is most important that the appropriate criterion be matched with each analysis situation.

It is not uncommon to hear a person state that he or she wants to maximize the program benefits for the minimum cost—to get the most for the least. Attempting to maximize benefits while minimizing costs is useless and inconsistent as a decision rule. Such a program alternative (maximum benefit, minimum cost) may, in fact, exist among a set of alternatives. However, program

Table 11-2
Example—Net Gain

Alternative	Cost	Benefit	Net Gain
A	100	110	10
B	100	120	20

benefits are, theoretically, infinite and the lowest possible cost is zero. Using that criterion does not yield consistent results; analysts using this approach usually become hopelessly confused and turn to the first feasible solution. If such a maximum benefit-minimum cost alternative actually exists, it will be revealed by using one of the three identified criteria.

Consider these three criteria relative to the cost and benefit estimates in Table 11-3. Alternative A exhibits the maximum benefit-cost ratio, B exhibits the maximum total benefit, and C exhibits the minimum cost. Note that the net benefit cannot be determined, because costs and benefits are measured in different terms. The question of which criterion to use depends on the purpose of the analysis. The benefit-cost criterion clearly relates to the efficiency of the use of resources, creating the most benefit per dollar of expenditure. However, the maximum benefit and minimum cost criteria are not particularly meaningful unless they are accompanied by explicit cost and benefit constraints. In the example above, a budget constraint of $1,000, coupled with a maximum benefit criterion, would lead to A as the preferable solution. That is, alternative A would create the maximum benefit, given a budget of $1,000. Likewise, a benefit constraint (minimum acceptable level of benefit) of 150 units, coupled with a minimum cost criterion, would lead to B as the solution. Therefore, it is important that explicit constraints and criteria are treated as integral parts of the program evaluation process.

Scale of Alternatives

The relative size or scale of alternatives is an important consideration that is often overlooked in the evaluation process. Consider the figures in Table 11-4. Alternative A exhibits the highest ratio of benefit to cost, but B exhibits the maximum net gain. However, the alternatives are of different scales. A decision between the two alternatives requires that a realistic constraint be placed on the cost or benefit (minimum acceptable benefit or maximum acceptable cost). The ratio does not facilitate a decision relative to maximum gain unless the alternatives are of an identical scale (that is, input scale).

Table 11-3
Application of Criteria

Alternative	$ Cost	Units of Benefit	B/C Ratio
A	1,000	100	0.10
B	2,000	180	0.09
C	500	40	0.08

Table 11–4
Scale Effects

Alternative	$ Cost	$ Benefit	B/C Ratio	$ Net Gain
A	100	300	3:1	200
B	1,000	2,000	2:1	1,000

Now, consider that the alternatives *A* and *B* in Table 11–4 are simply two different scales of the same alternative, *X,* and that program *X* is to be compared to a program *Y* (Figure 11-1). It shows the relationships between program inputs and outputs (costs and benefits) for each alternative. Note that program *X* (*A–B*) exhibits a continuous function that includes both *A* and *B,* as shown in Table 11–4. It is obvious that the costs, benefits, and ratios for each program (*X* and *Y*) depend on the scale at which the programs are evaluated. Program *X* yields the greatest benefit at an input, or cost, scale of less than $750; program *Y* appears best at a scale of greater than $750. Both programs yield equal bene-

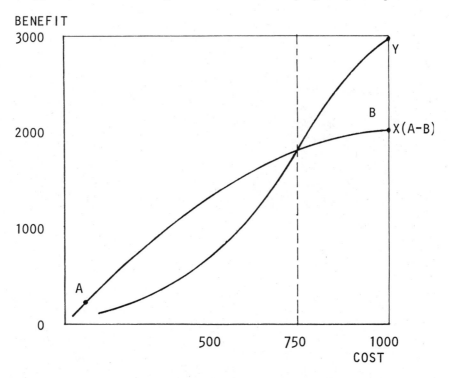

Figure 11-1. Evaluation of Programs of Different Scales

fits at $750. The analyst should be aware of scalar effects where they exist, and set explicit budget and acceptable benefit constraints. Ratios should be compared among alternatives at the same point on the cost scale. The interpretation of the benefit-cost ratio is uncertain to the extent that the above practice is not followed. Scalar alternatives are covered in detail in Chapter 12, Marginal Analysis.

An Example Analysis

The following is an example of a program analysis that includes many of the elements covered in Chapters 10 and 11. Although it is overly simplified in terms of situational assumptions, it should demonstrate the structure and process of analysis at the local government level.

Assume a medium-size city with a management–planning system similar to the one displayed in Figure 4-2 of this text. The city is in the program planning phase of the management cycle. The comprehensive plan includes a program of summer recreation. The city manager has the responsibility for developing this summer program, including the related elements of the fiscal program to be considered in the budgeting process for the coming fiscal year. To carry out this task, the manager assembles a multidisciplinary team consisting of the city planner, the head of the parks and recreation department, a budget analyst, a university-based recreational specialist, and several interested community representatives. It is important that the task be approached from a variety of viewpoints; each member will contribute from his or her area of expertise.

Definition of the Problem: Goals and Objectives

The city manager assembles the group and outlines the task to be undertaken. Work schedules and a completion date are set. The analysis group agrees that the first step in developing a program proposal is to determine the purpose—the goals and objectives—of the program. Here the group can refer to documents previously prepared within the city's management system. The most immediate document is the city's comprehensive plan, including the fiscal components of that plan. Such a plan should identify recreational goals and objectives, as well as identify general capital and operating fiscal resources to be applied to recreational activities. In this example situation, the general goal is stated as "the provision of an adequate level of recreational opportunity for every city resident." More specific objectives are identified: "the provision of a summer recreational program with a significantly expanded scope of activities appropriate to the outdoor climate and expanded free time of the city's residents, with special emphasis on the needs of the school age and senior citizens, and the provision of the highest level of recreational activity consistent with the resources available for that purpose." It is clear, then, that the summer program must be more extensive than the existing year-round program and that it must maximize benefits within the budget constraint. The city's fiscal program identifies a maximum budget amount of $300,000 for summer recreation. In addition, the city manager explains that the city budget is expected to be inordinately tight next year, and therefore the objective should be "to provide an adequate level of recreational activity (greater than the existing program) at the least possible cost"; there is no assurance that the city council will approve a budget as high as $300,000. The city planner suggests still another criterion—develop an "efficient" summer program that maximizes the ratio of benefits to costs. The analysis group agrees to disagree, and investigate alternative program designs under all three criteria (for purposes of illustration).

Identification of Alternatives: Inputs, Activities, Outputs

The next task, given the set of objectives, involves identifying the alternatives to be considered. These alternatives are to be analyzed and displayed in a general descriptive systems format (Figure 10-1, A General Systems Model), including inputs, activities, and outputs. In this case, inputs include the land, labor, and capital required to operate the summer program, measured in dollars of budget allocation. Activities are the sets of actions that are carried out by the parks department while conducting the program, articulated as a certain quantity and mix of specific recreational activities (the program design). The outputs are the actual recreational activities that are utilized by the community residents that can be measured by quantity, quality, or value. The first part of the program development task involves the identification of alternative program activities. One alternative is to do nothing—to continue the existing year-round program into the summer season. Other alternatives may be formulated via the expertise of the assembled team of experts. Each member can scan the available literature and the current and past experiences of other cities to generate alternatives. In this example, the team identifies three major determinants of recreational program design: geographic distribution, duration, and extensiveness. That is, a summer program of recreation can be:

1. centralized in several locations or decentralized to all of the community's existing parks
2. operated four or eight hours per day
3. planned to accommodate a light or an extensive schedule of activities

Of course, there are many other applicable design factors, but these three are considered to be most important. If a general program can be selected on the basis of these factors, then the parks department can develop a more specific design. This process of suboptimization serves to simplify the analysis.

Alternative general program designs are identified by inspecting all the possible combinations of the three important variables (Figure 11-2). Each path of the tree represents a distinct program design—a distinct combination of design variables. Assume that alternative A represents the existing year around program.

The outputs (benefits) of the program alternatives include both the estimated quantity and quality dimensions of the recreational activity. Quantity might be measured as user hours of activity; quality measurement is more difficult. Some part of the quality dimension may be reflected in the quantity measure; a high quality program simply may attract more participants. Quality, itself, may be measured in terms of: (a) absolute input quantities, (b) relative input quantities, or (c) input performance indicators. For example, absolute input quantities may include the number of activities offered, the number of staff, or the acres of park; relative input quantities include the number of activities per resident, the number of staff per resident, or the acres per resident; and input performance indicators include the percentage of trained staff. However, the highest order of output measure is value, as perceived by the residents, which combines both quantity and quality dimensions. The most direct estimate of this value is the market price for equivalent activities. For example, typical

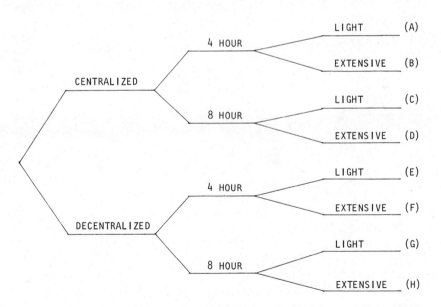

Figure 11-2. Identification of Alternatives

summer rates for private tennis courts may be $3 per hour, tennis instruction $10 per hour, music concerts $3, and so forth for the various activities included in the summer program. The total benefit of a proposed program can be estimated to the extent that each market value can be estimated. Total value is simply the number of user hours multiplied by the market rates, summed over all the activities. Program costs and benefits can be measured in common values; net consequences can be determined. In this example, the analysis team agrees to use this dollar value measure of benefits. Market equivalents are used where appropriate, and intuitively reasonable estimates are used where no market equivalents exist.

Identification of Constraints

The next task involves the identification of constraints that exist relative to program alternatives. The program objective calls for a "significantly expanded scope of activities" that can be interpreted as a constraint of "output greater than the existing program." In addition, the fiscal program identifies a budget constraint of $300,000, and the team members agree that the summer program should be at least as efficient in the use of the city's resources as the existing program.

External Effects and Uncertainty

The analysis team notes that an "extensive" program design and/or a "centralized" program location tend to attract participants from outside the city, which has the effect of reducing the benefits available to city residents. For example, a centralized, extensive tennis program is so attractive that nonresidents will travel into the city to use the facilities and services otherwise available to residents. This effect is estimated (from past experience) to be a 10 percent reduction in benefits to residents for either a centralized or extensive program, and 15 percent for both. The team also notes that decentralized programs offer greater recreational opportunities to school age children and senior citizens because of their increased accessibility and reduced travel effort, while centralized programs tend to create a critical mass of activities that attract the participation of persons who might otherwise overlook less extensive programs. Resolving the trade-off between these two factors would require analysis efforts beyond the capabilities of the analysis team. Therefore, the team accepts as reasonable the position that the net effect of the trade-off is zero. However, the important question of accessibility will be presented in the final analysis as an intangible factor. The team also determines that the major uncertain factor is the budget allocation by the city council. Although there is a budget constraint of $300,000, the council might actually allocate a lesser sum. Therefore, the analysis team decides to investigate program alternatives under various budget assumptions (sensitivity analysis).

The System Description

A simple system model is constructed to illustrate and clarify the major elements of the analysis (Figure 11-3).

Relationship Between Cost and Benefit

The next step of the analysis involves estimating the cost and benefit of each of the alternatives. First, however, the scope of the analysis must be selected—economic or financial. The financial burden of the program is important; financial feasibility must be determined. This question will be resolved as part of the city's budgeting process when the city council makes its allocation decision. The economic question should be based on a consideration of all the costs and benefits accruing directly or indirectly (via city government) to the residents of the

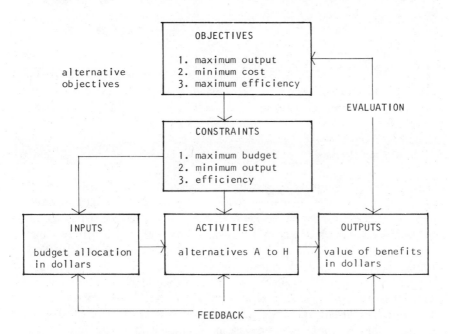

Figure 11-3. Example—System Model

community. Effects occurring outside the city are not to be included. Therefore, the analysis will be of the "limited economic" type. In this example, the program alternatives will be financially feasible if the budget resources are allocated and economically desirable if total benefits exceed total costs as they accrue to city residents.

The identification of costs and benefits is facilitated by a simple checklist of costs and benefits: direct (capital and operating), indirect, property value, secondary, and intangible. In this example, the relevant costs include the direct operating expenses (for materials, supplies, personnel, and so on), and the relevant benefits include the estimated value of the recreational activity to the residents. There are no associated capital investment requirements, and direct costs accruing to the users (such as travel or private equipment purchases) are considered to be negligible or, at least, equal among alternatives.[4] Likewise, indirect, property value, and secondary costs and benefits are considered to be negligible or nonexistent.

The direct costs can be estimated from the personnel, material, and supply requirements (quantities) of each of the alternative program designs. The benefits are estimated from the quantity of user hours, multiplied by the appropriate market rates, and modified by the resident/nonresident user factor. For example, a program element of group tennis lessons with 10 participants, 160 hours of instruction, a market rate of $2 per hour, and 85 percent resident users would have a value of:

$$10 \times 160 \times \$2 \times 0.85 = \$2,750 \tag{11.1}$$

Values for all the activities can be estimated in a similar manner, and summed to yield the total estimated value for each program design. Assume that this estimation process has been completed with the results as shown in Table 11-5.

Evaluation and Decision

Using the estimates displayed in Table 11-5, the analysis team proceeds with the evaluation process. The alternatives must be compared to one another via the application of a decision criteria. Recall that the basic decision criteria is "maximum net benefit"—which can be used when both costs and benefits are measured in common terms (such as dollars) and the scale of the inputs (costs) are identical. Although the former condition is satisfied in this example, the input scales are identical only for alternatives C and F ($240,000). A simple comparison of these two, with all other factors aside, would yield a decision for F, with the largest net benefit. However, all the alternatives must be compared and another criterion must be used—maximum benefit, minimum cost, or maximum efficiency. All three will be used for purposes of this example.

Table 11-5
Example—Program Estimates

Alternative	Design	Estimated Cost ($)	Estimated Benefit ($)	Benefit-Cost Ratio	Outcome
A	C-4-L	100,000	140,000	1.40	existing program, eliminated by minimum benefit constraint
B	C-4-E	200,000	190,000	0.95	economically undesirable
C	C-8-L	240,000	324,000	1.35	eliminated by the minimum efficiency constraint
D	C-8-E	280,000	450,000	1.61	
E	D-4-L	125,000	185,000	1.48	*minimum cost selection*
F	D-4-E	240,000	440,000	1.83	*maximum efficiency selection*
G	D-8-L	290,000	480,000	1.65	*maximum benefit selection*
H	D-8-E	375,000	600,000	1.60	eliminated by maximum budget constraint

Constraints: (a) maximum budget of $300,000
(b) minimum benefit greater than existing program (A)
(c) minimum efficiency at least as great as existing program (A)

First, however, the constraints must be applied to eliminate infeasible solutions. Program design *A*, the existing year-round alternative, is eliminated because the selection is limited to programs that exceed the existing program's level of benefit. Alternative *B* can be eliminated because it is economically undesirable; the cost exceeds the benefit.[5] Alternative *C*, as well as *B*, can be eliminated because the benefit-cost ratio falls below the ratio of the existing program. Alternatives *D*, *E*, *F*, and *G* appear to be feasible because they do not violate the stated constraints. However, alternative *H* can be eliminated because it violates the maximum budget constraint.

If the maximum benefit criterion is applied to the four feasible alternatives (*D*, *E*, *F*, *G*), *G* appears to be the best program with a maximum benefit of $480,000 within the maximum budget constraint of $300,000. If a minimum cost criterion is utilized, alternative *E* appears most satisfactory with a minimum cost of $125,000 within the minimum benefit constraint of "greater than the existing program." If an efficiency criterion is utilized, alternative *F* appears best with a benefit-cost ratio of 1.83 within both budget and benefit constraints.

The decision among alternatives depends on the application of realistic constraints and the selection of an appropriate decision criterion. This example was constructed to demonstrate and create conflict among three criteria. This will not be the case in all situations. It is possible that a single alternative may satisfy any or all the criteria. That is, a single program design may provide a maximum level of benefit at a minimum cost and maximum efficiency. However, there is no assurance that such a solution exists. Therefore, the decision criterion must be preselected to facilitate a decision. In this example analysis, a decision for a singular program cannot be reached until a single criterion is selected. This selection is not as difficult as it may seem; real world constraints often dictate the appropriate criteria. In situations with a fixed budget allocation, the task involves maximizing benefits within that budget. Where the public service levels (quantity and quality) are fixed, the task often involves minimizing the cost for that service. Likewise "efficiency" is useful in many analysis situations where productivity enhancement is desired.

Assume that the analysis team in this example accepts the maximum benefit criterion and program alternative *G*. It appears that a decentralized, eight-hour, light program of activities yields the highest level of benefits within the budget constraint. A more detailed program can be designed within this general program selection. Recall, however, that the actual budget to be allocated by the council is uncertain. The maximum benefit choice changes with the level of budget (Table 11-6).

If the city council allocates a sum that is more or less than the assumed budget constraint, then an alternative other than *G* may provide the maximum level of benefit. For example, *B* yields the highest level of benefit if only $200,000 is allocated. In this example, the selection of program design is highly sensitive to the budget allocation variable.

Table 11-6
Sensitivity to Budget

Level of Budget	Maximum Benefit Selection
$100,000	A
$150,000	E
$200,000	B
$250,000	F
$300,000	G
$400,000	H

In summary, this example is not meant to provide a hard algorithm for program analysis. Rather, it presents a simplified, orderly process for structuring a program analysis. The important conceptual elements should be present in any analysis; the conduct of details may vary considerably with context. One important variation would occur where benefits and costs are not measured in the same units (dollars). Assume the previous example with costs in dollars and benefits in user hours. Obviously, net benefits and economic desirability can not be ascertained. However, the analysis would be similar in every other way. The reader should review the example to demonstrate this fact.

Distributional Impact

Explicit consideration of the distributional impact of local public programs is often a major concern in program analysis. Three methods were suggested in Chapter 10; set the distributional impact as an objective, a constraint, or an intangible. All these require that the incidence of program costs and benefits be estimated as they accrue to groups of persons (by geographic area, age, sex, race, and so on). Costs assumed by the local governmental unit are assigned via the incidence of the related local tax or user charge mechanisms; benefits accrue primarily to direct users of the program output.

The following example treats distributional impact as an objective. Assume that the analysis involves the evaluation of three program alternatives with the evaluation criterion of maximum net benefit (Table 11-7). Alternative A appears to yield the highest net benefit without regard to distributional incidence. Assume, however, that the benefits and costs accrue to three groups of equal size, as shown in Table 11-8.

Although program A yields the highest net benefit, it does not yield the highest benefit to all three groups. Rather, program A favors group Z. Alternative B favors group X with a net cost to group Z. Such a dramatic pattern of distribution can have a major impact on the analysis; "who pays and who

Table 11-7
Example–Costs and Benefits without Distributional Consideration

Program	Per Capita Cost ($)	Per Capita Benefit ($)	Net Benefit ($)
A	2.00	3.00	1.00
B	3.00	3.00	0
C	4.00	4.50	0.50

Table 11-8
Example–Incidence of Costs and Benefits

Program	Net Effect, Group			Total Net Benefit ($)
	X	Y	Z	
A	+0.20	+0.30	+0.50	+1.00
B	+0.70	+0.30	−1.00	0
C	+0.10	+0.30	+0.10	+0.50

receives" is an important factor. Maximizing benefits is not particularly useful if the benefits fall to unintended targets. Internalizing these impacts can be accomplished by assigning weights to costs and benefits accruing to particular groups. Program benefits to one group may be inherently more important than benefits to another group. For example, a community low-cost medical care program may be directed towards a certain geographic area's low-income residents rather than to the community at large. Unfortunately, there are no readily acceptable rules for assigning weights; they may be based solely on intuitive-subjective measures. However, when weights are assigned to groups, they constitute an explicit statement of distributional objectives and facilitate the evaluation of alternatives relative to distributional impact.

Assume, for this example, that the following weights are assigned: 4 for X, 2 for Y, and 1 for Z. That is, the impact of $1 on group X is four times as great as $1 on Z, twice as great as Y, and so on. These weights are applied to the figures in Table 11-8 to yield the figures in Table 11-9. The pattern of incidence for weighted effects varies considerably from the unweighted patterns. Alternatives can be compared to one another in terms of the distributional objectives that have been articulated as weights. Here, program B yields the maximum weighted benefit; B is the best program in terms of satisfying distributional objectives.

The difficulty in this method is the determination of the actual weights to be used. The identification of appropriate groups and the selection of objective measures (total or per capita effects) are also of concern, but these can be derived within the purpose and context of the particular analysis effort. How-

Table 11-9
Example—Incidence of Weighted Effects

| | Net Weighted Effects | | | Total Net |
Program	X	Y	Z	Weighted Benefit
A	+0.80	+0.60	+0.50	+1.90
B	+2.80	+0.60	−1.00	+2.40
C	+0.40	+0.60	+0.10	+0.20

ever, the weighted approach does provide a consistent method for internalizing distributional objectives. Another acceptable method involves setting distributional impacts as constraints. For example, a constraint could hold that not less than a certain portion of the benefit can accrue to a particular group. Last, the estimated distributional consequences of a program alternative can be held aside as an intangible for the consideration of the final decisionmakers.

Multiple Objectives

This example considers the situation of evaluating alternatives that have more than one objective. Like the previous "distributional" example, each goal must be weighted relative to its importance. Assume that city officials are considering two sites for a small park. Both are of equal size and cost. However, they do vary in some hard to measure ways. Both sites have historical significance, both have aesthetic appeal, and both are reasonably well located with respect to the community. The task is to pick the best park. The analyst suggests that they rank each site on an intuitive scale of 1 to 10 for each of the three characteristics, that the importance of each characteristic be specified, and that a weighted single rating be constructed. The officials attach the following weights:

1. historical significance, 1.0
2. aesthetic appeal, 2.0
3. location, 2.0

Table 11-10
Example—Weighted Objective

Site	Historical (×1.0)	Aesthetic (×2.0)	Location (×2.0)	Weighted Rating
A	7	10	6	39
B	4	4	8	28

Then they collectively rank the sites (1 to 10 scale) relative to these features with the results as shown in Table 11-10.

The weighted rating then reflects a combined measure of the three objectives and their associated importance. Site *A* appears to be the best site. In this example, intuitive judgments were used in the absence of more objective measures. Although good objective measures would normally be preferred over subjective judgments, a structured subjective consideration is often better than a poor objective measure. Thus, subjective measures have their place in the analysis effort.

Notes

1. The concept of opportunity cost is covered in Chapter 1.

2. More detailed treatment of benefits and costs can be found in Roland N. McKean, *Efficiency in Government Through Systems Analysis* (New York: Wiley, 1958), Chapter 8; and in L. Douglas James and Robert R. Lee, *Economics of Water Resources Planning* (New York: McGraw-Hill, 1971), p. 163.

3. McKean, *Efficiency,* Chapter 9.

4. Effects that are equal among alternatives need not be considered in the decision; see Chapter 12, Marginal Analysis.

5. The question of economic undesirability rests on an evaluation of net benefit or loss—which implies that both costs and benefits are measured in identical terms.

12

Marginal Analysis

Marginal Concepts

Marginal analysis deals with the consideration of differences among alternatives rather than the inherent characteristics of any singular alternative. That is, choices among alternative courses of action are made by comparing the probable consequences of each alternative—by identifying the similarities and differences among alternatives. The differences determine the decision. This concept is so important that it has become an integral part of the analyst's thinking in both simple and complex problem situations.[1] Readers with a mathematical background will recognize marginal analysis as a part of calculus.[2] However, in this context it is more important that the reader develop an appreciation for the more basic concepts and be able to structure problems with a marginal content.

Alternatives can be structured as discrete courses of action or as varying scales of the same activity. Discrete alternatives take the form of "doing A," "doing B," "doing nothing," and so on. For example, the choice among three alternative building designs could be considered as a choice among discrete alternatives. Scalar alternatives generally take the form of increments along an input or output scale. For example, one might consider the fire stations in a city as an input to a fire protection program. The number of fire stations in operation at a given time represents one point on a scale of numbers of stations. If the planning-management decision involves a selection of the number of fire stations, then the choice is among scalar alternatives.

Consider another example of discrete alternatives. A city manager must select a type of road paving material from among three types currently available on the market. Assume that the cost is measured in dollars per ton, and that the benefit is measured in the expected months of service before repaving. The characteristics of each type are shown in Table 12-1. As in the previous chapter,

Table 12-1
Example—Discrete Alternatives

Type	Cost	Benefit	Benefit/Cost
A	25	30	1.2
B	45	48	1.06
C	15	20	1.33

241

the possible decision criteria include maximum benefit, minimum cost, or maximum benefit-cost ratio. In this case, *B* exhibits the maximum total benefit, and *C* exhibits both the minimum cost and the highest efficiency ratio.

Notice that the decision among the three alternatives cannot be made on the consideration of the inherent characteristics of each type. That is, the fact that type *C* costs $15 and lasts 20 months means nothing, in and of itself. Rather, the decision is facilitated by the differences between *C* and the other alternatives. Alternative *C* costs $10 less than *A* and $30 less than *B;* the benefit-cost ratio for *C* is 0.13 greater than *A,* and 0.27 greater than *B.* In this example, if the assumption is made that the critical constraint on road quality is the labor cost of repaving, then the absolute cost or the benefit-cost ratio for the paving material is not very important; the durability is important. If the appropriate criterion is maximum benefit, alternative *B* would be selected, not because it was expected to last 48 months, but because it was expected to last 18 months longer than the next best alternative. This all leads to the general marginal rule that "decisions among alternatives should be made with consideration of the differences among the alternatives." This intuitively simple and reasonable observation is presented here because, although it forms the basis for the techniques of marginal analysis, it is often overlooked in analysis situations. The internalization of marginal thinking is a prerequisite to much of the material of this text, and thus to sound management and planning analysis.

"Marginal" is an adjective pertaining to a border or edge. Mathematically, it refers to the quantitative differences between increments of inputs or outputs. Consider an example analysis of the assignment of police officers to traffic duty. The number of officers assigned represents the program input; the number of citations issued represents the output (Table 12-2). Assume that this table exhibits estimates derived from a city's past experience. The assignment of zero officers yields zero total citations. If one officer is assigned to this particular program, the estimated total number of citations issued is 25. The marginal effect of the assignment of this first officer to the program, or contribution to the total, is 25. The total, average, and marginal figures (25) are the same at this

Table 12-2
Example—Scalar Alternatives

Officers Assigned	Total Citations Issued	Average Citations	Marginal Citations
0	0	—	0
1	25	25	25
2	60	30	35
3	75	25	15

point. If a second officer is assigned for a total of two officers (input), the estimated total (output) is 60. The marginal contribution of the second officer is 35; the total has increased by 35; and the average has dropped to 30. Likewise, a third officer yields a marginal contribution of 15 citations and a total of 75 citations. This does not mean that the third officer writes only 15 citations; he may have written 25 citations while the first officer dropped from 25 to 15. The marginal figure shows only the additional output generated by one additional unit of input; it does not necessarily relate individual units of input to individual units of output. If the problem is one of deciding how many officers to assign, then each number becomes an alternative to be evaluated. Each alternative is a scalar increment of the same program activity. A rational decision will depend on the rules of marginal analysis.

Marginal Rules

As previously stated, the general marginal rule requires that decisions be made on consideration of the marginal differences among alternatives. This is easily accomplished with discrete alternatives (Table 12-1). However, additional attention is required with scalar alternatives (Table 12-2). There are two basic marginal rules applicable to maximizing net benefit for scalar alternatives:

Rule 1. Resources permitting, the scale of an activity should be expanded so long as its net marginal yield is positive, to the point where the net marginal yield is zero.

Rule 2. Where more than one activity exists, each activity should be expanded as per Rule 1; where that is not possible (because of limited resources) all activities should be expanded to a point where the net marginal yields are equal.

The first rule simply holds that a program activity, or course of action, is worth doing if the resulting net yield of that activity is positive, and that the scale, or the resources committed to that activity, should be increased so long as the marginal yield is positive, up to the point where the marginal yield is zero. Stopping short of this zero point is foregoing additional yield that could be obtained from increasing the scale. At the zero point, the marginal contribution obtained from additional input is zero; there is no more benefit to be obtained. Beyond this point, there is nothing to gain and possibly something to lose. Rule 2 applies when more than one activity exists and the problem is one of allocating resources among the various activities to maximize the total yield from all the activities taken together. If sufficient resources are available, then each activity can be expanded to the point of zero marginal returns, and the total yield across all activities would be maximized. However, if resources are constrained so that this cannot be achieved, then resources should be allocated so that the marginal yields for all activities are equal. This ensures the maximum total yield, given the level of input resources. If this were not the case, with one activity exhibiting a higher marginal yield than another, then the total yield could be increased by transferring resources out of the lower yield activity to the higher yield activity. Resources are optimally allocated only when marginal yields are equal.

Marginal Products

Consider the relationship between the level of input and the level of output (disregarding the cost of the inputs) for the following simplified example. Assume that there exists two police districts to which officers are assigned for the purpose of issuing traffic citations. The general task is to assign officers to the districts in such a way as to maximize the total citations issued. Inputs are "officers assigned"; outputs are "citations issued." Further, assume that the current situation is as shown in Table 12-3.

Now assume that one additional officer becomes available for assignment to this division, and the question becomes where to assign the officer. Given the situation shown in Table 12-3, it is tempting to assign the new officer to district A because the average number of citations is highest there, or perhaps to B to have equal inputs in each district. However, if the objective is to maximize the total citations issued, then the real concern is the marginal contribution of the new officer rather than the existing total or average figures. (Decisions among alternatives should be made with consideration of the marginal differences among alternatives.) Therefore, a rational decision depends on a closer look at the relationship between increments of input and level of output for each of these districts. Assume that estimates of output levels can be generated from the personal experience of the officers and from departmental records, so that Tables 12-4 and 12-5 can be formulated.

Table 12-3
Example—Marginal Product

District	Total Officers Assigned	Total Citations Per Week	Average Citation Per Officer
A	5	80	16.0
B	4	48	12.0
Total	9	128	14.2

Table 12-4
District *A*

Number of Officers Assigned	Total Citations	Average Citations	Marginal Citations
0	0	–	–
1	25	25	25
2	60	30	35
3	75	25	15
4	80	20	5
5[a]	80	16	0
6	75	12.5	–5
7	70	10	–5

[a]Currently assigned.

Table 12-5
District *B*

Number of Officers Assigned	Total Citations	Average Citations	Marginal Citations
0	0	–	–
1	10	10	10
2	22	11	12
3	36	12	14
4[a]	48	12	12
5	55	11	7
6	60	10	5

[a]Currently assigned.

District *A* shows the highest total and average figures, but with a declining, and eventually negative, marginal yield for successive officer assignments. District *B* exhibits lower totals and averages, and yet marginal yields for successive officers appear positive. The rational assignment of an additional officer will depend on the application of the two marginal rules. Rule 1 requires that an activity be expanded as long as its marginal yield is positive, to the point where the marginal yield is zero. At that point there is no more benefit to be captured. District *A* is already at that point with five officers assigned, so an additional officer would not contribute to a larger total; if the estimates are correct (Table 12-4), such assignment would actually lower the total. The assignment of an additional officer in District *B* is estimated to yield a marginal increase of seven citations, and thus an increase of seven in the total number of citations. Therefore, Rule 1 requires that the additional officer be assigned to District *B*. However, Rule 2 requires some additional action. It holds that where multiple

Table 12-6
Assignment of Successive Units of Input

Officers	Marginal Yield A	B	Total Yield
1	25	–	25
2	35	–	60
3	15	–	75
4	–	10	85
5	–	12	97
6	–	14	111
7	–	12	123
8	–	7	130
9	5	–	135
10	–	5	140
Total	4	6	140

activities exist, and where all activities cannot be expanded to the point where marginal yields are zero, the marginal yields should be equalized. The assignment of the officer to District B leaves B with a marginal return of 7, and A with a marginal return of zero. Therefore, an additional officer should be transferred to District B, leaving four officers in A and six officers in B, each with a marginal yield of five citations. The total number of citations, given the available resources, is then at its maximum point. This can be checked by considering the total citations under each condition: 128 citations with the existing situation, 135 with an additional officer assigned to B, and 140 with both the additional officer and the reassignment of one officer from A to B. Table 12-6 can be used to follow the correct assignment of successive officers from zero to ten.

That is, if only one officer is available, he or she should be assigned to District A for an expected yield of 25 citations. The second and third officers should be assigned to A; the fourth through the eighth should be assigned to B; and the ninth and tenth have equal effects in either district. Such an assignment is consistent with the marginal rules, and yields the maximum total output at any point on the input scale. If an eleventh officer became available, that officer would be assigned to B, where there is some chance of a positive marginal contribution.

Mathematical and Graphic Relationships

A graphic representation of the previous example is shown in Figures 12-1 and 12-2 (two dimensional graphs of Tables 12-4 and 12-5). Figure 12-1, District

NUMBER OF CITATIONS

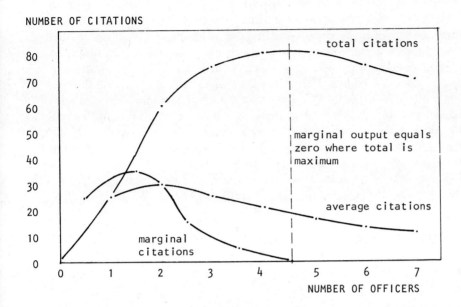

Figure 12-1. District *A*

NUMBER OF CITATIONS

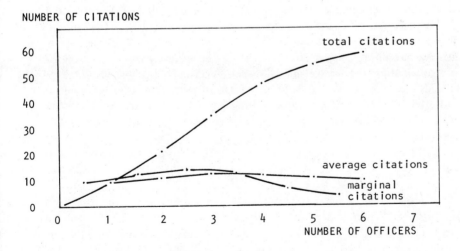

Figure 12-2. District *B*

A, shows a somewhat typical total product curve with an initial economy of scale. The data for such a curve would have to be estimated from past experience or technical design characteristics. In this case, citation data might be derived from an analysis of the departmental records. The shape of the total product curve might be a function of the total number of violations in the district and the relative organization efficiency of various team sizes. The average and marginal data are also plotted. Notice that the marginal data are plotted at the mid-points of the input scale. This is because the marginal number represents the change that occurs when moving from one unit of input to another. This relationship is seldom shown in table formats, and therefore presents some confusion. The marginal number always occurs "between" increments of input.

Figure 12-2 shows a similar set of curves for District *B,* with a lower total output apparently occurring at some higher level of input. Relationships among total, average, and marginal figures are illustrated by several additional rules:

Rule 3. The first unit of input yields equal total, average, and marginal output.

Rule 4. The total output is always the sum of the preceding marginal outputs.

Rule 5. Where the marginal output equals the average output, the average will remain the same. Where the marginal output exceeds the average, the average will rise. Where the marginal output is less than the average, the average will fall.

Each reader should ensure that these rules are demonstrated in Tables 12-4 and 12-5 and Figures 12-1 and 12-2. In addition, notice that the marginal output curve crosses the average output curve at the highest point on the average curve. This relationship follows directly from rule 5; the average rises when the marginal figure is above the average, and falls when the marginal figure is below the average. Notice also that the total output is maximum when the marginal output is zero. This, of course, follows directly from rule 1—the scale of an activity (inputs) should be expanded to the point where the marginal yield is zero (to maximize total yield).

Graphically, the average output at a given point on a total output curve is the slope of a line from that point to the origin (Figure 12-3). In this figure, the average output at three units of input is the slope of the line drawn from the origin to that point on the total product curve, or four divided by three, or 1.33. The marginal output at a point on the total output curve is the slope of the curve at that point. In Figure 12-3, the marginal output obtained from increasing the inputs from two to three units is two divided by one, or 2.00.

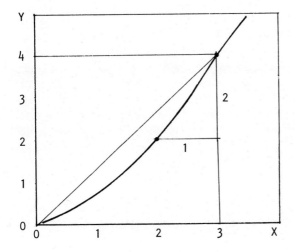

$$\text{MARGINAL} = \frac{2}{1} = 2.00$$

$$\text{AVERAGE} = \frac{4}{3} = 1.33$$

Figure 12-3. Marginal Curve Graphics

Marginal Costs

This section considers the relationship between the level of program inputs and program costs. Assume the situation of the previous example with five officers assigned to District *A*, and given the input-output relationships as shown in Table 12-4 and Figure 12-1. Further, assume that the total costs are composed of fixed costs and variable costs as shown in Table 12-7.

The data in Table 12-7 are displayed graphically in Figure 12-4. The fixed cost represents the input that does not vary with the level of output. Variable costs are directly related to the level of output. Total cost equals the fixed cost plus the variable cost. Marginal and average figures are calculated as with previous examples. Notice that the relationships of marginal rules 3, 4, and 5 hold as with the previous examples.

Table 12-7
Example—Program Costs

Officers	Fixed Cost	Variable Cost	Total Cost	Average Cost	Marginal Cost
0	0	0	0	—	—
1	300	200	500	500	500
2	300	450	750	375	250
3	300	750	1050	350	300
4	300	1100	1400	350	350
5	300	1500	1800	360	400

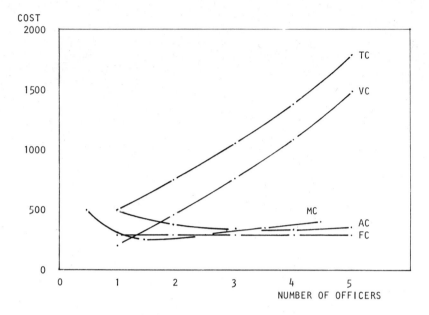

Figure 12-4. Cost Curves

Optimum Allocation

Thus far, the basic marginal concepts with examples of marginal output (relationship between level of inputs and level of outputs) and marginal cost (level of inputs and level of cost) have been presented. In the framework of program evaluation, it is also useful to consider the relationship between cost and the level of output. Recall that the first marginal rule (for maximum benefit) requires that the scale of an activity be expanded to the point where the net marginal yield equals zero. The net marginal yield is zero where the marginal costs equal the marginal benefits. This is nothing more than the basic profit-maximizing rule of equating marginal costs with marginal revenues.[3] If inputs and outputs can be measured in common terms (such as dollars), then marginal analysis can be used to determine the point of maximum net benefit.

Again, assume the data from the previous example of police District A. Also assume that the existing citation fines are $10, and that the schedule of fines is the subject of the analysis. The first step of analysis involves converting both input (cost) data and output (revenue) data into a common framework (Table 12-8). These cost and revenue figures are drawn from the previous tables and presented graphically in Figure 12-5. The curves have been "smoothed" to simulate a larger body of data. Predictably, there are initial economies of scale (falling average cost) and eventual diseconomies of scale (increasing cost as the

Table 12-8
Example—Cost and Revenue

Officers	Citations	Total Cost	Average Cost (per citation)	Marginal Cost	Total Revenue ($)	Average Revenue ($)	Marginal Revenue ($)	Net Total ($)
0	0	0	0	0				
1	25	500	20.00	20.00	250	10	10	−250
2	60	750	12.50	7.14	600	10	10	−150
3	75	1050	14.00	20.00	750	10	10	−300
4	80	1400	17.50	70.00	800	10	10	−600

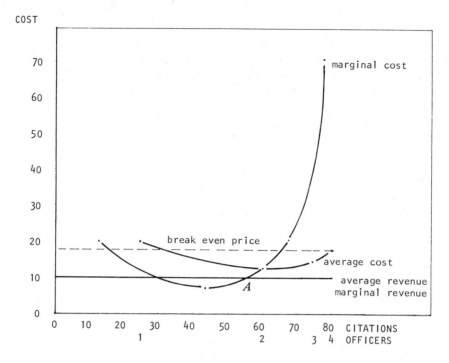

Figure 12-5. Marginal Cost and Revenue

number of citations approaches the number of violations in the subject district). On the revenue side, the average and marginal revenues remain the same (at $10 per citation). The city appears to be losing money at the current rate of 80 citations ($600 per month). Financially, the city would be best off (maximum net benefit or minimum net loss) at the point where marginal cost equals marginal revenue. This occurs at point *A*. However, the number of officers is not divisible; the nearest point is two officers and 60 citations (with a $150 per month loss). The city can operate as a monopoly and set the price (fine) at any point. The rationale for raising the fine can be based on the belief that regulatory costs should be paid by those individuals being regulated; in this case, these are the persons cited with violations. For example, a rational "break-even" price could be set at $17.50, where the average revenue covers the average cost. Alternately, the public purpose might be better served with an even higher fine to yield a positive net revenue and possibly decrease the "demand" (occurrence of) for traffic violations.

Summary

It should be clear from these simple examples that management decisions relating to the allocation of limited resources among competing programs depend, in great measure, on the concept of marginal analysis. It is the differences among projects that facilitate decisions; marginal analysis provides a useful structure for handling these differences. The basic marginal rules and graphic relationships should provide an intuitive understanding; the higher mathematics of calculus provide the mechanics for more complex analysis situations. The primary concern here is to demonstrate a way of thinking rather than a quantitative algorithm.

Notes

1. See William J. Baumol, *Economic Theory and Operations Analysis* (Englewood Cliffs, N.J.: Prentice-Hall, 1965). Chapter 3, as well as Chapter 1 of this text.

2. Mathematically, the marginal figure is expressed as the change in Y with respect to the change in X; or dy/dx, the "first derivative" in calculus. See Baumol, ibid., p. 45 for the rules of differentiation.

3. Refer again to the rules of maximum profit presented in Chapter 1 of this text.

13

Investment Analysis

Investment

Chapter 10 presented a basic "systems" format as an approach to analysis problems; Chapters 11 and 12 addressed the more specific task of program evaluation. The evaluation process in the latter chapters involved the application of one of several criteria to estimates of the costs and benefits associated with each of the alternatives. The costs and benefits were assumed to accrue over a relatively short time period. That is, the periods in which costs were paid and benefits received were considered to be immediate or unimportant. However, many public sector programs and projects accrue consequences over relatively long periods of time, and the chronology of costs and benefits becomes important. Analysis of these time situations is termed "investment analysis." Investment is the initial allocation of resources to purchase or construct some productive asset or to set up some program with the expectation of a return of benefits over some period of time. This chapter deals specifically with investment analysis techniques.

Time Horizon, Time Streams, and Discounting

One of the initial questions of investment analysis is selecting a time period for the analysis. That is, if resources are invested in an asset that yields benefits in future years, how many years should benefits be counted? An "expected life" can be technically or historically estimated for certain capital items. For example, a city hall structure might be expected to last twenty-five years before major renovation, a police vehicle may last an average of three years before maintenance costs exceed the cost of repurchase, and a certain road paving may last six years. Such time periods should be used when they can be so identified. Often, because alternatives to be evaluated do not exhibit specific horizons, the analyst must set arbitrary but reasonable limits. Estimates too far into the future are subject to greater uncertainty and increased cost of analysis. For example, the purchase of land for a neighborhood park may theoretically yield benefits until doomsday. Attempts to include such very long-range benefits would be impractical and unnecessary because such benefits would yield only marginal values when discounted to current values. Some reasonable limit must be set. The most important principle is that all alternatives under consideration must be

255

analyzed within the same time frame. That is, all the alternatives being evaluated must be considered over the same number of years. For example, the costs and benefits associated with the alternatives of leasing or purchasing an item of equipment would be estimated for an equal number of future years—such as five or ten years. It would be incorrect to count the benefits of "purchase" accruing for ten years, while counting the benefits of "lease" for only five years. Benefits and costs for each alternative can be arranged visually in a table format with reference to the time period in which they accrue—in a "time stream." A calendar of fiscal years is normally used for this purpose to coincide with the local government's planning and budget cycle. However, any equal periods can be used including quarters and months. The time streams can be displayed as shown in Table 13-1. T_0 represents the present time or the time at which the decision is to be made; T_1 represents the time after one year has elapsed; T_2 represents the time after two years have elapsed, and so on. Estimated costs and benefits can be displayed along with the net effect for each period. This format is useful for presentation purposes as well as for the detailed analysis.

The typical investment situation involves allocating resources (land, labor, and/or capital) in the current period in the anticipation of benefits returned in future periods. Some amount of current consumption is foregone in order to increase future consumption. However, people generally prefer current consumption to future consumption. There exists a time preference in society whereby benefits today are valued more highly than the same benefits promised for some future period. For example, if offered $100 today or next January 1, most people would opt for the former alternative. This preference indicates that differential values are placed on benefits relative to the time at which they are incurred. This preference and differential value leads to the mechanism of "interest," which is the compensation for postponing current consumption. That is, a person who wants to increase his or her level of current consumption borrows money from a person who wants to postpone current consumption in favor of increasing future consumption. The borrower pays interest to the lender as compensation; the interest rate is the price (rental payment) of money.

The general equations for principal and interest are shown in equations (13.1) and (13.2):

Table 13-1
Time Stream Display

Time	T_0	T_1	T_2	.... T_n
Benefits				
Costs				
Net				

where P = principal amount
        n = number of years (or time periods)
        P_n = principal in year n (or time period n)

     i or r = interest rate
       I = interest

$$I = Pi \tag{13.1}$$

$$P_n = P_0 (1 + i)^n \tag{13.2}$$

Thus, if \$100 is invested for one year at an interest rate of 5 percent per year, compounded (applied) once, the interest generated is \$5.00. The principal plus interest equals \$105.

$$I = Pi$$

$$I = (100)(0.05)$$

$$I = 5$$

$$P_n = P_0 (1 + i)^n$$

$$P_1 = 100 (1 + 0.05)^1$$

$$P_1 = 105$$

If the \$100 principal in the example above were left invested for three years at 7 percent per year, compounded annually, the principal would grow to \$122.50.

$$P_n = P_0 (1 + i)^n$$

$$P_3 = 100 (1 + 0.07)^3$$

$$P_3 = 122.50$$

Thus, the future value of principal sums can be determined by using equation 13.2 and an assumed interest rate. Likewise, the present value of future sums can be determined. The current value of some future sum is termed the "present value" or "discounted present value." Present value is determined via an equation and an assumed "discount rate" (Equation 13.3):

where
$$PV = P_n \left(\frac{1}{1+i} \right)^n \qquad (13.3)$$

$$PV = \text{discounted present value}$$

For example, the present value of $100, received three years hence, with a discount rate of 7 percent, is $81.60.

$$PV = P_n \left(\frac{1}{1+i} \right)^n$$

$$PV = 100 \left(\frac{1}{1.07} \right)^3$$

$$PV = 81.60$$

Thus, the value of money can be determined with reference to the time preference of society. Future values of present sums and present values of future sums can be determined via the interest and discount rates (equations 13.2 and 13.3).

These values can be calculated with other than the annual compounding assumption. For example, $1,000 invested for two years at an interest rate of 8 percent per year, compounded quarterly, would be $1171.66.

$$P_n = P_0 (1 + i)^n$$

$$P_8 = 1000 (1 + 0.02)^8$$

$$P_8 = 1171.66$$

That is, an interest rate of 8 percent per year, compounded four times per year, invested for two years, is equivalent to 2 percent compounded eight times. Present and future values can also be calculated with the assumption of "continuous" compounding (using equations 13.4 and 13.5).

$$P_n = P_0 e^z \qquad (13.4)$$

$$PV = P_n e^{-z} \qquad (13.5)$$

where
$$e = 2.718281 \text{ (a constant)}$$

$$z = (i)(n)$$

For example, $100 invested for three years at an interest rate of 7 percent per year, compounded continuously, yields a future sum of $123.37.

$$P_n = P_0 e^z$$

$$P_3 = 100 \, (2.718)^{[(0.07)(3)]}$$

$$P_3 = 271.8^{(0.21)}$$

$$P_3 = 123.37$$

Likewise, $123.37 received three years hence, continuously discounted at a rate of 7 percent per year, yields a present value of $100.

$$PV = P_n e^{-z}$$

$$PV = 123.37 \, (2.718)^{-[(0.07)(3)]}$$

$$PV = 123.37 \, (0.8106)$$

$$PV = 100.$$

Notice that quarterly or continuous compounding yields marginally higher future values and lower present values than annual compounding. These differences are not large enough to warrant using one or the other in analysis situations; however, the single method selected should be used throughout the analysis. The continuous compounding method is often used for its simplicity and adaptability to an infinite number of interest rates and time period increments (for example, 6.125 percent for 3.25 years).

The tables in appendixes A and B eliminate much of the need for calculation. Appendix A provides values for $(1 + i)^n$ and $\dfrac{1}{1+i}^n$ for various values of n (1 to 50) and i (0.01 to 0.20). Appendix B provides values of e^z and e^{-z} for various values of z (0.01 to 10.0). These tables can be used to calculate present and future values for most analysis situations. In addition, many electronic calculators provide present value, future value, and e^z functions.

The evaluation of investment alternatives requires that costs and benefits accruing in future time periods be converted to present values. A management decision made today must be made with respect to today's values. Therefore, the future consequences of alternative investments should be converted to present values, and the present values compared among alternatives. Consider the example analysis of a project that exhibits the following estimates of benefits and costs in a three-year time stream (Table 13-2).

Table 13–2
Time Stream I

Time	T_0	T_1	T_2	T_3
Benefits	0	+50	+40	+20
Costs	−100	0	0	0
Net	−100	+50	+40	+20

There is an initial investment of $100 with $50, $40, and $20 in returns after one, two, and three years, respectively. If these future values were not converted to present values, the analysis would show a total net benefit of $10. The project would appear to be economically desirable. If however, the appropriate discount rate were 10 percent and these future values were converted to present values, the results would differ. The present value of the time stream is calculated by summing the discounted present value of each figure in the stream.

$$PV = P_0 + P_1 \left(\frac{1}{1+i}\right)^1 + P_2\left(\frac{1}{1+i}\right)^2 \ldots P_n\left(\frac{1}{1+i}\right)^n$$

(13.6)

$$PV = -100 + 50 \left(\frac{1}{1.1}\right)^1 + 40 \left(\frac{1}{1.1}\right)^2 + 20 \left(\frac{1}{1.1}\right)^3$$

$$PV = -100 + 45.45 + 33.05 + 15.02$$

$$PV = -6.48$$

When so discounted, the present value of the investment is a negative $6.48; the project is economically undesirable.

Criteria

The previous section presented the mechanics of calculating the present values of investment time streams. This section addresses the evaluation of investments, or alternative investments, via the application of decision criteria. Many elements (such as estimating costs and benefits) of this type of analysis are similar to the methods presented in Chapters 10, 11, and 12. However, there are essentially two investment criteria applicable here: "maximize discounted present value," and "maximize internal rate of return."

Present Value

A decision among investment alternatives requires a judgment as to whether or not an alternative is worth doing. An investment that exhibits a time stream of costs and benefits with a positive discounted present value results in a net benefit (increase in net worth) to the investor. Therefore, it is worth doing. A project with a negative discounted present value results in a net loss and, therefore, is not worth doing. Any project or program exhibiting a positive present value is economically desirable. Assuming unlimited resources, a person or institution would want to undertake all such projects and reject any project with a negative present value. However, the luxury of financing an infinite number of promising projects and programs is seldom the case. When resources are limited, the available resources must be allocated among a limited set of alternatives to satisfy a variety of economic goals and objectives. The allocation of such an investment budget among projects is discussed later in this chapter.

The more practical analysis problem involves selecting the best investment from a set of mutually exclusive, but economically desirable, alternatives (for example, three designs for a particular program, two uses for a parcel of land, or several starting dates for a project). The present value criterion is fairly direct in such situations; it selects the alternative with the highest discounted present value. Another situation arises in cost-effectiveness analysis where the benefits from mutually exclusive alternatives are not measured, but are assumed to be equal or at least satisfactory for all alternatives. In this case, the present value criterion selects the alternative with the least negative present value (that is, the least cost alternative).

The typical investment analysis of mutually exclusive alternatives, assuming a maximum benefit objective and present value criterion, includes the following steps:

1. identification of alternatives to be evaluated
2. selection of a time horizon for the analysis
3. estimation of costs and benefits in the time stream (technical and financial data, measured in dollars)
4. selection of an appropriate discount rate
5. calculation of the discounted present value for each alternative
6. determination of economic desirability (rejection of alternatives with negative present values)
7. determination of financial feasibility
8. selection of the alternative with the highest discounted present value from among alternatives that are both desirable and feasible

For example, consider a situation in which a local government is faced with three alternatives relative to data processing operations. The alternatives are:

A. continue with the existing manual system (the do nothing alternative),
B. purchase a small computer system,
C. lease a small computer system.

Assume that steps 1 thru 5 above have been completed, with the estimates as shown in Table 13-3 (time frame of five years, discount rate of 6 percent). As indicated in Table 13-3, the existing manual system is expected to produce a stable level of benefits with rising costs. Alternative B, the purchase of a computer system, requires a large initial investment, but yields a higher level of benefits and lower future costs. Alternative C, the lease of a computer system, yields the higher level of benefits with a lower initial investment, but requires a somewhat higher level of future costs. Because these estimated costs and benefits accrue in present and future time periods, a valid comparison depends on the discounted present values of the alternatives. Each alternative exhibits a positive present value, so all are economically desirable. Alternative B, the purchase of equipment, yields the highest present value—the highest net benefit.

Table 13-3
Example Problem—PV Criterion[a]

(A) continue existing system

Time	T_0	T_1	T_2	T_3	T_4	T_5	Total
Benefits	0	+40.0	+40.0	+40.0	+40.0	+40.0	+200.0
Costs	0	−20.0	−30.0	−40.0	−50.0	−60.0	−200.0
Net	0	+20.0	+10.0	0	−10.0	−20.0	0
PV	0	+18.8	+8.9	0	−7.9	−14.9	+4.9

(B) purchase new system

Time	T_0	T_1	T_2	T_3	T_4	T_5	Total
Benefits	0	+60.0	+80.0	+100.0	+100.0	+100.0	+440.0
Costs	−250.0	−10.0	−10.0	−10.0	−10.0	−10.0	−300.0
Net	−250.0	+50.0	+70.0	+90.0	+90.0	+90.0	+140.0
PV	−250.0	+47.1	+62.3	+75.5	+71.2	+67.2	+73.3

(C) lease new system

Time	T_0	T_1	T_2	T_3	T_4	T_5	Total
Benefits	0	+60.0	+80.0	+100.0	+100.0	+100.0	+440.0
Costs	−130.0	−40.0	−40.0	−40.0	−40.0	−40.0	−330.0
Net	−130.0	+20.0	+40.0	+60.0	+60.0	+60.0	+110.0
PV	−130.0	+18.8	+35.6	+50.3	+47.5	+44.8	+67.0

[a]Figures in $1,000.

However, both economic desirability and financial feasibility must be considered. Alternative B requires a substantial initial investment. Recall from Chapter 11 that the maximum benefit criterion is usually accompanied by a maximum budget constraint. For example, if the budget for program initiation in the above example were $150,000, then alternative B would have to be rejected, and alternative C would become the maximum benefit alternative. Likewise, a minimum cost objective with a minimum level of benefit constraint might well yield another result. The general evaluation principles of Chapter 11 apply throughout investment analysis.

Note that alternative A is not an "investment." Rather, it is the continuation of an ongoing operation where costs are expected to rise for a given level of service. The first two years of this option appear economically desirable and financially feasible (positive net return without initial investment). Therefore, one might consider the additional options of waiting one or more years before purchase or lease of a new system.

Internal Rate of Return

Another related criterion for the evaluation of investment alternatives is the "internal rate of return" (IRR). The IRR is defined as "that discount rate at which the discounted present value of the time stream equals zero." Consider the following example. One hundred dollars invested for 10 years at 6 percent yields $182.21.

$$P_{10} = P_0 e^z$$

$$P_{10} = 100\,(e)^{[(10)(0.06)]} \tag{13.7}$$

$$P_{10} = 182.21$$

The time stream for this investment is shown in Table 13-4. This time stream, when discounted at 6 percent, yields a discounted present value of zero. Thus,

Table 13-4
Time Stream II

	T_0	T_{10}
Benefit		+182.21
Cost	−100	
Net	−100	
PV@0.06	−100	+100

the IRR of the investment is 6 percent. The IRR can be utilized as an investment evaluation criterion in the following manner: An investment alternative is economically desirable if the IRR exceeds the cost of capital to the investor. In most cases, the cost of capital will be the interest rate that the investor must pay for capital to be invested. That is, it is economically desirable to borrow money at 7 percent for investment in a project that returns (IRR) 9 percent. Therefore, an IRR that is higher than the cost of capital indicates an economically advantageous investment. However, the borrower's interest rate may not be the appropriate interest rate in some cases. The more critical measure is the "opportunity cost of capital"—that benefit (or net return) foregone by not allocating capital to the next best investment alternative. If limited resources are invested in a particular activity, then those funds are not available for investment in another activity. The opportunity cost of receiving benefits from the first investment is the loss of benefits from the second. For example, assume that there are two investment opportunities with IRR's of 12 and 10 percent respectively. If a person invests in the first, the 10 percent from the second is lost. If more capital were available, the 10 percent return could be captured. Therefore, additional capital is worth just under 10 percent to the investor. Ten percent is the opportunity cost of capital in this example.

Where a decision must be made among a number of mutually exclusive, economically desirable alternatives, the IRR criterion selects the alternative with the highest internal rate of return. A typical analysis of mutually exclusive alternatives would include the following steps:

1. identification of alternatives to be evaluated
2. selection of a time horizon for the analysis
3. estimation of the costs and benefits in the time stream
4. calculation of the internal rate of return (IRR)
5. determination of economic desirability and financial feasibility
6. selection of the alternative with the highest IRR.

The calculation of the IRR is essentially an iterative or trial and error process of trying interest rates and converging on the zero value for the discounted present value of the time stream. Consider again alternatives B and C of the previous example (Table 13-3). The calculation of rates of return for these mutually exclusive alternatives is shown in Table 13-5. The trial discount rates yield an IRR of 15 percent for alternative A, and 20 percent for alternative B. The application of the IRR criterion would lead to the selection of C as the best project. Recall that the PV criterion selected B rather than C; there is a conflict among criteria.

Table 13-5
Example Problem—IRR Criterion

(B) purchase new system

	T_0	T_1	T_2	T_3	T_4	T_5	PV
Net (in 1,000)	−250	+50.0	+70.0	+90.0	+90.0	+90.0	140.0
6%	−250	+47.1	+62.3	+75.5	+71.2	+67.2	+73.3
20%	−250	+41.6	+48.6	+52.0	+43.4	+36.1	28.3
14%	−250	+43.8	+53.8	+60.7	+53.2	+46.7	+8.2
15%	−250	+43.4	+52.9	+59.1	+51.4	+44.7	+1.5

IRR is approximately 15 percent.

(C) lease new system

	T_0	T_1	T_2	T_3	T_4	T_5	PV
Net (in 1,000)	−130	+20.0	+40.0	+60.0	+60.0	+60.0	110.0
6%	−130	+18.8	+35.6	+50.3	+47.5	+44.8	+67.0
15%	−130	+17.3	+30.2	+39.4	+34.3	+29.8	+21.0
20%	−130	+16.6	+27.7	+34.7	+28.9	+24.1	+2.0

IRR is approximately 20 percent.

Conflicts between PV and IRR Criteria

The internal rate of return is a familiar investment term and, therefore, intuitively attractive. However, there are some problems with its use in the evaluation of mutually exclusive program alternatives. For example, the IRR is useless in the evaluation of alternatives without a net cost in the time stream (no investment); such a situation yields an infinitely high IRR which has no practical meaning beyond the fact that it has a positive value. However, the *PV* criterion can still be used in such situations. The IRR is also generally unsatisfactory in the evaluation of alternatives with varying positive and negative net values in the time stream. Such cases can yield multiple or meaningless IRR values. Note that the IRR for alternative *A* in the previous example (Table 13-3) would be zero. Finally, the IRR and *PV* criteria may simply disagree, as with alternatives *B* and *C* in the previous example (*B* exhibited the highest *PV*, but the lowest IRR of the two alternatives). This conflict can be examined by plotting the *PV* and IRR on the graph in Figure 13-1. As shown, alternative *B* exhibits the highest present value at discount rates from zero to approximately 8 percent; alternative *C* exhibits the highest *PV* from that crossover to 20 percent. The best approach to a dual solution is to rely on the *PV* criterion at the appropriate discount rate. If the real opportunity cost of capital in the above example is less than 8 percent,

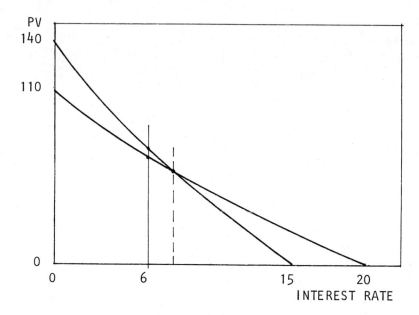

Figure 13-1. Conflict Between *PV* and IRR

alternative *B* would yield the greatest net benefit; if the cost of capital is above 8 percent, alternative *C* would yield the highest net benefit.

Benefit Cost Criterion

As discussed in Chapter 11, the benefit cost criterion (maximize the ratio of benefits to costs) is often used in investment analysis. If the discounted present values of benefits exceed costs in the time stream, the ratio exceeds 1.0, and the project is deemed economically desirable. The benefit-cost ratio thus employed is a useful and intuitively understandable measure. However, it can present problems when used to evaluate mutually exclusive alternatives. That is, the alternative with the highest benefit-cost ratio may not yield the largest net benefit when benefits are discounted at the appropriate discount rate. This results from the problems associated with alternatives of different scales as previously discussed.

Interest Rates and Inflation

The selection of an appropriate interest or discount rate is an important question for which there is no fully satisfactory answer. Unsettled theoretical questions about rates leave the practitioner in a state of confusion, and the field of practice with little uniformity among analyses. If the rate utilized is too low, future project benefits will appear correspondingly high, more investment alternatives will appear feasible, and more investment will be undertaken. If the rate is too high, the reverse will hold, and short-run projects will appear relatively more attractive than long-run projects.

The discount rate should equal the opportunity cost of capital. This determination is not a major problem for private sector firms, because the opportunity cost of capital is the price that the firms must pay for capital—the market rate of interest. That is, if a firm borrows money at a 9 percent interest rate for investment in a project, that 9 percent is the cost of capital, and should be used as the discount rate or the rate of comparison for the IRR criterion. Likewise, if an individual borrows from his own savings account (paying 6 percent) to invest in a small business, the cost of capital is the 6 percent foregone by not leaving the capital in a savings account. The public sector situation is more complicated. Resources invested in the public sector have been withdrawn from private consumption and investment via taxes. Therefore, the return on public investment should be at least equal to the return foregone in the private sector. Advocates of this view suggest a public rate equal to a weighted average of private rates. However, market rates may not be fully appropriate. Social opportunity costs may differ from private opportunity costs (because of social values, externalities, public goods, and the like). Also, private interest rates reflect tax effects that do not apply to public investment returns and often reflect a risk factor that is less important in public investment. Adjustments should be made for these factors.

As a practical matter, several approaches can be utilized by local government:

1. Use a weighted average of the current interest rates on bonds issued by the unit of local government, or an average of prevailing local rates.
2. Use, for particular projects, a market rate utilized in similar but private sector projects adjusted for tax effects.
3. Use a weighted average of the above (1) and (2).
4. Use several rates and sensitivity analysis.

In any case, a local government should be consistent by using the same rate for the entire analysis being conducted at a given time.

There is yet another approach that should theoretically, if not practically, be considered. Every unit of local government operates under a constrained budget, and many are forced to operate under severe fiscal conditions. Many worthwhile projects are foregone because of financial infeasibility rather than economic desirability or undesirability. In such situations, the "opportunity cost of capital" is not the bond or market rate, but the benefit foregone by not having additional capital. For example, a city may be able to sell bonds at 7 percent for investment in projects yielding 15 percent (IRR) in public benefits. However, if the city cannot sell the bonds because of a legal debt limit, the projects cannot be undertaken (financial infeasibility). Therefore, the real value of capital to the city is just less than 15 percent. If possible, the city would borrow at 14 percent to receive 15 percent in benefits for a net gain. The opportunity cost of capital in such a situation is the IRR of the best project that cannot be undertaken because of a constrained budget. Thus, a highly constrained capital budget indicates a high discount rate. Cities with such severe budgets might use an artificially high (higher than the bond rate) discount rate, which has the effect of placing a high value on short-term projects that return benefits rather quickly.

Inflation, the general increase in price levels, need not be considered in the context of program-investment analysis. Decisions among alternative are made via consideration of the differences among alternatives, and general price inflation would affect all alternatives in the same way. In addition, decisions are based on present rather than future values, and expectations of rates of inflation are built into the market interest rates. To the extent that inflation was already in the discount rate, adding an inflation rate to the discount rate would constitute a double counting of inflation. However, inflation can affect the evaluation of alternatives if the price of a particular resource is expected to rise differently than the general price increase. For example, a labor-intensive alternative, where labor costs were expected to increase beyond the general price inflation, might be adjusted to reflect the differential inflation effect. Where estimates of future costs and/or benefits are based on current prices, a price index can be used to convert values from one period to another.

The Capital Budget

This section provides a framework for the organization and selection of a group of investment projects or programs for a capital budget. Assume that a number of projects have been analyzed, the present values have been calculated, and the economic desirability of each has been determined. Choices among mutually exclusive alternatives and other interdependent projects have been made to yield a set of capital projects that are economically desirable and, taken individually, financially feasible. The task is to organize them into a capital budget—to include in the budget that group of projects that will yield the largest total net benefit.

However, this framework is not necessarily useful for the construction of actual capital budgets at the local government level. Like any other public sector decision, political, social, and other factors must be considered. The actual capital budget is particularly influenced by factors of timing, response to crisis situations, and financing opportunities. Nevertheless, this type of analysis is ex-

Table 13-6
Example–Ranking of Projects by IRR

Project	IRR (%)	Initial Cost ($)	Total Budget ($)
A	18	20,000	20,000
B	16	30,000	50,000
C	12	20,000	70,000
D	10	40,000	110,000
E	8	20,000	130,000
F	7	30,000	160,000
G	4	20,000	180,000

tremely important to the intuitive understanding of sound investment practice. The first step of the process requires that all the economically desirable projects be ranked by their internal rates of return. Table 13-6 shows such a ranking. The second step involves accepting projects into the budget in order of IRR ranking (Figure 13-2). That is, *A* appears to be the best project (by IRR criterion) and is placed first in the budget. Other projects are accepted into the budget until the budget constraint is reached. This budget constraint is shown here as the dashed

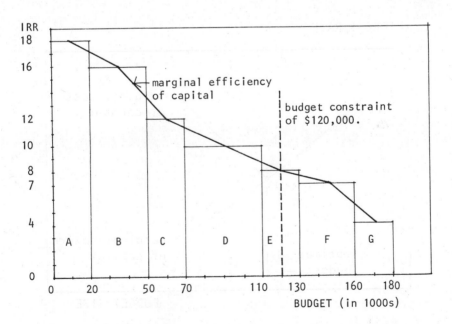

Figure 13-2. Example–The Capital Budget

line at $120,000. Thus, projects *A* through *D* would comprise the capital budget, with $10,000 left uncommitted. When such a sum is left uncommitted, the analyst should check for possible substitutions that would use the full budget amount and yield a higher total net benefit. Assume that there are no such substitutions in this example; therefore, the uncommitted sum might be invested in short-term securities. All other things being equal, this capital budget would yield the highest possible net benefit.

However, closer inspection reveals that "all other things" may not be equal. Consider, on Figure 13-2, the line that joins the IRR values for each project. This line represents the marginal efficiency of capital—the rate of return at each successive unit of the budget. For example, the marginal return on a dollar invested at the $35,000 point in the budget is 16 percent, while the return is 10 percent at $90,000, and so on. Also, plotting the marginal cost of capital allows a comparison of marginal cost and marginal return on investment. The marginal cost of capital would be the opportunity cost of capital used for the present value analysis. That line on the graph might be horizontal if the governmental unit can borrow a sufficient sum at a given interest rate, or it may be an increasing function of the amount of capital borrowed. An example comparison is shown in Figure 13-3.

Recall from Chapter 1 that the maximum benefit (profit maximum) is obtained where "marginal benefits equal marginal costs," and from Chapter 12 that

INTEREST RATE

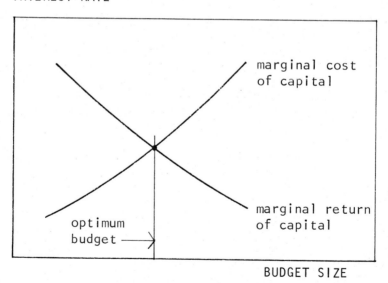

Figure 13-3. Example—Marginal Cost and Return

the scale of an activity should be increased until the "net marginal benefit is zero." These statements are identical in meaning; if marginal benefits equal marginal costs, the net marginal benefit is zero. In Figure 13-3, returns exceed costs up to point X on the budget, while costs exceed returns beyond that point. The maximum benefit is obtained at point X, the optimum budget size. Therefore, a local government should expand its capital budget (scale of investment) to a point where the marginal return on investment equals the opportunity cost of capital. This would create the largest possible net benefit. However, the reality of the local government situation is that costs occur in dollar terms, while benefits occur in a variety of ways. Financial feasibility rather than economic desirability is the constraining factor. Most local governments simply do not have the resources to invest in all the desirable capital projects available at a given time. Local governments with severe budget constraints tend to underinvest, while concentrating on much needed current consumption items (public services).

Returning to the capital budget example (Figure 13-2), assume that the discount rate (opportunity cost of capital) was set at 6 percent. Therefore, projects E and F should be included in the budget; both return more than 6 percent in benefits. The optimum size for the budget would be $160,000, where marginal returns equal marginal costs. However, the budget constraint of $120,000 prohibits taking advantage of these additional projects. That is, returns as high as 8 percent are foregone because of a lack of capital. Therefore, the real opportunity cost of capital is 8 percent, rather than the assumed 6 percent. Six percent was used to evaluate the original list of projects and to facilitate the determination of economic desirability and selection of mutually exclusive alternatives.

The budget analysis has revealed an opportunity cost of 8 percent caused by a constrained budget. In this situation, the analyst should return to the original list of investment projects, and calculate new present values at 8 percent. Projects that appeared desirable at 6 percent may appear undesirable at 8 percent, and so on. There may be some switchovers in the final list of projects for the capital budget. If such changes occur, a still different opportunity cost of capital may be revealed. Theoretically, this process would be reiterated until a stable capital budget was formulated. The stable budget would then yield the maximum total net benefit. The result of all this analysis is to present and support the idea that the appropriate discount rate for local government is the opportunity cost of capital, which may vary significantly from the market or municipal bond rates.

Short-Term Investment

Investment analysis, as presented in previous sections of this chapter, has dealt with the expenditure of public funds in projects or programs that are expected to yield substantial benefits in future time periods. In addition to this major public investment function, local units of government can invest idle cash funds in short-term securities for the purpose of generating interest revenue.

This investment opportunity is created because of the inevitable variance that exists between revenues and expenditures during the fiscal year. At certain times, revenues will be received at a faster rate than expenditures are disbursed, and surplus cash will accumulate. At other times, the reverse will hold, and the surplus cash will diminish. When cash resources are insufficient to cover expenditures, local governments must borrow short-term money (for example, in anticipation of future tax receipts). Likewise, when excess cash exists, local governments can invest in short-term securities that earn interest revenue. Thus, cash management should be an element in the overall fiscal management system. Although practices vary among states and cities, and many local governments overlook short-term investment potential, there is evidence that local governments are becoming more active in this area.

Short-term securities are traded in the money market. There exists a number of markets for short-term securities (1 to 90 days) where individuals, banks, corporations, and governments (including the Federal Reserve Bank) participate in buying and selling money. Local banks provide local governments with services in this area; they buy and sell securities, provide timely investment advice, and hold the securities in safekeeping. Trading is normally carried out by the bank's "money man" and the appropriate local government official via the telephone; cash and securities need not be transported.

Short-term investments offer a high degree of safety and are considered to be essentially free of risk. The market includes both new and previously purchased (secondary) issues. Thus, the market offers investments of almost any size and duration—for a high degree of flexibility. For example, $300,000 invested for 90 days, $65,000 for 15 days, or any other short-term combination can be arranged because of the mix of securities on the market at any given time. The types of securities include United States Treasury obligations (U.S. Treasury Bills, Bonds, Notes, and Certificate of Indebtedness), federal agency issues (Federal, Intermediate Credit Banks, Banks for Cooperatives, Federal Land Banks, Federal Home Loan Banks, and Federal National Mortgage Association), savings and loan association shares, bank certificates of deposit and time deposits, and repurchase agreements (a simultaneous agreement to purchase a security at a given price and sell the security at a specific future time for a given price).

Given the existence of surplus cash at certain times in the fiscal year and a flexible short-term investment market, local governments should place considerable emphasis on an efficient cash management program. In establishing such a program, the first step involves investigating the state and local laws governing the investment of public monies. If necessary, local ordinances should be enacted to allow the finance or investment officer to invest surplus cash. The program should ensure both safety and liquidity. Speculation is prohibited; all persons and institutions that are involved in the program should be aware of security provisions (safekeeping, collateral, insurance, and bond requirements).

"Liquidity" is the ease and timeliness with which securities are converted to needed cash. A certain sum of cash should be retained to provide for normal fluctuations in cash requirements and emergencies; securities should be converted to cash as cash is needed. Finally, the objective of the cash program is to maximize the yield to local governments. In addition, some local governments prefer to invest in local institutions (such as banks or savings and loans) to make more money available for loans to local residents. Implementation of a cash investment program requires that the management system be aware of how much cash is available and for what period of time. The sum of cash available at any given time should be derived from the accounting system, or the accounting system should be so designed as to produce such information. Determination of the time that the cash will be available for investment purposes will depend on an analysis of previous patterns and trends in cash accumulation. Once the pattern has been established, the investment plan can be formulated. For example, a particular local government might find that it generally has $200,000 of cash surplus for five months after taxes are received, and an additional $80,000 for eleven months of the fiscal year. These funds could then be invested in the appropriate short-term securities. Large units of government with substantial sums of cash and varying durations may require an active day-by-day investment operation.

Example Problems

1. Find the future value (10 years hence) of $10,000 invested today at an interest rate of 6 percent per year (a) assuming annual compounding, (b) assuming quarterly compounding, and (c) assuming continuous compounding.

(a)
$$P_n = P_0 (1 + i)^n$$

$$P_{10} = 10,000 (1 + 0.06)^{10}$$

$$P_{10} = 17,908.00 \text{ (using Appendix A)}$$

(b) Six percent per year compounded quarterly for 10 years is equivalent to 1.5 percent per quarter compounded 40 times.

$$P_n = P_0 (1 + i)^n$$

$$P_{40} = 10,000 (1 + 0.015)^{40}$$

$$P_{40} = 10,000 \, (1.814)$$

$$P_{40} = 18,140.00$$

(c) $\quad P_n = P_0 e^z$, where $z = (n)(i)$

$$P_{10} = 10,000 e^{(10)(0.06)}$$

$$P_{10} = 10,000 \, (1.8221) \text{ (from Appendix B)}$$

$$P_{10} = 18,221.00$$

2. Given a discount rate of 0.10, find the present value of $1,000 received 15 years hence (a) assuming annual compounding and (b) assuming continuous compounding.

(a) annual

$$PV = P_n \left(\frac{1}{1 + i} \right)^n$$

$$PV = 1000 \; \overline{\frac{1}{1 + .10}}^{\,15}$$

$$PV = 1000 \, (0.2394) \text{ (from Appendix A)}$$

$$PV = 239.40$$

(b) continuous

$$PV = P_n e^{-z}, \text{ where } z = (n)(i)$$

$$PV = 1000 e^{(15)(0.10)}$$

$$PV = 1000 \, (0.2231) \text{ (from Appendix B)}$$

$$PV = 223.10$$

3. Given a discount rate of 7 percent and annual compounding, find the present value of an investment that requires an initial cost of $12,000 and returns $4,000 for each of five years.

	T_0	T_1	T_2	T_3	T_4	T_5	Total
Net	−12,000	+4,000	+4,000	+4,000	+4,000	+4,000	+8,000
PV	−12,000	+3,738	+3,494	+3,265	+3,052	+2,852	+4,401

Present value of the time stream is $4,401.

4. Find the IRR (internal rate of return) for the investment in problem 3.

	T_0	T_1	T_2	T_3	T_4	T_5	Total
	−12,000	+4,000	+4,000	+4,000	+4,000	+4,000	
PV@.07	−12,000	+3,738	+3,494	+3,265	+3,052	+2,852	+4,401
PV@.12	−12,000	+3,572	+3,189	+2,847	+2,542	+2,270	+2,420
PV@.20	−12,000	+3,333	+2,778	+2,315	+1,929	+1,608	−37

IRR is approximately 20 percent.

5. Assume that two mutually exclusive alternative investments have the following time streams:

	T_0	T_1	T_2	T_3	T_4
Alternative A	−500	−500	+200	+400	+700
Alternative B	−1,000	+700	+300	+100	+100

(a) Calculate the PV (at a discount rate of 6 percent) and IRR for each alternative:

$$PV_a = -500 + (0.9434)(-500) + (0.8900)(300) + (0.8396)(400) \\ + (0.7921)(700)$$

$$PV_a = -500 - 471 + 178 + 336 + 554$$

$$PV_a = +97$$

$$PV_b = -1000 + (0.9434)(700) + (0.8900)(300) + (0.8396)(100) \\ + (0.7921)(100)$$

$$PV_b = -1000 + 660 + 267 + 84 + 79$$

$$PV_b = +90$$

(A)	T_0	T_1	T_2	T_3	T_4	Total
	−500	−500	+200	+400	+700	
PV@0.10	−500	−455	+165	+301	+478	−11
PV@0.045	−500	−457	+166	+305	+487	+1

IRR_a is approximately 9.5 percent.

(B)	T_0	T_1	T_2	T_3	T_4	Total
	−1,000	+700	+300	+100	+100	
PV@0.10	−1,000	+636	+248	+75	+68	+27
PV@0.12	−1,000	+625	+239	+71	+64	−1

IRR_b is approximately 12 percent.

(b) Which, if any, project should be selected as "best"? Both alternatives exhibit a positive present value at a discount rate of 6 percent; both are economically desirable. Because they are mutually exclusive, only one can be selected. Alternative A exhibits the higher discounted present value, while alternative B exhibits the higher internal rate of return. This apparent conflict between criteria is illustrated in the following graph.

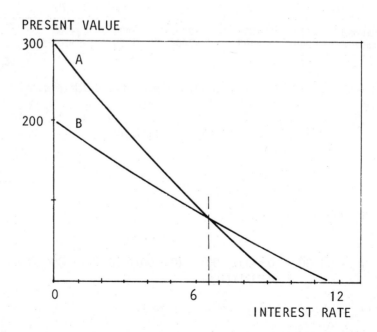

It appears that A has the highest PV up to approximately 6.5 percent, where B exhibits a higher PV. Therefore, the PV criterion at the appropriate opportunity cost of capital should be used. Below 6.5 percent, A is best; above that point, B is best. One might also consider financial feasibility in that A requires a larger initial investment than B.

References

James, L. Douglas, and Lee, Robert R. *Economics of Water Resources Planning*. New York: McGraw-Hill, 1971.

Jones, John A., and Howard, S. Kenneth. *Investment of Idle Funds by Local Governments: A Primer*. Washington: Municipal Finance Officers Association, 1973.

McKean, Roland N. *Efficiency in Government Through Systems Analysis*. New York: Wiley, 1958.

$$n, (1 + i)^n, \left(\frac{1}{1 + i} \right)^n \text{ for } n = 1 \text{ to } 50, i = 0.01 \text{ to } 0.20$$

n	i = .010		i = .015		i = .020		i = .025	
1	1.0100	.9901	1.0150	.9852	1.0200	.9804	1.0250	.9756
2	1.0201	.9803	1.0302	.9707	1.0404	.9612	1.0506	.9518
3	1.0303	.9706	1.0457	.9563	1.0612	.9423	1.0769	.9286
4	1.0406	.9610	1.0614	.9422	1.0824	.9238	1.1038	.9060
5	1.0510	.9515	1.0773	.9283	1.1041	.9057	1.1314	.8839
6	1.0615	.9420	1.0934	.9145	1.1262	.8880	1.1597	.8623
7	1.0721	.9327	1.1098	.9010	1.1487	.8706	1.1887	.8413
8	1.0829	.9235	1.1265	.8877	1.1717	.8535	1.2184	.8207
9	1.0937	.9143	1.1434	.8746	1.1951	.8368	1.2489	.8007
10	1.1046	.9053	1.1605	.8617	1.2190	.8203	1.2801	.7812
11	1.1157	.8963	1.1779	.8489	1.2434	.8043	1.3121	.7621
12	1.1268	.8874	1.1956	.8364	1.2682	.7885	1.3449	.7436
13	1.1381	.8787	1.2136	.8240	1.2936	.7730	1.3785	.7254
14	1.1495	.8700	1.2318	.8118	1.3195	.7579	1.4130	.7077
15	1.1610	.8613	1.2502	.7999	1.3459	.7430	1.4483	.6905
16	1.1726	.8528	1.2690	.7880	1.3728	.7284	1.4845	.6736
17	1.1843	.8444	1.2880	.7764	1.4002	.7142	1.5216	.6572
18	1.1961	.8360	1.3073	.7649	1.4282	.7002	1.5597	.6412
19	1.2081	.8277	1.3270	.7536	1.4568	.6864	1.5986	.6255
20	1.2202	.8195	1.3469	.7425	1.4859	.6730	1.6386	.6103
21	1.2324	.8114	1.3671	.7315	1.5157	.6598	1.6796	.5954
22	1.2447	.8034	1.3876	.7207	1.5460	.6468	1.7216	.5809
23	1.2572	.7954	1.4084	.7100	1.5769	.6342	1.7646	.5667
24	1.2697	.7876	1.4295	.6995	1.6084	.6217	1.8087	.5529
25	1.2824	.7798	1.4509	.6892	1.6406	.6095	1.8539	.5394
26	1.2953	.7720	1.4727	.6790	1.6734	.5976	1.9003	.5262
27	1.3082	.7644	1.4948	.6690	1.7069	.5859	1.9478	.5134
28	1.3213	.7568	1.5172	.6591	1.7410	.5744	1.9965	.5009
29	1.3345	.7493	1.5400	.6494	1.7758	.5631	2.0464	.4887
30	1.3478	.7419	1.5631	.6398	1.8114	.5521	2.0976	.4767
35	1.4166	.7059	1.6839	.5939	1.9999	.5000	2.3732	.4214
40	1.4889	.6717	1.8140	.5513	2.2080	.4529	2.6851	.3724
45	1.5648	.6391	1.9542	.5117	2.4379	.4102	3.0379	.3292
50	1.6446	.6080	2.1052	.4750	2.6916	.3715	3.4371	.2909

n	i = .030		i = .035		i = .040		i = .045	
1	1.0300	.9709	1.0350	.9662	1.0400	.9615	1.0450	.9569
2	1.0609	.9426	1.0712	.9335	1.0816	.9246	1.0920	.9157
3	1.0927	.9151	1.1087	.9019	1.1249	.8890	1.1412	.8763
4	1.1255	.8885	1.1475	.8714	1.1699	.8548	1.1925	.8386
5	1.1593	.8626	1.1877	.8420	1.2167	.8219	1.2462	.8025
6	1.1941	.8375	1.2293	.8135	1.2653	.7903	1.3023	.7679
7	1.2299	.8131	1.2723	.7860	1.3159	.7599	1.3609	.7348
8	1.2668	.7894	1.3168	.7594	1.3686	.7307	1.4221	.7032
9	1.3048	.7664	1.3629	.7337	1.4233	.7026	1.4861	.6729
10	1.3439	.7441	1.4106	.7089	1.4802	.6756	1.5530	.6439
11	1.3842	.7224	1.4600	.6849	1.5395	.6496	1.6229	.6162
12	1.4258	.7014	1.5111	.6618	1.6010	.6246	1.6959	.5897
13	1.4685	.6810	1.5640	.6394	1.6651	.6006	1.7722	.5643
14	1.5126	.6611	1.6187	.6178	1.7317	.5775	1.8519	.5400
15	1.5580	.6419	1.6753	.5969	1.8009	.5553	1.9353	.5167
16	1.6047	.6232	1.7340	.5767	1.8730	.5339	2.0224	.4945
17	1.6528	.6050	1.7947	.5572	1.9479	.5134	2.1134	.4732
18	1.7024	.5874	1.8575	.5384	2.0258	.4936	2.2085	.4528
19	1.7535	.5703	1.9225	.5202	2.1068	.4746	2.3079	.4333
20	1.8061	.5537	1.9898	.5026	2.1911	.4564	2.4117	.4146
21	1.8603	.5375	2.0594	.4856	2.2788	.4388	2.5202	.3968
22	1.9161	.5219	2.1315	.4692	2.3699	.4220	2.6337	.3797
23	1.9736	.5067	2.2061	.4533	2.4647	.4057	2.7522	.3634
24	2.0328	.4919	2.2833	.4380	2.5633	.3901	2.8760	.3477
25	2.0938	.4776	2.3632	.4231	2.6658	.3751	3.0054	.3327
26	2.1566	.4637	2.4460	.4088	2.7725	.3607	3.1407	.3184
27	2.2213	.4502	2.5316	.3950	2.8834	.3468	3.2820	.3047
28	2.2879	.4371	2.6202	.3817	2.9987	.3335	3.4297	.2916
29	2.3566	.4243	2.7119	.3687	3.1187	.3207	3.5840	.2790
30	2.4273	.4120	2.8068	.3563	3.2434	.3083	3.7453	.2670
35	2.8139	.3554	3.3336	.3000	3.9461	.2534	4.6673	.2143
40	3.2620	.3066	3.9593	.2526	4.8010	.2083	5.8164	.1719
45	3.7816	.2644	4.7024	.2127	5.8412	.1712	7.2482	.1380
50	4.3839	.2281	5.5849	.1791	7.1067	.1407	9.0326	.1107

n	i = .050		i = .055		i = .060		i = .065	
1	1.0500	.9524	1.0550	.9479	1.0600	.9434	1.0650	.9390
2	1.1025	.9070	1.1130	.8985	1.1236	.8900	1.1342	.8817
3	1.1576	.8638	1.1742	.8516	1.1910	.8396	1.2079	.8278
4	1.2155	.8227	1.2388	.8072	1.2625	.7921	1.2865	.7773
5	1.2763	.7835	1.3070	.7651	1.3382	.7473	1.3701	.7299
6	1.3401	.7462	1.3788	.7252	1.4185	.7050	1.4591	.6853
7	1.4071	.7107	1.4547	.6874	1.5036	.6651	1.5540	.6435
8	1.4775	.6768	1.5347	.6516	1.5938	.6274	1.6550	.6042
9	1.5513	.6446	1.6191	.6176	1.6895	.5919	1.7626	.5674
10	1.6289	.6139	1.7081	.5854	1.7908	.5584	1.8771	.5327
11	1.7103	.5847	1.8021	.5549	1.8983	.5268	1.9992	.5002
12	1.7959	.5568	1.9012	.5260	2.0122	.4970	2.1291	.4697
13	1.8856	.5303	2.0058	.4986	2.1329	.4688	2.2675	.4410
14	1.9799	.5051	2.1161	.4726	2.2609	.4423	2.4149	.4141
15	2.0789	.4810	2.2325	.4479	2.3966	.4173	2.5718	.3888
16	2.1829	.4581	2.3553	.4246	2.5404	.3936	2.7390	.3651
17	2.2920	.4363	2.4848	.4024	2.6928	.3714	2.9170	.3428
18	2.4066	.4155	2.6215	.3815	2.8543	.3503	3.1067	.3219
19	2.5270	.3957	2.7656	.3616	3.0256	.3305	3.3086	.3022
20	2.6533	.3769	2.9178	.3427	3.2071	.3118	3.5236	.2838
21	2.7860	.3589	3.0782	.3249	3.3996	.2942	3.7527	.2665
22	2.9253	.3418	3.2475	.3079	3.6035	.2775	3.9966	.2502
23	3.0715	.3256	3.4262	.2919	3.8197	.2618	4.2564	.2349
24	3.2251	.3101	3.6146	.2767	4.0489	.2470	4.5331	.2206
25	3.3864	.2953	3.8134	.2622	4.2919	.2330	4.8277	.2071
26	3.5557	.2812	4.0231	.2486	4.5494	.2198	5.1415	.1945
27	3.7335	.2678	4.2444	.2356	4.8223	.2074	5.4757	.1826
28	3.9201	.2551	4.4778	.2233	5.1117	.1956	5.8316	.1715
29	4.1161	.2429	4.7241	.2117	5.4184	.1846	6.2107	.1610
30	4.3219	.2314	4.9840	.2006	5.7435	.1741	6.6144	.1512
35	5.5160	.1813	6.5138	.1535	7.6861	.1301	9.0623	.1103
40	7.0400	.1420	8.5133	.1175	10.2857	.0972	12.4161	.0805
45	8.9850	.1113	11.1266	.0899	13.7646	.0727	17.0111	.0588
50	11.4674	.0872	14.5420	.0688	18.4201	.0543	23.3067	.0429

n	i = .070		n	i = .075		n	i = .080		n	i = .085	
1	1.0700	.9346	1	1.0750	.9302	1	1.0800	.9259	1	1.0850	.9217
2	1.1449	.8734	2	1.1556	.8653	2	1.1664	.8573	2	1.1772	.8495
3	1.2250	.8163	3	1.2423	.8050	3	1.2597	.7938	3	1.2773	.7829
4	1.3108	.7629	4	1.3355	.7488	4	1.3605	.7350	4	1.3859	.7216
5	1.4026	.7130	5	1.4356	.6966	5	1.4693	.6806	5	1.5037	.6650
6	1.5007	.6663	6	1.5433	.6480	6	1.5869	.6302	6	1.6315	.6129
7	1.6058	.6227	7	1.6590	.6028	7	1.7138	.5835	7	1.7701	.5649
8	1.7182	.5820	8	1.7835	.5607	8	1.8509	.5403	8	1.9206	.5207
9	1.8385	.5439	9	1.9172	.5216	9	1.9990	.5002	9	2.0839	.4799
10	1.9672	.5083	10	2.0610	.4852	10	2.1589	.4632	10	2.2610	.4423
11	2.1049	.4751	11	2.2156	.4513	11	2.3316	.4289	11	2.4532	.4076
12	2.2522	.4440	12	2.3818	.4199	12	2.5182	.3971	12	2.6617	.3757
13	2.4098	.4150	13	2.5604	.3906	13	2.7196	.3677	13	2.8879	.3463
14	2.5785	.3878	14	2.7524	.3633	14	2.9372	.3405	14	3.1334	.3191
15	2.7590	.3624	15	2.9589	.3380	15	3.1722	.3152	15	3.3997	.2941
16	2.9522	.3387	16	3.1808	.3144	16	3.4259	.2919	16	3.6887	.2711
17	3.1588	.3166	17	3.4194	.2925	17	3.7000	.2703	17	4.0023	.2499
18	3.3799	.2959	18	3.6758	.2720	18	3.9960	.2502	18	4.3425	.2303
19	3.6165	.2765	19	3.9515	.2551	19	4.3157	.2317	19	4.7116	.2122
20	3.8697	.2584	20	4.2479	.2354	20	4.6610	.2145	20	5.1120	.1956
21	4.1406	.2415	21	4.5664	.2190	21	5.0338	.1987	21	5.5466	.1803
22	4.4304	.2257	22	4.9089	.2037	22	5.4365	.1839	22	6.0180	.1662
23	4.7405	.2109	23	5.2771	.1895	23	5.8715	.1703	23	6.5296	.1531
24	5.0724	.1971	24	5.6729	.1763	24	6.3412	.1577	24	7.0846	.1412
25	5.4274	.1842	25	6.0983	.1640	25	6.8485	.1460	25	7.6868	.1301
26	5.8074	.1722	26	6.5557	.1525	26	7.3964	.1352	26	8.3401	.1199
27	6.2139	.1609	27	7.0474	.1419	27	7.9881	.1252	27	9.0490	.1105
28	6.6488	.1504	28	7.5759	.1320	28	8.6271	.1159	28	9.8182	.1019
29	7.1143	.1406	29	8.1441	.1228	29	9.3173	.1073	29	10.6528	.0939
30	7.6123	.1314	30	8.7550	.1142	30	10.0627	.0994	30	11.5582	.0865
35	10.6766	.0937	35	12.5689	.0796	35	14.7853	.0676	35	17.3796	.0575
40	14.9745	.0668	40	18.0442	.0554	40	21.7245	.0460	40	26.1330	.0383
45	21.0024	.0476	45	25.9048	.0386	45	31.9204	.0313	45	39.2951	.0254
50	29.4570	.0339	50	37.1897	.0269	50	46.9016	.0213	50	59.0863	.0169

n	i = .090		n	i = .095		n	i = .100		n	i = .105	
1	1.0900	.9174	1	1.0950	.9132	1	1.1000	.9091	1	1.1050	.9050
2	1.1881	.8417	2	1.1990	.8340	2	1.2100	.8264	2	1.2210	.8190
3	1.2950	.7722	3	1.3129	.7617	3	1.3310	.7513	3	1.3492	.7412
4	1.4116	.7084	4	1.4377	.6956	4	1.4641	.6830	4	1.4909	.6707
5	1.5386	.6499	5	1.5742	.6352	5	1.6105	.6209	5	1.6474	.6070
6	1.6771	.5963	6	1.7238	.5801	6	1.7716	.5645	6	1.8204	.5493
7	1.8280	.5470	7	1.8876	.5298	7	1.9487	.5132	7	2.0116	.4971
8	1.9926	.5019	8	2.0669	.4838	8	2.1436	.4665	8	2.2228	.4499
9	2.1719	.4604	9	2.2632	.4418	9	2.3579	.4241	9	2.4562	.4071
10	2.3674	.4224	10	2.4782	.4035	10	2.5937	.3855	10	2.7141	.3684
11	2.5804	.3875	11	2.7137	.3685	11	2.8531	.3505	11	2.9991	.3334
12	2.8127	.3555	12	2.9715	.3365	12	3.1384	.3186	12	3.3140	.3018
13	3.0658	.3262	13	3.2537	.3073	13	3.4523	.2897	13	3.6619	.2731
14	3.3417	.2992	14	3.5629	.2807	14	3.7975	.2633	14	4.0464	.2471
15	3.6425	.2745	15	3.9013	.2563	15	4.1772	.2394	15	4.4713	.2236
16	3.9703	.2519	16	4.2719	.2341	16	4.5950	.2176	16	4.9408	.2024
17	4.3276	.2311	17	4.6778	.2138	17	5.0545	.1978	17	5.4596	.1832
18	4.7171	.2120	18	5.1222	.1952	18	5.5599	.1799	18	6.0328	.1658
19	5.1417	.1945	19	5.6088	.1783	19	6.1159	.1635	19	6.6663	.1500
20	5.6044	.1784	20	6.1416	.1628	20	6.7275	.1486	20	7.3662	.1358
21	6.1088	.1637	21	6.7251	.1487	21	7.4002	.1351	21	8.1397	.1229
22	6.6586	.1502	22	7.3639	.1358	22	8.1403	.1228	22	8.9944	.1112
23	7.2579	.1378	23	8.0635	.1240	23	8.9543	.1117	23	9.9388	.1006
24	7.9111	.1264	24	8.8296	.1133	24	9.8497	.1015	24	10.9823	.0911
25	8.6231	.1160	25	9.6684	.1034	25	10.8347	.0923	25	12.1355	.0824
26	9.3992	.1064	26	10.5869	.0945	26	11.9182	.0839	26	13.4097	.0746
27	10.2451	.0976	27	11.5926	.0863	27	13.1100	.0763	27	14.8177	.0675
28	11.1671	.0895	28	12.6939	.0788	28	14.4210	.0693	28	16.3736	.0611
29	12.1722	.0822	29	13.8998	.0719	29	15.8631	.0630	29	18.0928	.0553
30	13.2677	.0754	30	15.2203	.0657	30	17.4494	.0573	30	19.9926	.0500
35	20.4140	.0490	35	23.9604	.0417	35	28.1024	.0356	35	32.9367	.0304
40	31.4094	.0318	40	37.7194	.0265	40	45.2592	.0221	40	54.2614	.0184
45	48.3273	.0207	45	59.3793	.0168	45	72.8905	.0137	45	89.3928	.0112
50	74.3575	.0134	50	93.4773	.0107	50	117.3908	.0085	50..	147.2698	.0068

n	i = .110		i = .115		i = .120		i = .125	
1	1.1100	.9009	1.1150	.8969	1.1200	.8929	1.1250	.8889
2	1.2321	.8116	1.2432	.8044	1.2544	.7972	1.2656	.7901
3	1.3676	.7312	1.3862	.7214	1.4049	.7118	1.4238	.7023
4	1.5181	.6587	1.5456	.6470	1.5735	.6355	1.6018	.6243
5	1.6851	.5935	1.7234	.5803	1.7623	.5674	1.8020	.5549
6	1.8704	.5346	1.9215	.5204	1.9738	.5066	2.0273	.4933
7	2.0762	.4817	2.1425	.4667	2.2107	.4523	2.2807	.4385
8	2.3045	.4339	2.3889	.4186	2.4760	.4039	2.5658	.3897
9	2.5580	.3909	2.6636	.3754	2.7731	.3606	2.8865	.3464
10	2.8394	.3522	2.9699	.3367	3.1058	.3220	3.2473	.3079
11	3.1518	.3173	3.3115	.3020	3.4785	.2875	3.6532	.2737
12	3.4985	.2858	3.6923	.2708	3.8960	.2567	4.1099	.2433
13	3.8833	.2575	4.1169	.2429	4.3635	.2292	4.6236	.2163
14	4.3104	.2320	4.5904	.2178	4.8871	.2046	5.2016	.1922
15	4.7846	.2090	5.1183	.1954	5.4736	.1827	5.8518	.1709
16	5.3109	.1883	5.7069	.1752	6.1304	.1631	6.5833	.1519
17	5.8951	.1696	6.3632	.1572	6.8660	.1456	7.4062	.1350
18	6.5436	.1528	7.0949	.1409	7.6900	.1300	8.3319	.1200
19	7.2633	.1377	7.9108	.1264	8.6128	.1161	9.3734	.1067
20	8.0623	.1240	8.8206	.1134	9.6463	.1037	10.5451	.0948
21	8.9492	.1117	9.8350	.1017	10.8038	.0926	11.8632	.0843
22	9.9336	.1007	10.9660	.0912	12.1003	.0826	13.3461	.0749
23	11.0263	.0907	12.2271	.0818	13.5523	.0738	15.0144	.0666
24	12.2392	.0817	13.6332	.0734	15.1786	.0659	16.8912	.0592
25	13.5855	.0736	15.2010	.0658	17.0001	.0588	19.0026	.0526
26	15.0799	.0663	16.9491	.0590	19.0401	.0525	21.3779	.0468
27	16.7386	.0597	18.8982	.0529	21.3249	.0469	24.0502	.0416
28	18.5799	.0538	21.0715	.0475	23.8839	.0419	27.0564	.0370
29	20.6237	.0485	23.4948	.0426	26.7499	.0374	30.4385	.0329
30	22.8923	.0437	26.1967	.0382	29.9599	.0334	34.2433	.0292
35	38.5749	.0259	45.1461	.0222	52.7996	.0189	61.7075	.0162
40	65.0009	.0154	77.8027	.0129	93.0509	.0107	111.1990	.0090
45	109.5302	.0091	134.0815	.0075	163.9875	.0061	200.3842	.0050
50	184.5648	.0054	231.0698	.0043	289.0021	.0035	361.0989	.0028

286

i = .130

n		
1	1.1300	.8850
2	1.2769	.7831
3	1.4429	.6931
4	1.6305	.6133
5	1.8424	.5428
6	2.0820	.4803
7	2.3526	.4251
8	2.6584	.3762
9	3.0040	.3329
10	3.3946	.2946
11	3.8359	.2607
12	4.3345	.2307
13	4.8980	.2042
14	5.5348	.1807
15	6.2543	.1599
16	7.0673	.1415
17	7.9861	.1252
18	9.0243	.1108
19	10.1974	.0981
20	11.5231	.0868
21	13.0211	.0768
22	14.7138	.0680
23	16.6266	.0601
24	18.7881	.0532
25	21.2305	.0471
26	23.9905	.0417
27	27.1093	.0369
28	30.6335	.0326
29	34.6158	.0289
30	39.1159	.0256
35	72.0685	.0139
40	132.7815	.0075
45	244.6414	.0041
50	450.7358	.0022

i = .135

n		
1	1.1350	.8811
2	1.2882	.7763
3	1.4621	.6839
4	1.6595	.6026
5	1.8836	.5309
6	2.1378	.4678
7	2.4264	.4121
8	2.7540	.3631
9	3.1258	.3199
10	3.5478	.2819
11	4.0267	.2483
12	4.5704	.2188
13	5.1874	.1928
14	5.8877	.1698
15	6.6825	.1496
16	7.5846	.1318
17	8.6085	.1162
18	9.7707	.1023
19	11.0897	.0902
20	12.5869	.0794
21	14.2861	.0700
22	16.2147	.0617
23	18.4037	.0543
24	20.8882	.0479
25	23.7081	.0422
26	26.9087	.0372
27	30.5413	.0327
28	34.6644	.0288
29	39.3441	.0254
30	44.6556	.0224
35	84.1114	.0119
40	158.4289	.0063
45	298.4102	.0034
50	562.0732	.0018

i = .140

n		
1	1.1400	.8772
2	1.2996	.7695
3	1.4815	.6750
4	1.6890	.5921
5	1.9254	.5194
6	2.1950	.4556
7	2.5023	.3996
8	2.8526	.3506
9	3.2519	.3075
10	3.7072	.2697
11	4.2262	.2366
12	4.8179	.2076
13	5.4924	.1821
14	6.2613	.1597
15	7.1379	.1401
16	8.1372	.1229
17	9.2765	.1078
18	10.5752	.0946
19	12.0557	.0829
20	13.7435	.0728
21	15.6676	.0638
22	17.8610	.0560
23	20.3616	.0491
24	23.2122	.0431
25	26.4619	.0378
26	30.1666	.0331
27	34.3899	.0291
28	39.2045	.0255
29	44.6931	.0224
30	50.9501	.0196
35	98.1001	.0102
40	188.8834	.0053
45	363.6789	.0027
59	700.2326	.0014

i = .145

n		
1	1.1450	.8734
2	1.3110	.7628
3	1.5011	.6662
4	1.7188	.5818
5	1.9680	.5081
6	2.2534	.4438
7	2.5801	.3876
8	2.9542	.3385
9	3.3826	.2956
10	3.8731	.2582
11	4.4347	.2255
12	5.0777	.1969
13	5.8140	.1720
14	6.6570	.1502
15	7.6222	.1312
16	8.7275	.1146
17	9.9929	.1001
18	11.4419	.0874
19	13.1010	.0763
20	15.0006	.0667
21	17.1757	.0582
22	19.6662	.0508
23	22.5178	.0444
24	25.7829	.0388
25	29.5214	.0339
26	33.8020	.0296
27	38.7033	.0258
28	44.3153	.0226
29	50.7410	.0197
30	58.0985	.0172
35	114.3384	.0087
40	225.0191	.0044
45	442.8400	.0023
50	871.5138	.0011

n	i = .150		i = .155		i = .160		i = .165	
1	1.1500	.8696	1.1550	.8658	1.1600	.8621	1.1650	.8584
2	1.3225	.7561	1.3340	.7496	1.3456	.7432	1.3572	.7368
3	1.5209	.6575	1.5408	.6490	1.5609	.6407	1.5812	.6324
4	1.7490	.5718	1.7796	.5619	1.8106	.5523	1.8421	.5429
5	2.0114	.4972	2.0555	.4865	2.1003	.4761	2.1460	.4660
6	2.3131	.4323	2.3741	.4212	2.4364	.4104	2.5001	.4000
7	2.6600	.3759	2.7420	.3647	2.8262	.3538	2.9126	.3433
8	3.0590	.3269	3.1671	.3158	3.2784	.3050	3.3932	.2947
9	3.5179	.2843	3.6580	.2734	3.8030	.2630	3.9531	.2530
10	4.0456	.2472	4.2249	.2367	4.4114	.2267	4.6053	.2171
11	4.6524	.2149	4.8798	.2049	5.1173	.1954	5.3652	.1864
12	5.3502	.1869	5.6362	.1774	5.9360	.1685	6.2504	.1600
13	6.1528	.1625	6.5098	.1536	6.8858	.1452	7.2818	.1373
14	7.0757	.1413	7.5188	.1330	7.9875	.1252	8.4833	.1179
15	8.1371	.1229	8.6842	.1152	9.2655	.1079	9.8830	.1012
16	9.3576	.1069	10.0302	.0997	10.7480	.0930	11.5137	.0869
17	10.7613	.0929	11.5849	.0863	12.4677	.0802	13.4135	.0746
18	12.3755	.0808	13.3806	.0747	14.4625	.0691	15.6267	.0640
19	14.2318	.0703	15.4546	.0647	16.7765	.0596	18.2051	.0549
20	16.3665	.0611	17.8501	.0560	19.4608	.0514	21.2089	.0471
21	18.8215	.0531	20.6168	.0485	22.5745	.0443	24.7084	.0405
22	21.6447	.0462	23.8124	.0420	26.1864	.0382	28.7853	.0347
23	24.8915	.0402	27.5033	.0364	30.3762	.0329	33.5348	.0298
24	28.6252	.0349	31.7664	.0315	35.2364	.0284	39.0681	.0256
25	32.9189	.0304	36.6901	.0273	40.8742	.0245	45.5143	.0220
26	37.8568	.0264	42.3771	.0236	47.4141	.0211	53.0242	.0189
27	43.5353	.0230	48.9456	.0204	55.0004	.0182	61.7732	.0162
28	50.0656	.0200	56.5321	.0177	63.8004	.0157	71.9657	.0139
29	57.5754	.0174	65.2946	.0153	74.0085	.0135	83.8401	.0119
30	66.2118	.0151	75.4153	.0133	85.8499	.0116	97.6737	.0102
35	133.1755	.0075	155.0134	.0065	180.3141	.0055	209.6077	.0048
40	267.8635	.0037	318.6245	.0031	378.7211	.0026	449.8181	.0022
45	538.7691	.0019	654.9212	.0015	795.4437	.0013	965.3093	.0010
50	1083.6570	.0009	1346.1670	.0007	1670.7036	.0006	2071.5533	.0005

i = .170			i = .175			i = .180			i = .185		
1	1.1700	.8547	1	1.1750	.8511	1	1.1800	.8475	1	1.1850	.8439
2	1.3689	.7305	2	1.3806	.7243	2	1.3924	.7182	2	1.4042	.7121
3	1.6016	.6244	3	1.6222	.6164	3	1.6430	.6086	3	1.6640	.6010
4	1.8739	.5337	4	1.9061	.5246	4	1.9388	.5158	4	1.9718	.5071
5	2.1924	.4561	5	2.2397	.4465	5	2.2878	.4371	5	2.3366	.4280
6	2.5652	.3898	6	2.6316	.3800	6	2.6996	.3704	6	2.7689	.3612
7	3.0012	.3332	7	3.0922	.3234	7	3.1855	.3139	7	3.2812	.3048
8	3.5115	.2848	8	3.6333	.2752	8	3.7589	.2660	8	3.8882	.2572
9	4.1084	.2434	9	4.2691	.2342	9	4.4355	.2255	9	4.6075	.2170
10	4.8068	.2080	10	5.0162	.1994	10	5.2338	.1911	10	5.4599	.1832
11	5.6240	.1778	11	5.8941	.1697	11	6.1759	.1619	11	6.4700	.1546
12	6.5801	.1520	12	6.9256	.1444	12	7.2876	.1372	12	7.6669	.1304
13	7.6987	.1299	13	8.1375	.1229	13	8.5994	.1163	13	9.0853	.1101
14	9.0075	.1110	14	9.5616	.1046	14	10.1472	.0985	14	10.7661	.0929
15	10.5387	.0949	15	11.2349	.0890	15	11.9737	.0835	15	12.7578	.0784
16	12.3303	.0811	16	13.2010	.0758	16	14.1290	.0708	16	15.1180	.0661
17	14.4265	.0693	17	15.5111	.0645	17	16.6722	.0600	17	17.9148	.0558
18	16.8789	.0592	18	18.2256	.0549	18	19.6732	.0508	18	21.2290	.0471
19	19.7484	.0506	19	21.4151	.0467	19	23.2144	.0431	19	25.1564	.0398
20	23.1056	.0433	20	25.1627	.0397	20	27.3930	.0365	20	29.8103	.0335
21	27.0335	.0370	21	29.5662	.0338	21	32.3238	.0309	21	35.3253	.0283
22	31.6292	.0316	22	34.7403	.0288	22	38.1421	.0262	22	41.8604	.0239
23	37.0062	.0270	23	40.8198	.0245	23	45.0076	.0222	23	49.6046	.0202
24	43.2973	.0231	24	47.9633	.0208	24	53.1090	.0188	24	58.7815	.0170
25	50.6578	.0197	25	56.3568	.0177	25	62.6686	.0160	25	69.6560	.0144
26	59.2696	.0169	26	66.2193	.0151	26	73.9490	.0135	26	82.5424	.0121
27	69.3455	.0144	27	77.8077	.0129	27	87.2598	.0115	27	97.8127	.0102
28	81.1342	.0123	28	91.4240	.0109	28	102.9665	.0097	28	115.9081	.0086
29	94.9270	.0105	29	107.4232	.0093	29	121.5005	.0082	29	137.3511	.0073
30	111.0646	.0090	30	126.2223	.0079	30	143.3706	.0070	30	162.7610	.0061
35	243.5034	.0041	35	282.6997	.0035	35	327.9972	.0030	35	380.3138	.0026
40	533.8685	.0019	40	633.1617	.0016	40	750.3781	.0013	40	888.6563	.0011
45	1170.4788	.0009	45	1418.0905	.0007	45	1716.6834	.0006	45	2076.4695	.0005
50	2566.2138	.0004	50	3176.0935	.0003	50	3927.3556	.0003	50	4851.9609	.0002

n	i = .190		i = .195		i = .200	
1	1.1900	.8403	1.1950	.8368	1.2000	.8333
2	1.4161	.7062	1.4280	.7003	1.4400	.6944
3	1.6852	.5934	1.7065	.5860	1.7280	.5787
4	2.0053	.4987	2.0393	.4904	2.0736	.4823
5	2.3864	.4190	2.4369	.4104	2.4883	.4019
6	2.8398	.3521	2.9121	.3434	2.9860	.3349
7	3.3793	.2959	3.4800	.2874	3.5832	.2791
8	4.0214	.2487	4.1586	.2405	4.2998	.2326
9	4.7854	.2090	4.9695	.2012	5.1598	.1938
10	5.6947	.1756	5.9385	.1684	6.1917	.1615
11	6.7767	.1476	7.0965	.1409	7.4301	.1346
12	8.0642	.1240	8.4804	.1179	8.9161	.1122
13	9.5964	.1042	10.1340	.0987	10.6993	.0935
14	11.4198	.0876	12.1102	.0826	12.8392	.0779
15	13.5895	.0736	14.4717	.0691	15.4070	.0649
16	16.1715	.0618	17.2936	.0578	18.4884	.0541
17	19.2441	.0520	20.6659	.0484	22.1861	.0451
18	22.9005	.0437	24.6958	.0405	26.6233	.0376
19	27.2516	.0367	29.5114	.0339	31.9480	.0313
20	32.4294	.0308	35.2662	.0284	38.3376	.0261
21	38.5910	.0259	42.1430	.0237	46.0051	.0217
22	45.9233	.0218	50.3609	.0199	55.2061	.0181
23	54.6487	.0183	60.1813	.0166	66.2474	.0151
24	65.0320	.0154	71.9167	.0139	79.4968	.0126
25	77.3881	.0129	85.9404	.0116	95.3962	.0105
26	92.0918	.0109	102.6988	.0097	114.4754	.0087
27	109.5892	.0091	122.7251	.0081	137.3705	.0073
28	130.4112	.0077	146.6565	.0068	164.8446	.0061
29	155.1893	.0064	175.2545	.0057	197.8135	.0051
30	184.6753	.0054	209.4291	.0048	237.3762	.0042
35	440.7006	.0023	510.3600	.0020	590.6680	.0017
40	1051.6674	.0010	1243.7014	.0008	1469.7710	.0007
45	2509.6504	.0004	3030.7884	.0003	3657.2603	.0003
50	5988.9133	.0002	7385.7590	.0001	9100.4336	.0001

e, e^z, e^{-z} for $e = 0.01$ to 10.00

x	e^x	e^{-x}
.01	1.0101	.9900
.02	1.0202	.9802
.03	1.0305	.9704
.04	1.0408	.9608
.05	1.0513	.9512
.06	1.0618	.9418
.07	1.0725	.9324
.08	1.0833	.9231
.09	1.0942	.9139
.10	1.1052	.9048
.11	1.1163	.8958
.12	1.1275	.8869
.13	1.1388	.8781
.14	1.1503	.8694
.15	1.1618	.8607
.16	1.1735	.8521
.17	1.1853	.8437
.18	1.1972	.8353
.19	1.2092	.8270
.20	1.2214	.8187
.21	1.2337	.8106
.22	1.2461	.8025
.23	1.2586	.7945
.24	1.2712	.7866
.25	1.2840	.7788
.26	1.2969	.7711
.27	1.3100	.7634
.28	1.3231	.7558
.29	1.3364	.7483
.30	1.3499	.7408
.31	1.3634	.7334
.32	1.3771	.7261
.33	1.3910	.7189
.34	1.4049	.7118
.35	1.4191	.7047
.36	1.4333	.6977
.37	1.4477	.6907
.38	1.4623	.6839
.39	1.4770	.6771
.40	1.4918	.6703
.41	1.5068	.6637
.42	1.5220	.6570
.43	1.5373	.6505
.44	1.5527	.6440
.45	1.5683	.6376
.46	1.5841	.6313
.47	1.6000	.6250
.48	1.6161	.6188
.49	1.6323	.6126
.50	1.6487	.6065
.51	1.6653	.6005
.52	1.6820	.5945
.53	1.6989	.5886
.54	1.7160	.5827
.55	1.7333	.5769
.56	1.7507	.5712
.57	1.7683	.5655
.58	1.7860	.5599
.59	1.8040	.5543
.60	1.8221	.5488
.61	1.8404	.5434
.62	1.8589	.5379
.63	1.8776	.5326
.64	1.8965	.5273
.65	1.9155	.5220
.66	1.9348	.5169
.67	1.9542	.5117
.68	1.9739	.5066
.69	1.9937	.5016
.70	2.0138	.4966
.71	2.0340	.4916
.72	2.0544	.4868
.73	2.0751	.4819
.74	2.0959	.4771
.75	2.1170	.4724
.76	2.1383	.4677
.77	2.1598	.4630
.78	2.1815	.4584
.79	2.2034	.4538
.80	2.2255	.4493
.81	2.2479	.4449
.82	2.2705	.4404
.83	2.2933	.4360
.84	2.3164	.4317
.85	2.3396	.4274
.86	2.3632	.4232
.87	2.3869	.4190
.88	2.4109	.4148
.89	2.4351	.4107
.90	2.4596	.4066
.91	2.4843	.4025
.92	2.5093	.3985
.93	2.5345	.3946
.94	2.5600	.3906
.95	2.5857	.3867
.96	2.6117	.3829
.97	2.6379	.3791
.98	2.6645	.3753
.99	2.6912	.3716
1.00	2.7183	.3679
1.01	2.7456	.3642
1.02	2.7732	.3606
1.03	2.8011	.3570
1.04	2.8292	.3535
1.05	2.8577	.3499
1.06	2.8864	.3465
1.07	2.9154	.3430
1.08	2.9447	.3396
1.09	2.9743	.3362
1.10	3.0042	.3329
1.11	3.0344	.3296
1.12	3.0649	.3263
1.13	3.0957	.3230
1.14	3.1268	.3198
1.15	3.1582	.3166
1.16	3.1899	.3135
1.17	3.2220	.3104
1.18	3.2544	.3073
1.19	3.2871	.3042
1.20	3.3201	.3012
1.21	3.3535	.2982
1.22	3.3872	.2952
1.23	3.4212	.2923
1.24	3.4556	.2894
1.25	3.4903	.2865
1.26	3.5254	.2837
1.27	3.5609	.2808
1.28	3.5966	.2780
1.29	3.6328	.2753
1.30	3.6693	.2725
1.31	3.7062	.2698
1.32	3.7434	.2671
1.33	3.7810	.2645
1.34	3.8190	.2618
1.35	3.8574	.2592
1.36	3.8962	.2567
1.37	3.9354	.2541
1.38	3.9749	.2516
1.39	4.0149	.2491
1.40	4.0552	.2466

1.41	4.0960	.2441	1.76	5.8124	.1720	2.11	8.2482	.1212	2.46	11.7048	.0854
1.42	4.1371	.2417	1.77	5.8709	.1703	2.12	8.3311	.1200	2.47	11.8224	.0846
1.43	4.1787	.2393	1.78	5.9299	.1686	2.13	8.4149	.1188	2.48	11.9413	.0837
1.44	4.2207	.2369	1.79	5.9895	.1670	2.14	8.4994	.1177	2.49	12.0613	.0829
1.45	4.2631	.2346	1.80	6.0496	.1653	2.15	8.5849	.1165	2.50	12.1825	.0821
1.46	4.3060	.2322	1.81	6.1104	.1637	2.16	8.6711	.1153	2.51	12.3049	.0813
1.47	4.3492	.2299	1.82	6.1719	.1620	2.17	8.7583	.1142	2.52	12.4286	.0805
1.48	4.3929	.2276	1.83	6.2339	.1604	2.18	8.8463	.1130	2.53	12.5535	.0797
1.49	4.4371	.2254	1.84	6.2965	.1588	2.19	8.9352	.1119	2.54	12.6797	.0789
1.50	4.4817	.2231	1.85	6.3598	.1572	2.20	9.0250	.1108	2.55	12.8071	.0781
1.51	4.5267	.2209	1.86	6.4237	.1557	2.21	9.1157	.1097	2.56	12.9358	.0773
1.52	4.5722	.2187	1.87	6.4883	.1541	2.22	9.2073	.1086	2.57	13.0658	.0765
1.53	4.6182	.2165	1.88	6.5535	.1526	2.23	9.2999	.1075	2.58	13.1971	.0758
1.54	4.6646	.2144	1.89	6.6194	.1511	2.24	9.3933	.1065	2.59	13.3298	.0750
1.55	4.7115	.2122	1.90	6.6859	.1496	2.25	9.4877	.1054	2.60	13.4637	.0743
1.56	4.7588	.2101	1.91	6.7531	.1481	2.26	9.5831	.1044	2.61	13.5991	.0735
1.57	4.8066	.2080	1.92	6.8210	.1466	2.27	9.6794	.1033	2.62	13.7357	.0728
1.58	4.8550	.2060	1.93	6.8895	.1451	2.28	9.7767	.1023	2.63	13.8738	.0721
1.59	4.9037	.2039	1.94	6.9588	.1437	2.29	9.8749	.1013	2.64	14.0132	.0714
1.60	4.9530	.2019	1.95	7.0287	.1423	2.30	9.9742	.1003	2.65	14.1540	.0707
1.61	5.0028	.1999	1.96	7.0993	.1409	2.31	10.0744	.0993	2.66	14.2963	.0699
1.62	5.0531	.1979	1.97	7.1707	.1395	2.32	10.1757	.0983	2.67	14.4400	.0693
1.63	5.1039	.1959	1.98	7.2427	.1381	2.33	10.2779	.0973	2.68	14.5851	.0686
1.64	5.1552	.1940	1.99	7.3155	.1367	2.34	10.3812	.0963	2.69	14.7317	.0679
1.65	5.2070	.1920	2.00	7.3891	.1353	2.35	10.4856	.0954	2.70	14.8797	.0672
1.66	5.2593	.1901	2.01	7.4633	.1340	2.36	10.5910	.0944	2.71	15.0293	.0665
1.67	5.3122	.1882	2.02	7.5383	.1327	2.37	10.6974	.0935	2.72	15.1803	.0659
1.68	5.3656	.1864	2.03	7.6141	.1313	2.38	10.8049	.0926	2.73	15.3329	.0652
1.69	5.4195	.1845	2.04	7.6906	.1300	2.39	10.9135	.0916	2.74	15.4870	.0646
1.70	5.4739	.1827	2.05	7.7679	.1287	2.40	11.0232	.0907	2.75	15.6426	.0639
1.71	5.5290	.1809	2.06	7.8460	.1275	2.41	11.1340	.0898	2.76	15.7998	.0633
1.72	5.5845	.1791	2.07	7.9248	.1262	2.42	11.2459	.0889	2.77	15.9586	.0627
1.73	5.6407	.1773	2.08	8.0045	.1249	2.43	11.3589	.0880	2.78	16.1190	.0620
1.74	5.6973	.1755	2.09	8.0849	.1237	2.44	11.4730	.0872	2.79	16.2810	.0614
1.75	5.7546	.1738	2.10	8.1662	.1225	2.45	11.5883	.0863	2.80	16.4446	.0608

2.81	16.6099	.0602
2.82	16.7769	.0596
2.83	16.9455	.0590
2.84	17.1158	.0584
2.85	17.2878	.0578
2.86	17.4615	.0573
2.87	17.6370	.0567
2.88	17.8143	.0561
2.89	17.9933	.0556
2.90	18.1741	.0550
2.91	18.3568	.0545
2.92	18.5413	.0539
2.93	18.7276	.0534
2.94	18.9158	.0529
2.95	19.1060	.0523
2.96	19.2980	.0518
2.97	19.4919	.0513
2.98	19.6878	.0508
2.99	19.8857	.0503
3.00	20.0855	.0498
3.05	21.1153	.0474
3.10	22.1980	.0450
3.15	23.3361	.0429
3.20	24.5325	.0408
3.25	25.7903	.0388
3.30	27.1126	.0369
3.35	28.5027	.0351
3.40	29.9641	.0334
3.45	31.5004	.0317
3.50	33.1155	.0302
3.55	34.8133	.0287
3.60	36.5982	.0273
3.65	38.4747	.0260
3.70	40.4473	.0247
3.75	42.5211	.0235

3.80	44.7012	.0224
3.85	46.9931	.0213
3.90	49.4024	.0202
3.95	51.9354	.0193
4.00	54.5982	.0183
4.05	57.3975	.0174
4.10	60.3403	.0166
4.15	63.4340	.0158
4.20	66.6863	.0150
4.25	70.1054	.0143
4.30	73.6998	.0136
4.35	77.4785	.0129
4.40	81.4509	.0123
4.45	85.6269	.0117
4.50	90.0171	.0111
4.55	94.6324	.0106
4.60	99.4843	.0101
4.65	104.5850	.0096
4.70	109.9472	.0091
4.75	115.5843	.0087
4.80	121.5104	.0082
4.85	127.7407	.0078
4.90	134.2898	.0074
4.95	141.1750	.0071
5.00	148.4132	.0067
5.05	156.0225	.0064
5.10	164.0219	.0061
5.15	172.4315	.0058
5.20	181.2722	.0055
5.25	190.5663	.0052
5.30	200.3368	.0050
5.35	210.6083	.0047
5.40	221.4064	.0045
5.45	232.7582	.0043
5.50	244.6919	.0041

5.55	257.2375	.0039
5.60	270.4264	.0037
5.65	284.2915	.0035
5.70	298.8674	.0033
5.75	314.1907	.0032
5.80	330.2995	.0030
5.85	347.2344	.0029
5.90	365.0375	.0027
5.95	383.7533	.0026
6.00	403.4288	.0025
6.10	445.8578	.0022
6.20	492.7490	.0020
6.30	544.5719	.0018
6.40	601.8450	.0017
6.50	665.1416	.0015
6.60	735.0952	.0014
6.70	812.4058	.0012
6.80	897.8473	.0011
6.90	992.2747	.0010
7.00	1096.6332	.0009
7.10	1211.9670	.0008
7.20	1339.4308	.0007
7.30	1480.2999	.0007
7.40	1635.9844	.0006
7.50	1808.0424	.0006
7.60	1998.1958	.0005
7.70	2208.3480	.0005
7.80	2440.6019	.0004
7.90	2697.2823	.0004
8.00	2980.9580	.0003
8.10	3294.4678	.0003
8.20	3640.9500	.0003
8.30	4023.8722	.0002
8.40	4447.0667	.0002
8.50	4914.7689	.0002

8.60	5431.6591	.0002
8.70	6002.9118	.0002
8.80	6634.2437	.0002
8.90	7331.9734	.0001
9.00	8103.0839	.0001
9.10	8955.2919	.0001
9.20	9897.1283	.0001
9.30	10938.0187	.0001
9.40	12088.3805	.0001
9.50	13359.7268	.0001
9.60	14764.7802	.0001
9.70	16317.6061	.0001
9.80	18033.7441	.0001
9.90	19930.3699	.0001
10.00	22026.4658	.0000

Bibliography

Advisory Commission on Intergovernmental Relations. *A Handbook for Inter-governmental Agreements and Contracts.* Washington: Government Printing Office, 1967.

Advisory Commission on Intergovernmental Relations. *American Federalism: Into the Third Century.* Washington: Government Printing Office, 1974.

Advisory Commission on Intergovernmental Relations. *Federal Approaches to Aid State and Local Capital Financing.* Washington: Government Printing Office, 1970.

Advisory Commission on Intergovernmental Relations. *State and Local Finances: Significant Features and Suggested Legislation.* Washington: Government Printing Office, 1974.

Anthony, Robert. *Planning and Control Systems: A Framework for Analysis.* Cambridge: Harvard University Press, 1965.

Banovetz, James M. *Managing the Modern City.* Washington: International City Management Association, 1971.

Baumol, William J. *Economic Theory and Operations Analysis.* Englewood Cliffs, N.J.: Prentice Hall, 1965.

Bell, Daniel. "The Revolution of Rising Entitlements." *Fortune* (April 1975), pp. 93–103.

Book, Samuel H. "Costs of Commuters to the Central City as a Basis for Commuter Taxation." Ph.D. dissertation, Columbia University, 1970.

Borut, Donald J. "Implementing PPBS: A Practitioner's Viewpoint," in *Financing the Metropolis,* ed. John P. Crecine. Beverly Hills: Sage Publications, 1970.

Brown, Rex V., Kahr, Andrew S., and Peterson, Cameron. *Decision Analysis for the Manager.* New York: Holt, Rinehart and Winston, 1974.

Burkhead, Jesse. *Government Budgeting.* New York: Wiley, 1956.

Catanese, Anthony J. *Scientific Methods of Urban Analysis.* Urbana: University of Illinois Press, 1972.

Catanese, Anthony J., and Steiss, Alan Walter. *Systemic Planning: Theory and Application.* Lexington, Mass.: D.C. Heath, 1970.

Doyle, Arthur Conan. *A Study in Scarlet. The Complete Sherlock Holmes.* Garden City, N.Y.: Doubleday, 1930.

Drake, Alvin W., Keenen, Ralph L., and Morse, Philip M. (eds.). *Analysis of Public Systems.* Cambridge: The MIT Press, 1972.

Dror, Yehezkel. "The Planning Process: A Facet Design," in *Planning Programming Budgeting,* ed. Fremont J. Lyden and Ernest G. Miller. Chicago: Markham, 1968.

Due, John F., and Friedlaender, Ann F. *Government Finance: Economics of the Public Sector.* Homewood, Ill.: Richard D. Irwin, 1973.

Freeman, Robert J., and Lynn, Edward S. *Fund Accounting.* Englewood Cliffs, N.J.: Prentice Hall, 1974.

Gans, Herbert J. *More Equality.* New York: Pantheon Books, 1968.

Greene, Kenneth V., Neenan, William B., and Scott, Claudia D. *Fiscal Interactions in a Metropolitan Area.* Lexington, Mass.: Lexington Books, 1974.

Gross, Bertram M. "The New Systems Budgeting." *Public Administration Review* (March–April 1969).

Hamburg, Morris. *Statistical Analysis for Decision Making.* New York: Harcourt, Brace and World, 1970.

Hatry, Harry P. "Criteria for Evaluation in Planning State and Local Programs," in *Decision-Making in Urban Planning,* ed. Ira M. Robinson. Beverly Hills: Sage Publications, 1972.

Hatry, Harry P. "Overview of Modern Program Analysis Characteristics and Techniques." Urban Institute Reprint. Washington: The Urban Institute, 1970.

Hatry, Harry P., Winnie, Richard E., and Fisk, Donald M. *Practical Program Evaluation for State and Local Government Officials.* Washington: The Urban Institute, 1973.

Hatry, Harry P., Blair, Louis, Fisk, Donald, and Kimmel, Wayne. *Program Analysis for State and Local Governments.* Washington: The Urban Institute, 1976.

Heilbrun, James. *Urban Economics and Public Policy.* New York: St. Martin's Press, 1974.

Herber, Bernard P. *Modern Public Finance: The Study of the Public Sector.* Homewood, Ill.: Richard D. Irwin, 1971.

Hinrichs, Harley H. and Taylor, Graeme M. *Systemic Analysis: A Primer on Benefit-Cost Analysis and Program Evaluation.* Pacific Palisades: Goodyear Publishing Company, 1972.

Hirsch, Werner Z. *The Economics of State and Local Government.* New York: McGraw-Hill, 1970.

International City Management Association. Report for the Department of Housing and Urban Development. *Applying Systems Analysis in Urban Government: Three Case Studies.* Washington: The Association, 1972.

International City Managers' Association. *Municipal Finance Administration,* 6th ed. Chicago: The International City Managers' Association, 1962.

James, L. Douglas, and Lee, Robert R. *Economics of Water Resources Planning.* New York: McGraw-Hill, 1971.

Jones, John A. and Howard, S. Kenneth. *Investment of Idle Funds by Local Governments: A Primer.* Washington: Municipal Finance Officers Association, 1973.

Kraemer, Kenneth L. *Policy Analysis in Local Government: A Systems Approach to Decision Making.* Washington: International City Management Association, 1973.

Krueckeberg, Donald A., and Silvers, Arthur L. *Urban Planning Analysis: Methods and Models.* New York: Wiley, 1974.

Lee, Robert D., Jr., and Johnson, Ronald W. *Public Budgeting Systems.* Baltimore: University Park Press, 1973.

Lindbloom, Charles E. "The Science of Muddling Through." *Public Administration Review.* Vol. 19 (Spring 1959).

Lipsey, Richard G., and Steiner, Peter O. *Economics.* New York: Harper and Row, 1966.

McKean, Roland N. *Efficiency in Government Through Systems Analysis.* New York: Wiley, 1958.

March, James G., and Simon, Herbert A. *Organizations.* New York: Wiley, 1958.

Meltsner, Arnold J., and Wildavsky, Aaron. "Second Thoughts of the Reform," in *Financing the Metropolis,* ed. John P. Crecine. Beverly Hills: Sage Publications, 1970.

Mendonsa, Arthur A. *Simplified Financial Management in Local Government.* Athens: Institute of Government, University of Georgia, 1969.

Mikesell, R.M., and Hay, Leon E. *Governmental Accounting.* Homewood, Ill.: Richard D. Irwin, 1969.

Municipal Finance Officers Association and Peat, Marwick, Mitchell and Company. *Study Guide to Governmental Accounting, Auditing and Financial Reporting.* Chicago: Municipal Finance Officers Association, 1974.

Munson, Michael J. "How to Keep Plans off the Shelf: An Organizational View of Planning, Management, and Implementation." Ph.D. dissertation, University of Michigan, 1972.

National Committee of Governmental Accounting. *Governmental Accounting, Auditing, and Financial Reporting.* Chicago: Municipal Finance Officers Association, 1968.

Neenan, William. *Political Economy of Urban Areas.* Chicago: Markham, 1972.

de Neufville, Richard, and Stafford, Joseph H. *Systems Analysis for Engineers and Managers.* New York: McGraw-Hill, 1971.

Pettengill, Robert B., and Uppal, Jogindar S. *Can Cities Survive?* New York: St. Martin's Press, 1974.

Rondinelli, Dennis A. "Revenue Sharing and American Cities: Analysis of the Federal Experiment in Local Assistance." *Journal of the American Institute of Planners,* vol. 41, no. 5 (September 1975), pp. 319-333.

Simon, Herbert. *Administrative Behavior.* New York: Free Press, 1957.

Smith, R.F. "Are Nonresidents Contributing Their Share to the Core City Revenues?" *Land Economics* (August 1972).

Steiner, Peter O. "The Public Sector and the Public Interest," in *Public Expenditures and Policy Analysis,* ed. Robert H. Haveman and Julius Margolis. Chicago: Markham, 1970.

Steiss, Alan W. *Public Budgeting and Management.* Lexington, Mass.: D.C. Heath, 1972.

Tax Foundation. *Facts and Figures on Government Finance,* 18th ed. New York: Tax Foundation, 1975.

Thompson, Wilbur. *A Preface to Urban Economics.* Baltimore: The Johns Hopkins Press, 1965.

Thompson, Wilbur. "The City as a Distorted Price System." *Psychology Today* (August 1968), pp. 28-33.

Tiebout, Charles M. "A Pure Theory of Local Expenditures," in *State and Local Finance,* ed. William E. Mitchell and Ingo Walter. New York: Ronald Press, 1970, p. 21.

U.S. Bureau of the Census. *City Government Finances in 1971-72.* Washington: Government Printing Office, 1973.

U.S. Bureau of the Census. *Historical Statistics on Governmental Finances and Employment,* Vol. 6, No. 4. Washington: Government Printing Office, 1972.

U.S. Bureau of the Census. *Historical Statistics of the United States, Colonial Times to 1957.* Washington: Government Printing Office, 1960.

U.S. Bureau of the Census. *Local Government Employment in Selected Metropolitan Areas and Large Counties, 1973.* Washington: Government Printing Office, 1974.

U.S. Bureau of the Census. *Statistical Abstract of the United States: 1974,* 95th ed. Washington: Government Printing Office, 1974.

U.S. Department of Housing and Urban Development. *Summary of the Housing and Community Development Act of 1974.* Washington: Government Printing Office, 1974.

Vincent, Phillip E. "The Fiscal Impact of Commuters" in *Fiscal Pressures on the Central City,* ed. Werner Z. Husch, et al. New York: Praeger, 1971.

Wildavsky, Aaron. *The Politics of the Budgetary Process.* Boston: Little, Brown, 1964.

Wingfield, Clyde J. "City Planning," in *Managing the Modern City,* ed. James M. Banovetz. Washington: International City Managers' Association, 1971.

Index

Index

Accounting: cash and accrual, 190-191; in local government, 183-186; procedure, 185-186; structure of, 184

Accounts, 186-187

Administration, role in public policy, 64

Administrative Revenues, 147

Administrators, roles of, 77-78

Ad Valorem taxes, 140

Allocation of resources, 3; and efficiency of taxes, 126-127; optimum, 250-252; policy, 43; rationale for, 35

Alternatives: complimentary, 215-216; do nothing, 214-215; examples of, 231-232; mutually exclusive, 214-215; scalar, 227-229, 241-243; structuring of, 197, 213-214

Analysis, investment, 255; marginal, 241-249; process of, 212; program, 67-68, 107, 202-208, 219; of service standards, 92

Anticipated fiscal policy, 102

Appropriations, 121

Assessment of tax, 129

Assessor, 78

Attorney, city, 78

Audit, 191-192

Auditor, 78

Authorizations, 121

Average cost pricing, 38-39, 252

Basic economic research, 81-82, 102

Benefit cost ratio, 199-200, 242, 266

Benefits, types of, 222-223

Bonds: coverage for, 181-182; funds, 184; general obligation and revenue, 169; ratings, 178-180; types of, 176-177, 222-223

Book, Samuel H., 159

Bookkeeping, 188-191

Budgeting, 99-100; accounts, 185-188; balancing, 103, 111-112; calendar, 100-102; documents, 103-104; management, 102-104; problems, 105-109; process, 100; systems, 109, 114; types and format, 114-117

Business tax, 143

Capital budget, 104, 117, 268-269

Capital programs, 95-97, 102, 117

Capitalism, 5

Capital stock tax, 143

Central economy, 6

Circuit breaker, 133

Cities, administrative structure of, 54; definition of, 53

City council, 77

City planner, 78

Collection cost, 43

Collective consumption, 35-36

Collective risk, 43

Combined budget, 114-115

Community Development, Title 1, 163

Compensation for externalities, 42

Competition, in markets, 8, 24-29

Complimentary alternatives, 215-216

Composite population models, 85-86

Comprehensive planning, 66-67

Consolidation of governments, 165-166

Constraints, in program analysis, 199, 210-212, examples of, 232

Content analysis, 65

Contracts, interlocal, 166-167

Controller, comptroller, accountant, 78

Cost: of collection, 43; estimation, 234; fixed, marginal, and variable, 22; internal versus external, 41; long run, 23-24; opportunity versus cash, 20; and production, 21-22; public versus private, 20; schedule and curves, 22-23; types of, 224-225

About the Author

James C. Snyder is assistant dean and associate professor at the school of Architecture and Urban Planning, University of Wisconsin-Milwaukee. A graduate of the Ohio State University (B. Architecture) and the University of Michigan (M. Architecture, M. City Planning, Ph.D., Urban and Regional Planning), Dr. Snyder has taught at the University of Michigan, Georgia Institute of Technology, and the University of Wisconsin-Milwaukee. Dr. Snyder has served as a consultant to numerous local governments in addition to his teaching and research interests.